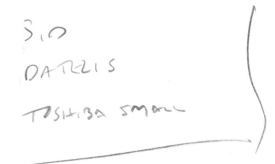

PRAISE FOR *UBUNTU FOR NON-GEEKS*

"A fast, crystal-clear topical tour of the amazing collective accomplishment embodied in Ubuntu. I learned something new in every chapter, and ended up with a computer that did more of what I wanted it to do, faster. This book should come with every Ubuntu Live CD—it's just the documentation I needed to take some of the mystery out of my machine."
—BOING BOING

"Highly recommended to all Ubuntu newcomers."
—PC WORLD

"This very nice book on Ubuntu Linux is clearly targeted at the neophytes who wish to take their first steps in installing and using Ubuntu. The author explains in a step-by-step manner the solutions to the problems that one might face in installing, configuring and using Ubuntu Linux."
—SLASHDOT

"This is a good, practical book that reads well and doesn't involve the victim in lots of superfluous stuff."
—UNIX REVIEW

"Grant makes it seem easy with his step-by-step instructions and plenty of screen shots."
—LINUX.COM

"With humor and pragmatism, Mr. Grant walks the novice explorer through all the basics of switching to this distribution of Linux, on to the practical level of getting things done."
—P2P FOUNDATION BLOG

"The best thing in Rickford Grant's *Ubuntu Linux for Non-Geeks* is plenty of practical examples."
—LINUX MAGAZINE

"Highly recommended for both new Linux users and new computer users in general."
—BLOGCRITICS

In loving memory of Dr. James Howard Cremin, who, along with his fam[...] gave me a place in which to find a sense of self during my early days of tun[...] and who managed to keep his cool when I blew out half the electricity in [...] house one Christmas morning. I miss you.

UBUNTU FOR NON-GEEKS

3RD EDITION

A Pain-Free, Project-Based, Get-Things-Done Guidebook

by Rickford Grant

NO STARCH
PRESS

San Francisco

UBUNTU FOR NON-GEEKS, 3RD EDITION. Copyright © 2008 by Rickford Grant.

 Printed on recycled paper in the United States of America

12 11 10 09 08   1 2 3 4 5 6 7 8 9

ISBN-10: 1-59327-180-8
ISBN-13: 978-1-59327-180-0

Publisher: William Pollock
Production Editor: Megan Dunchak
Cover and Interior Design: Octopod Studios
Developmental Editor: William Pollock
Technical Reviewer: Phil Bull
Copyeditor: Megan Dunchak
Compositor: Riley Hoffman
Proofreader: Kathleen Mish

For information on book distributors or translations, please contact No Starch Press, Inc. directly:

No Starch Press, Inc.
555 De Haro Street, Suite 250, San Francisco, CA 94107
phone: 415.863.9900; fax: 415.863.9950; info@nostarch.com; www.nostarch.com

The Library of Congress has cataloged the first edition as follows:

```
Grant, Rickford.
 Ubuntu Linux for non-geeks : a pain-free, project-based, get-things-done guidebook / Rickford Grant.
     p. cm.
 Includes index.
 ISBN 1-59327-118-2
1. Linux. 2. Operating systems (Computers)  I. Title.  QA76.76.O63.G7246 2006
005.4'32--dc22
```
                                                2006015576

BRIEF CONTENTS

CONTENTS IN DETAIL

3
A NEW PLACE TO CALL HOME
Getting to Know the Desktop

31

4
MORE THAN WEBBED FEET
The Internet, Linux Style

49

5
ROUNDING OUT THE BIRD
Downloading, Installing, and Updating Programs the Easy Way 67

6
A TIDY NEST
File and Disk Handling in Ubuntu 79

7
DRESSING UP THE BIRD
Customizing the Look and Feel of Your System   103

8
SIMPLE KITTEN WAYS
Getting to Know the Linux Terminal and
Command Line   131

9
ALIENS, TARBALLS, A GLASS OF WINE, AND A CUP OF JOE
More Ways to Install Programs
161

10
GUTENBIRD
Setting Up and Using Your Printer and Scanner   183

11
FONT FEATHERED FRENZY
Adding New Fonts to Your System   197

12
POLYGLOT PENGUINS
Linux Speaks Your Language
209

13
PENGUINS BACK AT WORK
Getting Down to Business in Linux
223

14
BRUSH-WIELDING PENGUINS
Linux Does Art
237

15
TUX ROCKS
Music à la Linux

253

ACKNOWLEDGMENTS

There are a good number of people who deserve thanks for the help and support they provided either while or before this book was written, and there are still others whose help will come after the book is released. I would like to acknowledge all of them now.

Starting with my family, I'd like to thank Sumire, as always, for her patience and kindness throughout the project. The same thanks go to my mother, Dixie Angelina Burckel-Testa, who helped out with the initial proofreading of my earlier manuscripts and always lends a hand when she can. Thanks go out again to my auntie and uncle, Danica Lucia and David Zollars, for their continuous support and help (and for getting me into this book-writing business in the first place); and to round out the clan, thanks are due to my cousin and friend, Stephanie Garrabrant-Sierra, who tries to keep me on track whenever I am on the verge (or in the midst) of stumbling.

In the production of any book, editors are so very important, and I would like to thank Phil Bull, the technical editor, who kept an eye on everything and pointed out a number of things that had missed my notice; Megan Dunchak, the very all-together (and decidedly cool) production manager, who had the unenviable task of managing me, a real but-I-sent-that-in-to-you-already . . . oh-I-guess-I-didn't kind of guy; and Riley Hoffman, who took a whole jumble of files, images, changes, and more changes and laid it all out, thus turning it into . . . well, a book.

Special thanks also go out to the other folks at No Starch Press, especially Leigh Poehler, who continues to help me with all sorts of things, including answers to a lot of absolutely inane questions; and last but not, as the saying goes, least, William Pollock for not only taking a chance on the completely unknown writer that I was, but also for turning me on to a great *pupuseria* in San Mateo. Of course, San Mateo, California is a bit far off for a quick lunch now that I am in North Carolina, but . . .

Speaking of North Carolina, it wouldn't be just of me to go on thanking people without mentioning a few of the people who have helped keep me sane since coming here. For my present state of relative decent mental well-being, I thank my colleagues Linda Sullivan, Eva Garner, Kay Miller, Bob Egan, and Ligia Henderson, who all helped me to keep my new-found world in better perspective.

Turning now to my friends and colleagues, let me thank Donald Hammang—cycle-pal, Windows expert, and keeper of the Great Saw (the inspiration for SawGear); Sheldon Rudolph—lifelong friend, artist, composer, and my original compu-buddy from the Atari XL600 days; Steven Young—hiker, environmentalist, birder, ultimate gadget-geek, and the inspiration for *Linux Made Easy* (not to mention the person who first brought Ubuntu to my attention); and Tracy Nakajima—my Mac connection and de facto life advisor. Thank you all very much.

And although I am no longer in Japan, thanks are still due to the gang back there: my former colleagues Setsu Uesaka, Toshiko Takagi, James Porcaro, and Andrezej Kozlowski for their indirect and, at times, very direct help while I was writing this book; and Enryo Nagata, Masayasu Tsuchida, and Seiichi Mizuta for their time, help, vision, and continued kindness.

Special thanks are also due to those people who provided me with support or helped direct me in ways they probably do not even realize—Dick Petrie, Kimberly Jo Burk, Peter and Cate Corvin-Brittin, Charlene Gawa, Leopi (Levy) Sanderson-Edmunds, and Olynxa Levy.

Finally, a special thanks to my sweet little black cat and dear feline friend, Muju, who, despite vociferously protesting as I spent *her* time writing this book, continues to listen to whatever I have to say and keeps me sane when I'm feeling down, though I admit to losing it a bit when she demands that I spin her around on my swivel chair at 4 AM. Such is life in service to one's cat. Meow.

INTRODUCTION

My computing life began long ago in the Commodore/Atari days. No doubt inspired by Alan Alda's television commercials at the time, I purchased my first machine, an Atari 600XL with a cassette drive for storage and 16KB of RAM—more than I thought I would ever need. Most of my time on that machine, I must admit, was spent playing cartridge-based games and transcribing pages and pages of machine code from the now-defunct magazine *Antic* to create even more games. Eventually, my interest in computers increased, especially after seeing my first (and actually *the* first) Macintosh at the UCLA bookstore. The very in-your-face nature of the Mac's operating system caused me to become an operating system maniac. To date, I have worked with a lot of different operating systems, including Mac OS up to and including OS X, every Windows version from 3.1 to XP, and even IBM's much forgotten OS/2.

Though tempted to join the Linux fray, I continued to steer away from it for a long time because I could not help but see it, as so many others do, as a system for never-seen-the-light-of-day-faced, late-night Dr Pepper–drinking,

Domino's-pizza-eating compu-geeks. However, when I moved to Japan and was suddenly surrounded by machines loaded with Japanese versions of Windows, I encountered numerous problems, such as language constraints. Since everything, including Help files, was written in Japanese, I ended up using only a fraction of the full potential of most software. Then there were those annoying Windows-type problems, such as the constant freezes and restarts and the gradual system slowdowns, which were eventually only remedied by reinstalling the system. Getting the software I needed to do the things I wanted to do also took its toll on my wallet, and I began to rethink my initial resistance to Linux. With Linux's multilingual support, system stability, and extensive and free software packages, there were plenty of incentives for me to get over my preconceived notions about the typical Linux user.

After a few failed attempts at getting Linux to work on the oddball, Frankenstein-like collection of junk that was my computer, I finally succeeded with a CD-based Knoppix distribution, which worked well enough to hook me in a little further. I moved on to Mandrake (now known as Mandriva) next, since that was claimed to be the most newbie-friendly version, and then tried out SuSE as well, which I found to be rather quirky. Eventually, I tried out Red Hat Linux and stuck to that because it just didn't give me any grief; and I, like most others, do not want any more grief than necessary.

I started off with my three desktop machines at work and home set up as dual-boot systems running both Linux and Windows, but I gradually found myself using only Linux. Although I had expected to encounter numerous limitations in Linux that would force me to return to Windows often, I instead found that I had actually increased my productivity. Other than lack of native support for Windows streaming media, I was actually able to do more due to the extensive software base that was now installed on my machine. Without having to fork out money that I could ill afford to spend, I was able to manipulate my digital images, rip songs from CDs, create vector drawings, create PDF files, and do a variety of other things that I wasn't able to do under Windows. It was only a matter of time before my dual-boot setups became full Linux-only setups. I ceased to be a Windows user.

Since those early Linux days, I have gone on to try out a number of other distributions including JAMD, Xandros, Damn Small Linux, and most recently Ubuntu. I am happy to report that things have continued to get easier and better, and those early frustrations I suffered trying to get things to work with this machine or that piece of hardware are becoming more and more a thing of the past. Best of all, with the advent of live CDs, which allow you to try Linux out before you actually install it, you don't even have to take a leap of faith to get started.

Who Is This Book For?

If you are standing in the aisle of your local bookstore reading this right now, you may well be wondering who this book is for. If you also happen to see my previous books, *Linux for Non-Geeks* and *Linux Made Easy* on the same shelf (or have at least heard about them), you might also be wondering what the differences among these books are. These questions are reasonable enough. To put it simply, there are two differences: the experience level of the target reader and the distribution covered in each book. *Linux for Non-Geeks*, based on Fedora Core 1, was my first book and was written with folks like my mother in mind—average computer users with some computer experience in the Windows or Mac worlds who had an interest in Linux but were afraid to give it a go. My second book, *Linux Made Easy*, was based on Xandros 3 and was written at a more basic level for those who just wanted a free and easy way out of the grasping tentacles of the Microsoft empire.

Ubuntu for Non-Geeks, as you might imagine, is based on Ubuntu Linux, and like the original *Linux for Non-Geeks*, it targets readers who are interested in Linux but feel the need for a jumping-off point of sorts. Although there are some similarities with its predecessor, *Ubuntu for Non-Geeks* is different in many ways. This is not only due to the inherent differences between the Debian-based Ubuntu and the RPM-based Fedora Core, but also due to the advances made by Linux as a whole. These advances have resulted in a system that is easier and more convenient to use than ever before.

If you are familiar with computers, but unfamiliar with Linux, or somewhat familiar with Linux but not with Ubuntu, you are essentially the reader for whom I have written this book. So to avoid any misunderstanding on your part (and at the risk of being redundant), I must re-emphasize that this is not a book for seasoned geeks or power users. It is instead an introductory guide that will provide new users with some hands-on experience in order to get them up, running, and comfortable with the Ubuntu distribution of Linux.

Version Compatibility

This third edition of *Ubuntu for Non-Geeks* was prepared for use with Ubuntu 8.04 (Hardy Heron) Desktop edition. Included with this book is a full working copy of that system on one CD, which functions not only as an install CD, but also as a live CD. This means that you can run Ubuntu directly off the CD without so much as touching your hard disk. You can thus give Ubuntu a try before making any hardware commitments. And since we're talking hardware, it is also worth pointing out that running a live CD session gives you the chance to see if Ubuntu works with the hardware you've got.

If you like what you see and all the hardware seems to work, you can go ahead and install the full shebang on your computer . . . and using the same disk, no less (instructions included in Chapter 2).

NOTE *The world of computers is exceedingly dynamic, and as such, there may be changes in the software or the links to the files for projects in this book after the book is released. I'll post any such changes at www.edgy-penguins.org/UFNG.*

Concept and Approach

As a language teacher, I have always enjoyed programming books, mathematics books, and old-fashioned foreign language–learning texts because of their straightforward, skill-based orientation, one in which each chapter builds upon the skills acquired in the previous chapter. I have tried to organize this book in that manner so that you will never be called upon to do something that you have not already learned. I also like such books because they not only teach you how to do something, but they also provide you with the chance to put those morsels of knowledge into practice with exercises. I have therefore included several exercises, or projects, in this book so that you will have opportunities to apply your knowledge. This book will serve as a reference text and will also provide a dynamic learning experience so you can learn by doing, as they say.

The projects throughout this book have a secondary purpose as well: By working through them, you will properly configure and round out your Ubuntu system so that it can do anything you want it to do. By the time you finish with this book, your system will have all the bases covered. If that is still not enough to satisfy you, you will be happy to know that you will have access to even more—an unbelievably greater amount more—via the online Ubuntu repositories, which you will learn how to use in Chapter 5. If your interest is already piqued, take a look at these chapter descriptions:

Chapter 1: Becoming a Penguinista—Welcome to the World of Linux
What's Linux? What's Ubuntu? What's a distribution? Can I . . .? Will my . . .? Chapter 1 holds the answers to these and many other questions you might have as it introduces you to the world of Linux and what it takes to get it up and running on your machine.

Chapter 2: Wading and Diving—Running and (If You Like) Installing Ubuntu
The Ubuntu Desktop CD that comes with this book works as both a live and an install CD. Chapter 2 tells you how to run a live Ubuntu session off the CD and, assuming you catch the Linux bug after doing that, how to install the full Ubuntu system on your hard disk as your sole operating system or in a dual-boot setup with Windows.

Chapter 3: A New Place to Call Home—Getting to Know the Desktop
Regardless of whether you are an émigré from the Windows or Mac worlds, the Desktop is something you are already quite familiar with. Chapter 3 will point out the differences between Ubuntu's GNOME desktop and the one on your previous operating system, and it will teach you a number of cool tricks you can use to customize the look and feel of things. A couple of nifty GNOME Easter eggs are also introduced.

Chapter 4: More Than Webbed Feet—The Internet, Linux Style
"Have computer, will cyber-travel" could well be the mantra of the Internet age, and that being the case, Chapter 4 is an indispensable part of your Ubuntu experience. In this chapter you will learn how to connect to the Internet and set up wireless connections, and you will meet the various software entities that allow you to interact with the Web.

Chapter 5: Rounding Out the Bird—Downloading, Installing, and Updating Programs the Easy Way

Ubuntu comes bundled with most of the software you need, but there is still much more available out there, free and waiting on the Web. Chapter 5 teaches you how to easily download and install applications using Advanced Package Tool (APT) and Synaptic. System and application updating is also covered.

Chapter 6: A Tidy Nest—File and Disk Handling in Ubuntu

From creating folders to copying files to browsing your system and network, all things file management are covered in Chapter 6. You will also learn how to work with USB storage devices, transfer files via Bluetooth, burn data CDs and DVDs, deal with CD-RW disks and multisession CDs, and create space-saving compressed archives of file folders.

Chapter 7: Dressing Up the Bird—Customizing the Look and Feel of Your System

Tired of looking at the same old desktop? Feeling nostalgic for the desktop in your previous operating system? Chapter 7 tells you how you can beat the déjà vu blues by changing the look and feel of just about every visual element of your system, and how to take control of Ubuntu's new visual effects engine, Compiz.

Chapter 8: Simple Kitten Ways—Getting to Know the Linux Terminal and Command Line

Many people still shy away from Linux because they perceive it as a system in which everything still needs to be done by typing commands. That perception is, as the saying goes, a load of squashed avocados. Still, there is a lot of cool stuff that can be done via the command Terminal, and Chapter 8 will tell you all about it as it tames your fears and piques your interest in commands. Really.

Chapter 9: Aliens, Tarballs, a Glass of Wine, and a Cup of Joe—More Ways to Install Programs

Ever wanted to compile your own application? Or maybe you'd like to convert an RPM to a DEB package? Maybe you'd like to figure out how to run Java applications. Or maybe you'd just like to learn a really easy way to install all of the most essential missing bits of your system? In Chapter 9 you will learn how to do all these things, and you will even find out how you can run some Windows applications from within Linux.

Chapter 10: Gutenbird—Setting Up and Using Your Printer and Scanner

Just about everyone with a computer has or needs a printer, and Chapter 10 tells you exactly how to get yours working with your new Linux system. Scanner usage and support are also discussed.

Chapter 11: Font Feathered Frenzy—Adding New Fonts to Your System

Whether you want to use the same fonts that your Windows-using friends are plugging into their documents or you just want to add a bit of flair to your own, Chapter 11 will tell you how to do it in Ubuntu.

Chapter 12: Polyglot Penguins—Linux Speaks Your Language

Need to jot off a note in Urdu? Write a book in Korean? Send a letter in Chinese to your friend in Chengdu? All of the basics you need to know to read and write in just about any language in the world are provided in Chapter 12.

Chapter 13: Penguins Back at Work—Getting Down to Business in Linux

Work can be a drag, especially when there are so many other things you could be doing. Still, wearing the ol' fingers to the bone is a part of life for just about everyone outside of a Jane Austen novel, so you'll be glad to know that Linux is a very capable system in this regard. Chapter 13 introduces you to the various productivity applications bundled with or available for your system.

Chapter 14: Brush-Wielding Penguins—Linux Does Art

Those of you with an artistic bent will find Chapter 14 especially useful. Working with your digital camera, modifying images, and building web albums are just some of the topic areas covered.

Chapter 15: Tux Rocks—Music à la Linux

Chapter 15 is the music lover's treasure trove. You will learn how to rip CDs, encode MP3 or Ogg Vorbis audio files, and even find out how to create your own mix-and-match audio CDs from those files. A number of audio ripping and playback applications are also covered.

Chapter 16: Pluggin' In the Penguin—Ubuntu and Your iPod

Need I say more? Have an iPod? Want to use it in Ubuntu? Chapter 16 tells you how.

Chapter 17: Couch Penguins—Video and DVD Playback in Ubuntu

Sitting in your dorm room trying to figure out how to play your DVD copy of *The Baxter* on your Ubuntu-ized computer? Just finished filming a video of your sibling talking while asleep and want to do some creative editing of the evidence? Chapter 17 covers these and other video-related topics.

Chapter 18: Defending the Nest—Security

Although Linux is about as safe and secure a system as you are likely to come across, some folks feel a bit more secure . . . well, feeling a bit more secure. Chapter 18 tells you how to add a few lines of defense to your system.

Appendix A: Ubuntu Desktop CDs for AMD64 Users

The CD bundled with this book is designed to work with i386 processors. It will also work with AMD64 processors, although not in 64-bit mode. Want to run Ubuntu with an AMD64 processor in 64-bit mode? It's easy enough to do. Appendix A shows you how to download Ubuntu Desktop CD images and burn them to disk.

Appendix B: Resources

Are you crazy for Ubuntu and want to say so? Check out a forum. Do you have a hardware compatibility question? Some websites seem to have all the answers. Are you looking for free downloads or do you want to read up on the other Linux distributions? Appendix B is a great place to start.

How to Use This Book

It is possible, of course, to use this book as a mere reference text that you only consult when you have a problem to solve, but that would negate the basic concept behind its design. Instead, I recommend that you go through the entire book chapter by chapter, doing the projects along the way. This will give you a much broader understanding of how things are done (and of how you can get things done), and it will reduce the chance for anxiety, confusion, and worse yet, mistakes.

It is best to read this book and complete its projects when you are relaxed and have time to spare. Nothing makes things go wrong more than working in a rush. And keep in mind that Linux and the projects in this book are fun, not just work exercises. The whole point of the Linux world, in my opinion, is that it offers all kinds of fun. So go ahead and enjoy it.

About the Conventions Used in This Book

There are only a few minor points worth noting about the conventions I have used here. I have put in **bold** type the items within your system that you need to click or directly manipulate in any way, such as buttons, tabs, and menus. Where words or phrases are defined, they have been set in *italics*. Any text that I ask you to input will be indicated by `monospace` font. I have also opted to use the more graphically suggestive term *folder* instead of *directory*—no doubt the legacy of my many years as a Mac user.

About the Projects in This Book

The projects and other information in this book are primarily geared toward users who have installed Ubuntu using the CD that comes with this book. Most of the information also applies to Ubuntu live sessions run from the CD. You should note, however, that some projects and actions cannot be performed in live sessions, as they require write access to your hard disk, and this is not possible during live sessions.

1

BECOMING A PENGUINISTA

Welcome to the World of Linux

Now we begin our project to get you up and running in the world of Linux. If you have already made the commitment and have Ubuntu installed on your machine, you are essentially ready to go. Others of you might have made the commitment psychologically, but have yet to act on that commitment. And some of you are probably reading these words in the aisle of a bookstore, wondering about Linux and about whether you should spend your money on this book or on a latté every morning for the next couple of weeks. For those in this last group, I can only say, "Get this book." Save the wear and tear on your stomach and nerves.

In any case, the first thing we need to do is get you up to snuff on what this Ubuntu thing is all about, why you might want to install and use it, and what you will need in order to do so. I expect you will have lots of questions along the way, and if you are like most people, a few doubts. I hope that by the time you finish this book and have your Linux system up and running, your doubts will be gone and your questions, for the most part, will be answered. Anyway, until you are ready to make the commitment, you can still follow along, because the CD that comes with this book contains, in addition to the Ubuntu installer, a live Ubuntu environment—meaning that you can have a taste of the Ubuntu Linux experience without having to even touch what you've got on your hard drive. You can kick back, put your worries in check, and go with the flow.

What Is Linux?

Your computer, despite being a collection of highly sophisticated parts, is really just . . . well, a collection of highly sophisticated parts. On its own, it can do nothing other than switch on and off and spin a disk or two. In order for it to do anything truly useful, it needs an operating system (OS) to guide it. The OS takes an essentially well-endowed but completely uneducated hunk of a machine and educates it, at least enough so that it will understand what you want it to do.

You already know of and have probably used at least one of the many operating systems that exist today. Windows, DOS, and the Mac OS are all such operating systems, and Linux is yet another. Linux is, however, different from these other operating systems, both in terms of its capabilities and its heritage. Linux was not created by a corporation or by some corporate wannabes out to make money. The Linux core, referred to as the *kernel*, was created by computer enthusiast Linus Torvalds, a member of Finland's Swedish ethnic minority, who wanted to create a system like Unix that would work on home computers, particularly his.

Rather than keeping his creation to himself, Torvalds opened it up to the world, so to speak, and compu-geeks around the globe worked to make it better and more powerful. It is this combination of applications built around the core of the Linux kernel that is the essence of all Linux distributions today.

Linux has acquired many fans and followers since its creation in 1991. Such devotees praise Linux for its many features, as well as for being robust, reliable, free, and open. Despite these positive characteristics, however, Linux is, on its own, just a text-based system. There is no pretty desktop, and there are no windows or charming little icons to make you feel safe and comfy once you are behind the keyboard. Powerful though it may be, Linux is still strictly a black-screen, command line–driven operating system. I guess you could think of it as DOS on steroids, though a Linux purist will surely cringe at the thought. Sorry.

Although you can use Linux by itself, accomplishing all your tasks by typing commands on a black screen (the most common way of doing things when Linux is used as a server), you don't have to. It is fair to say that with the advent of the Macintosh and its easy-to-use graphical user interface (GUI, pronounced *goo-ee*) in 1984, users of other operating systems began suffering something akin to GUI envy. They began clamoring for a GUI to call their own. The final result was Windows, which gave DOS a GUI and eased many command-wary users into the Microsoft world.

Similarly, many members of the Linux world felt the need and desire to go graphical. Various GUIs (called *window managers* and *desktop environments*) and a subsystem with which to handle them (somewhat confusingly referred to as the *X Window System*) were developed by the community at large to bring about the change. The graphical desktop environment, GNOME, that is included in your Ubuntu distribution is one example of the fruit of that development.

About the Penguin

You may have been wondering about the penguin in the chapter title, so I might as well explain that now. The penguin was chosen by Linus Torvalds as the Linux mascot, and what has come to be thought of as *the* Linux penguin was designed by Larry Ewing and is named Tux (see Figure 1-1). This explains not only the ornithological references and graphics throughout the book, but also why there are so many penguin icons in Linux distributions and so many programs that include *penguin* or *Tux*, such as TuxRacer, XPenguins, and Pingus. This, combined with the fact that Linux is a revolutionary OS, helps to explain why Linux users are sometimes referred to as *Penguinistas.*

Figure 1-1: Tux, the Linux mascot

Why Should I Use Linux?

People use Linux for different reasons. For many it is a matter of power, stability, multilingual capabilities, or even personal philosophy. However, for others, crass as it may sound, it is a matter of money. Just think for a moment about what it usually costs to get started with an operating system. Go to wherever it is you go to buy software, and take a walk down the aisles. Make a list in your head of all the things you want to buy and how much each costs: an office suite; a game or two; maybe a graphics program with which to make yourself look better in your digital photos; and a collection of all those firewall, antispam, antivirus, and anti-adware programs that you really need to protect yourself in the Windows world. Now do the math.

After you pick yourself up off the floor, you will understand that we are talking big bucks here. On the other hand, for the price of this book you will have all of the things you wanted and more in the Linux world. Despite the worries that many people have, making the move to Linux means not only savings for you, but also more computing versatility. You will not be hamstrung at some point along the way because you don't have this or that program when you need it most—you'll have it all from the get-go, or else be able to download it easily . . . and at no cost!

You might counter with the fact that there are a lot of freeware applications out there for other operating systems, but c'mon, let's face it—these are often rather limited in terms of their capabilities. The programs with a little more oomph are mostly shareware, and most shareware programs these days are limited in some way, or they only let you use them for a short time unless you are willing to pay for them. Sure, their costs are relatively low, but $25 here and $35 there eventually adds up to a considerable chunk of change. There is also the problem that some of these programs, unbeknownst to you, install backdoors, or keyloggers, or make your system a sudden garden of adware. Finally, at least in my experience, the majority of such programs are hardly worth the money asked. The only shareware programs I ever found worth buying were Lemke Software's GraphicConverter and Plasq's Comic Life, both for the Mac.

Is It All Just About Money?

While money is important to the average user, it is certainly not the only reason for taking the Linux plunge; there are a variety of other reasons as well. As I mentioned before, Linux is noted for its stability. Try running your present system for a month without restarting and see what happens. Linux has been known to run without a reboot for over a year without a hitch or decrease in performance. With its multilingual capabilities, Linux is also a perfect choice for language students or users in a multilingual environment.

In addition, Linux is infinitely customizable: You can get your system to look and act the way you want it to without being wizarded to death. And then there are the applications that come with most Linux distributions. In addition to their wide variety, most are well up to industry snuff, with some, such as Evolution and the GIMP, being sources of envy for those outside the Linux world.

Finally, with the advent of Microsoft's new Windows Vista system and its more demanding hardware requirements (especially if you want to take advantage of its most touted new features), you may find your present machine on the fast track to obsolescence. Turning it into a Linux machine will ensure it several more years of working life. Shame to put good hardware out to pasture so early, after all.

But Is Linux Really Ready for the Desktop?

Despite the advances Linux has made in recent years, this question still pops up quite often, and that's fair enough. But consider this: When you install a program on your present Windows system and get an error message saying that the program can't run because some DLL file is missing, or when you connect a piece of hardware and can't get it to run, no one asks if that operating system is ready for the desktop.

In my own experience, I have found no reason to doubt that Linux is ready. Sure, Linux has its occasional quirks, but so does every other operating system. Linux is ready and able. If my mother, hardly a computer wiz, can do the work she needs to do and can keep herself amused till the middle of the night using her Linux system (without blowing the whole thing up), then I think it's pretty safe to say that you'll do all right too.

What Is a Distribution?

An operating system consists of a lot of files that perform a lot of different functions. And because there is no Linux corporation to package and distribute the files that make up Linux, the task of getting Linux onto your computer in working order, along with the applications that you are likely to want, has fallen to a varied group of entities—companies, universities, user groups, and even private individuals. These entities create Linux system and application collections called *distributions*, or *distros*. You could bypass such distros and try to collect everything you'd need to set up a system all on your own, but you would undoubtedly lose your mind in the process. Most people, even the geekiest, opt for the distros.

The majority of these distros, whatever their ultimate target audience, basically consist of the same main elements: the core operating system (better known as the *Linux kernel*), some sort of installer program to get all the system parts and applications properly installed on your machine, the X Window System to provide graphical interface support, one or more graphical desktop environments, and a series of applications, such as word processors, audio players, and games, as well as all the files needed to make these things work.

There are, of course, a large number of distros. Some are geared toward specific audiences, such as businesses, educators, gamers, students, programmers, system administrators, and specific language users. What makes each distro different is the specific software that is bundled with the Linux kernel, as well as other convenience features like the package, or application, installation mechanism, and the installer for the system itself. Some distros are especially appropriate for home users due to their ease of installation. Ubuntu, a relative newcomer to the Linux world, is one of these, joining other distros that have long been popular in the ease-of-use arena, such as Mandriva, SUSE, and Fedora Core. There are also many other new distros, like Xandros and Linspire, that are specifically geared toward making the transition for Windows users easier. While many of these entities charge for their distros, most also provide them free for download.

What Is Ubuntu?

Ubuntu is a completely free, easy-to-use, and extremely popular Linux distribution that is geared toward the desktop user. It is one of the hottest Linux distros in the marketplace today. It is also one of the few Linux distros with what could be described as a social agenda behind it.

Ubuntu was the brainchild of South African millionaire entrepreneur Mark Shuttleworth, who is probably better known for being one of the first space tourists—the first African in space, to be exact. Shuttleworth invested over $10 million starting up the Ubuntu Foundation based on his belief in free software and in order to fix what he describes as "bug #1"—Microsoft's dominance of the desktop PC marketplace. As Shuttleworth states in his blog (available at https://wiki.ubuntu.com/MarkShuttleworth):

> I believe that free software brings us into a new era of technology, and holds the promise of universal access to the tools of the digital era. I drive Ubuntu because I would like to see that promise delivered as reality.

As you can see, it's a vision thing.

Befitting the nationality and goals of the man who brought it into being, the word *ubuntu* comes from the Zulu and Xhosa languages. *Ubuntu*, according to Wikipedia, is a concept meaning something along the lines of *humanity toward others* or *I am because we are*. If you're interested, the 2005 film *In My Country*, starring Juliette Binoche and Samuel L. Jackson, although not one of the greatest films ever produced, is on many levels a 100-minute examination of the concept of ubuntu.

Why Ubuntu Then?

With so many distros out there, you may wonder why you should opt for Ubuntu. Well, as they say, numbers don't lie, and Ubuntu's popularity is not without good cause. These traits are especially crowd pleasing:

Easy to install
It's fair to say that most Linux distributions these days are pretty easy to install (and definitely easier and faster to install than Windows). Ubuntu is right in line with these improvements, and the fact that you can install it with only a few mouse clicks while running the live CD means it is pretty much ready to go whenever you are.

Easy to use
Ubuntu is easy to use in that it is very Windows-like in operation, and yet it's more Linux-like than other Windows user–oriented distributions.

DEB based
Ubuntu is based on the *Debian* distribution, which means that it utilizes Debian's very convenient DEB package system for application handling and installation. The two preconfigured, graphical package installers that come with Ubuntu make installing applications even easier. There are so many packages available for Debian systems like Ubuntu that you are likely to find more software out there than you'll ever know what to do with.

Up to date
Some distros are updated at a snail's pace, while others strive to be so cutting edge that they are often plagued with bugs. Ubuntu, with its reasonable six-month release cycle, tries to stay as up to date as possible, while at the same time making sure that things are not released before they are ready for prime time. In this way, you are ensured of having an up-to-date yet less buggy distro at your disposal.

Dependable and robust

I know these terms come across as mere hype, but after you smack Ubuntu around a bit, you come to understand what they mean. Knock things down and around, and they bounce right back—this is very important for beginners who often have a knack for screwing things up. Nothing turns a new user off more than a twitchy system that has to be velvet gloved all the time.

Desktop user–oriented

A lot of Linux distributions, although quite capable in the desktop arena, cater more to geeks and developers, taking up valuable disk space with a lot of junk you'll probably never use. Ubuntu's purpose is to grab desktop market share from the Redmond folks, so the needs of the common end user are always in mind. The result is that Ubuntu's GNOME desktop environment is a very comfy place for the average desktop user to be.

Hardware Compatibility

Well, enough of this background babble; it's time to get things rolling. If you haven't installed Linux on your machine yet and are wondering whether you can, it is relatively safe to say that Ubuntu will run on most machines out there today. Of course, this statement comes with a major caveat: You just never know until you get up and running. There are so many minor parts to your machine that it is difficult to say whether each part will cooperate with your installation. Ignoring minor parts for the time being, there are video cards, sound chips, LAN cards, monitors, and so on, and they all need to be considered.

Diving In

If you are going to buy a new machine on which to run Ubuntu, then it is reasonable enough to do a bit of worrying and check things out first, but if you are going to install it on the machine you have, I recommend just diving in. After all, you don't really have to install anything the first time out. You have a live CD right here in this book, after all, so you can just pop that CD in your drive, boot up your machine, and, *biff, bam, zowie,* you'll be up and running (or not) in a minute or two. If everything seems to be going as it should . . . well, your worries are over, and you can go ahead and install the system when you're ready and willing. That is one of the Ubuntu advantages— not only do all the essentials fit on a single CD (compared to four or more for other distros), but that CD is both a live operating environment and the installer! You can't get much more convenient than that.

When Research Is Required

If things don't work out for you with the live CD, you can search the Web to see if you can identify what part of your hardware puzzle is causing your problems. (Or if you are looking to buy a machine on which to install Ubuntu, you can search for hardware that is supported by Linux.) Of course, before you can do this, you need to know what models of hardware you have. You should know at least what motherboard, central processing unit (CPU), monitor, and video card you have if you want to be able to find out anything of value. Identifying your CPU and monitor should be easy enough, but the motherboard and video card may require a bit more searching.

If you have no documentation that clearly states the make and model of these devices, you can find out most things you need to know from within Windows by going to the Windows Control Panel, double-clicking **System**, and then clicking the **Hardware** tab in that window. Once in the Hardware tab, click the **Device Manager** button, and see what you can find about your system components there. Sometimes the information there is rather limited, so you might instead want to try out a shareware application such as HWiNFO (www.hwinfo.com) or Sandra (www.sisoftware.net) to get more useful details, such as the specifications of your motherboard or the supported video modes for your present setup.

Both HWiNFO and Sandra should give you the information you need about your motherboard, but if they don't (or if you don't feel like bothering with them), you can always just open up the case of your computer and look at your board, though I wouldn't recommend doing so if you've got a laptop. Once inside, you needn't worry about damaging anything because you don't need to touch anything—so don't. You may need a flashlight to find it, but the model name and number should be stamped on there somewhere, either in the middle of the board or around the edges. Mine, for example, says quite clearly in the middle of the board, *AOpen MX46-533V*. You should be looking for similar information.

Once you have all your information, you can do a variety of things to check out your hardware's compatibility with Ubuntu. You can simply do a Yahoo! or Google search by entering your motherboard's make and model plus the word *Linux*. This works for other hardware devices too.

You can also post a question to the Ubuntu User Forums (at www .ubuntuforums.org) or one of the other various Linux forums or mailing lists on the Web. A listing of some of these is provided in Appendix B at the end of this book. Just write that you are a newbie and want to know if anyone has had any experience using Ubuntu with the board (or other hardware) in question. You will probably get quite a few responses. Linux users are usually rather evangelical in terms of trying to draw in new Penguinistas.

Hardware Requirements

All worries about compatibility aside, there are some minimum hardware requirements that you will need to meet:

- Any computer with an i386-based processor, or an Intel or AMD 64-bit processor
- About 4 gigabytes (GB) of hard disk space, though having at least 10GB would be a bit more comfy
- Sufficient memory (RAM)

The CD that comes with this book is designed to work on machines with i386-based processors (basically, all the Pentium chips, including Celeron, Xeon, and the new Core Duo, as well as processors from AMD). Though this CD will install Ubuntu on a computer with an AMD or Intel 64-bit processor, it will only run in 32-bit mode. To make full use of your 64-bit processor, you need to download the 64-bit version of Ubuntu.

As for RAM, the official specs tell you that you need a minimum of 256 megabytes (MB) to run Ubuntu. While you can no doubt get by with this, you'd get by much better with more. My basic rule of thumb, no matter what OS I am dealing with, is that you need the recommended (not the minimum) memory plus at least 128MB. Regardless of what the official specs say, put in more. You won't regret it.

Saying that the more memory you have, the better, may sound a bit simple, and perhaps even cavalier, but trust me on this one. When you have too little memory, no matter what system you are running, weird things happen: Applications seem to take years to open, or don't open at all; menus take forever to render their little icons; freezes and general system meltdowns just happen much more often. In other words, running your machine on too little RAM is sort of like trying to do jumping jacks in a broom closet. Sure, you could do it, but you would be all contorted, and you'd be smashing your hands into the walls every 1.4 seconds.

Fortunately, it is pretty hard to find a machine with less than 512MB of RAM these days (256MB, perhaps, on the really old beasties), but if you do happen to have such a machine, you can at least take solace in the fact that memory is relatively cheap, so go for it.

Good News for AMD64 Users

It is again important to mention that the CD that comes with this book is designed to work on machines with i386-based processors, which pretty much covers the vast majority of PCs out there. If your machine has an AMD64, you will be glad to know that it will also work, albeit not in 64-bit mode. Sorry, but no go.

Fortunately there is good news for those of you who were a bit disappointed by the content of that previous paragraph. Ubuntu is available in a native AMD64 version. Check Appendix A for information on how to get it. The information provided there will also be of use to i386 users who happen to lose or damage the disk that comes with this book.

Mixed News for Mac Users

Those of you with PowerPC Macs may be aware that previous Ubuntu releases have been available in PowerPC versions. Unfortunately, as of the Feisty Fawn release last year, this is no longer the case. This means that if you are a PowerPC Mac user, you will have to use one of the older Ubuntu releases or wait for an unofficial, community-supported release of Hardy Heron (more on that name in the following section) for PowerPCs (http://cdimage.ubuntu.com/ports).

Of course, if you are using one of the new Intel-based Macs, you're in luck because the disk that comes with this book will work on your Mac. After all, the *i* in *i386* stands for *Intel*.

Speaking Ubuntu

It's worth noting that there are a lot of weird phrases you are bound to come across when dealing with Ubuntu, especially when searching for information on the Net. In particular, I am referring to seven seemingly incongruous phrases: *Warty Warthog, Hoary Hedgehog, Breezy Badger, Dapper Drake, Edgy Eft, Feisty Fawn,* and *Gutsy Gibbon.* These are the unlikely code names of each of the releases of Ubuntu since its first appearance in 2004. The important one for you to remember is that of the current release (the one on the disk that comes with this book): *Hardy Heron.*

You are also likely to come across a few other variations of the Ubuntu theme. These are Kubuntu, a KDE-based version of Ubuntu; Edubuntu, a special version of Ubuntu designed for use in the classroom; Xubuntu, a lightweight version of Ubuntu based on the XFCE desktop; and Gobuntu, a new flavor of Ubuntu geared toward more experienced Linux users and open source software purists that contains only 100 percent open source, freely-licensed software.

Where Do I Go from Here?

Now that you know more about the world of Linux and Ubuntu, and you've got your disk in hand, it's time to get down to it. If you have already installed Ubuntu on your machine, just flip ahead to Chapter 3. If your machine is still Linuxless, though, it's time to take it out for a spin and see if you like it. So for now, strap yourself down in front of that computer, clip on your spurs, and go straight to the next chapter. It's time to become a Penguinista!

2

WADING AND DIVING
Running and (If You Like) Installing Ubuntu

As I have already mentioned, one of the great things about Ubuntu is that it comes on a live CD, which means that you can try it out before you install it . . . or never install it at all, if that's what you prefer. Better yet is the fact that, unlike earlier editions of Ubuntu, you don't need an additional installation CD if you do choose to install it—the Ubuntu Desktop CD functions as both a live and an install CD. And while in the good-better-best swing of things, the best point of all is that installation from the live CD is actually much, much easier than any other installation process you've ever dealt with, and, in fact, it gives you more than one way to go about it.

In this chapter, I will be covering the basics of starting up and running Ubuntu from the live CD, and then, assuming you've caught the Linux bug, the painless steps of installing Ubuntu on your hard disk as your sole operating system, in its own partition on your hard disk in a traditional dual-boot setup (with Windows in its own partition), or, for the slightly less adventurous, from within your Windows system. Whatever way you end up going about things, let's put this book to use and get Ubuntu up and running. . . .

Going in for a Dip

To get a taste of what Ubuntu is all about (and to check out your hardware to see if it's all comfy-cozy with Ubuntu), there is probably no better way to go than to run Ubuntu directly from the live CD. To do this, just place the Ubuntu Desktop CD in your disk drive and restart your machine. When the machine starts up again, it should boot up from the CD, and after a second or two, you should see the first Ubuntu startup screen, obscured by language selection menus. If the screen does not appear, and your machine instead boots up into your usual operating system, then it is very likely that your machine's BIOS needs to be changed so as to allow you to boot from CD.

You can access your machine's BIOS by restarting and then pressing whatever key the onscreen startup instructions assign to accessing the BIOS setup. This is usually DELETE or F1, but not all machines are the same. If the onscreen information passes by so fast that you miss it, you can check your user's manual to see what the correct key is. Once you get into the BIOS setup, change the boot sequence so that your CD drive is first.

Once your machine boots from the live CD, and you see the Ubuntu live session startup screen and language menus, either press ENTER to select the default of English for your session language, or use the arrow keys to select the language you want and then press ENTER. The language menu will disappear, and you will have an unobscured view of the startup screen. Press ENTER or just do nothing for about 30 seconds in order to start a live session . . . and remember, your hard disk will go untouched, so rest easy—you're not going to change, let alone hurt, anything.

If you would like to change the default keyboard layout, press F3, select your layout of choice using the cursor keys, and then press ENTER. Once you're done, press ENTER to start up the system.

NOTE *Special input mechanisms required for typing in certain languages (i.e., Chinese, Japanese, and Korean) are not supported in live CD sessions.*

From then on out, it is strictly autopilot time for you—all you have to do is wait. There will be some scrolling white text now and then, and an occasional period when things will go black for a few seconds, but eventually things will go totally graphical when the GNOME desktop environment begins its initialization process, and when that is done . . . well, you will be face to face with the Ubuntu desktop, meaning you're ready to roll—but I'll hold off on talking about that until Chapter 3.

Choices, Choices, Choices—Installation Options

If you have already installed Ubuntu on your machine, are satisfied running it from the live CD, or still haven't made up your mind what to do, you can skip the rest of this chapter and go on to the next one to get started working with the Ubuntu desktop. If, however, you haven't installed Ubuntu yet and are ready and raring to do so, then you had better stay right where you are and read on.

Going out for a Swim—Installing Ubuntu Inside Windows (the Wubi Installer)

It used to be that if you enjoyed Ubuntu enough to want to run it off your hard disk but were afraid to do it for fear of damaging the delicate state of your Windows setup, you were . . . well, out of luck. Things have changed, however, because there is now a new installation option called *Wubi* that lets you install Ubuntu directly on your Windows C: drive as if it were any other Windows program. Once installed, every time you start up your machine you will be able to choose between starting up into Windows or into Ubuntu from the Windows bootloader. Your Windows system stays as it is, you don't have to partition your hard disk, and if you want to get rid of Ubuntu later on for whatever reason, you can do so like you would with any other Windows application. It's a great way to go about things for the faint of heart.

Admittedly, this approach could be described as a half measure, in that it doesn't really give you the full head of steam you would normally get from a dedicated Ubuntu installation. But it is a pretty good compromise—it's definitely quicker and is much, much more useable and enjoyable than an Ubuntu live CD session. You also have the added benefit of being able to save files and settings to disk, which means you can follow along with anything described in this book. Pretty cool.

If this alternative installation approach doesn't seem appealing to you, move on to "Taking the Full Plunge—Installing Ubuntu Outside of Windows" on page 23. If you haven't made up your mind yet and would like to know a bit more about this Wubi installer, point your browser to http://wubi-installer.org. If, on the other hand, you've decided that the Wubi installer is the answer to your prayers, here's what you need to do:

1. Insert the Ubuntu live CD that comes with this book into your computer's disk drive while Windows is up and running. A window like the one in Figure 2-1 will automatically appear.

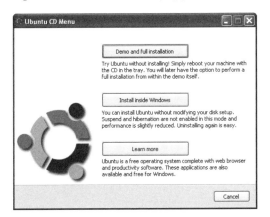

Figure 2-1: An Ubuntu live CD automatically launched in Windows

2. In that window, click the **Install inside Windows** button.

3. In the Ubuntu Setup Window that then appears (Figure 2-2), choose a username and a password for use within Ubuntu, and then click the **Install** button.

Figure 2-2: Choosing to install Ubuntu inside Windows

4. If your machine is not already connected to the Internet at this point, you will be told to get it connected. Do so if you need to, and click the **Retry** button if the warning window appears.

   At this point, Ubuntu will begin downloading the files it needs in order to create a bootable disk image within your Windows environment. Depending on your connection speed, this could take some time.

   After all is done, you will see a window like the one in Figure 2-3 asking you to reboot.

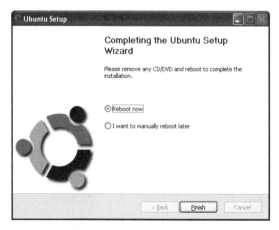

Figure 2-3: Ubuntu has completed the first phase of its inside-Windows installation.

5. Click the **Finish** button in that window, after which your machine will begin to reboot.

6. When the machine restarts, you will see the Windows bootloader, a black screen with white text, which allows you to decide whether to boot up in Windows or in Ubuntu. Use your down arrow key to select **Ubuntu**, and then press ENTER.

Your machine will then begin the Ubuntu startup process, which should be new territory for you. Once the Ubuntu desktop (or parts thereof) appears, Ubuntu will get to work setting things up for you, which might take a bit of time, depending on the speed of your machine. When it is done, you will be delivered to the login screen (Figure 3-1). When that happens, you can stay in Chapter 3, because you are done here.

Uninstalling Ubuntu when Installed Inside of Windows

If you decide that you do not want to keep Ubuntu on your machine, you can remove it from within Windows by going to the Windows Control Panel, selecting **Add or Remove Programs**, and then selecting **Wubi** for removal.

Taking the Full Plunge—Installing Ubuntu Outside of Windows

If you don't already have Windows installed on your machine, you can skip right over this section. If, on the other hand, you do, then you are going to have to decide whether or not you want to keep it.

It is possible to have both Windows and Linux installed on the same machine and for them to happily coexist. This is known as a *dual-boot setup*. It has also become incredibly easy to set up such a system. I started out with a dual-boot setup; however, I eventually found that I used the Linux side of things exclusively. Having so much disk space being taken up by a Windows system I didn't use seemed a waste of prime real estate, so eventually I just dumped the whole thing and went for a straight Linux-only setup. My feeling is that unless there is some application that you really need that is not available on the Linux side (probably some game), then go for the Linux-only setup and just forget about Windows. Linux has most of what you will need anyway, and because the applications in the OpenOffice.org office suite can read and write Microsoft Office files, you'll still be able to collaborate with Windows users, if that is of concern to you.

You may be thinking that if you do as I suggest and dump your Windows system when you install Linux, you might have to reinstall Windows if you don't like Linux or if you can't get it installed properly. That would be a considerable waste of time and energy, to be sure. However, believe it or not, there are advantages to my suggestion even if your no-go scenario turns out to be the case.

You may have noticed that your Windows system, as you've used it over time, has gotten sort of gunked up—it is no longer the quick little kitten it used to be. Menus don't pop open as quickly as they used to, things take longer to start up than they did before, and you find yourself asking, "What the Sam Habberdack is that?!" all the time as mysterious things happen with increasing frequency.

This is just the nature of the beast, and a very good way of getting things back to normal is to reinstall the whole thing. So even if you do decide to come back to Windows later, you'll be doing yourself a favor, because it should run better than before. It's a little more work up front, but in the long run, you'll be a happier camper.

If, on the other hand, you opt for a dual-boot setup, from which you can run both Windows and Linux, you will have the best of both worlds. Starting up in either system is easy. When you start up your machine, you will be greeted by the GRand Unified Bootloader (better known as GRUB) screen, from which you can choose to continue booting up Linux or choose Windows in its stead. After that, bootup proceeds as normal for the system you selected. This setup works fine, so you needn't worry.

So as you see, either way you decide to go, you can't really go wrong. Just be sure to back up your important files before starting the installation; proceed with common sense, patience, and a positive attitude; and you'll be fine. In short: Don't worry.

Getting Ready for Action

There is less you need to do to prepare for an Ubuntu installation than for many other Linux distributions. Once you've decided whether or not you want to go the dual-boot route, all you really need to have on hand is your single Ubuntu Desktop disk and, for guidance and security, this book. The only mental energy you'll probably need to expend is to come up with a username and user password, just as you do for most other operating systems.

Usernames and User Passwords

Your username is something that you will be using quite a bit. You will input it every time you boot up your system, so be sure it is something you can live with, especially in terms of typing. It can be just your first name, or your initials, or whatever you want it to be. It must, however, begin with a lowercase letter, followed by numbers and/or other lowercase letters. Mine, for example, is simply *rg*, but you could use something like *hope4u2pal*, though that would get rather tiring to type at login day after day. Think of your fingers when deciding upon your username.

You also need to come up with a user password, which you will also need to type every time you log in. You will need to use it when you install new software or change certain system settings, as well. It should be a minimum of eight characters in length and consist of numbers and letters (upper- and lowercase) for improved security. You can, of course, get by with fewer characters and only letters if you prefer. The installer will advise you if the password you enter is unacceptable, so don't worry too much. Be sure to write it down and keep the paper you've written it on in a safe place so you don't end up locking yourself out of your system.

If you have experience working with other Linux distributions, you may be surprised to learn that the root account is disabled by default in Ubuntu. There is, therefore, no installation step for inputting a root password. You can check the Forums (http://ubuntuforums.org) to learn ways of getting around this setup. You can also set up a root password later at any time after the system is installed, so if having a root account is of importance to you, don't worry.

Dual-Booters Take Note

If you are going to be creating a dual-boot setup, it is a good idea to first defragment your present Windows disk before moving on to installing Ubuntu. This will make the repartitioning phase of the installation process must faster and safer.

If you are using Windows Vista, your system is set up by default to automatically defragment your hard disk on a regular basis, so you should be good to go without any additional effort on your part. On other versions of Windows, however, you'll have to defragment your disk manually. In Windows XP, you can do this by double-clicking **My Computer**, right-clicking the icon for your hard disk, and selecting **Properties**. You can then defragment your hard disk by clicking the **Tools** tab in the Properties window and clicking the **Defragment Now** button. In Windows 2000, you can do this by going to the **Start** menu and selecting **Control Panel ▶ Administrative Tools ▶ Computer Management ▶ Disk Defragmenter**, while in Windows 98 and some other versions, you can do the same by selecting **Programs ▶ Accessories ▶ System Tools ▶ Disk Defragmenter**.

Doing the Deed

Well, now that we've covered all that prelim stuff, let's get down to the actual Linux installation. Set this book on your lap so you can follow along, and then get ready for action. It's time to do the deed!

Fortunately for you, the installation process is extremely easy, as there are very few steps in which you actually have to do anything. Most of what you will be doing is clicking buttons on your screen. Nothing hard about that, eh?

Of course, when you look at the directions and descriptions listed here, it may look like a long and cumbersome process. It is not. It will be over more quickly than you can imagine. As a beginner frequently referring to this text, you might take a bit longer, of course, but don't worry. All in all, the whole process is faster and easier than that for Windows or Mac OS X. And keep in mind that with Windows and OS X, you are installing the operating system with just a few bundled applications. In an Ubuntu installation, on the other hand, you are installing not only the operating system itself, but also most of the applications you will ever want or need to use. You will thus be getting a lot done in one fell swoop.

One more thing before we start. Some people approach installing a system with a good deal of trepidation. The process makes them nervous, as if the house is going to go up in smoke if they click the wrong thing somewhere along the line. Needless to say, there is no need for such concern. As long as you have backed up your data, you will be okay. If you screw up the installation the first time out, so what? Just start over again. No harm done, as you have nothing to harm. Just make sure that you give yourself more time than you need for the process. Don't start installing one hour before you have to be at work or before you have to meet your friend downtown. Rushing makes people do weird things. Make things easy on yourself by giving yourself plenty of time and, as I mentioned before, by backing up any data you would mourn the loss of.

If you're ready, here are the steps:

1. **Start 'er up**   If you haven't already done so, boot up your machine from the Ubuntu Desktop CD.

2. **Start the installation**   Double-click the **Install** icon on the Ubuntu live desktop to start the installation. This will bring up the first page of the installation wizard (Figure 2-4).

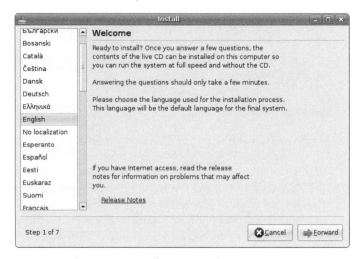

Figure 2-4: The opening installation wizard screen

3. **Welcome (choose language)**   Choose the language you want to use during and after the installation process, and then click the **Forward** button. No matter what language you choose, you will always have the option of booting up in English once the system is installed. You can also add support for other languages later.

4. **Where are you? (choose location)**   The Ubuntu installer will select the default location for the installation language you have chosen. If your location is different, select the one appropriate for you by clicking directly on the wizard map (Figure 2-5). Once your selection is made, click **Forward**.

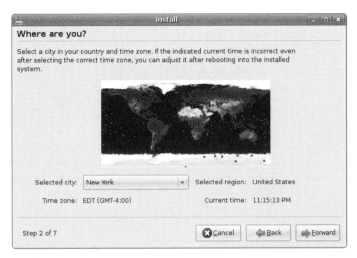

Figure 2-5: Choosing your geographic location in the Ubuntu installation wizard

5. **Keyboard layout**   The default keyboard layout for the installation language you have chosen will appear in the next wizard screen. If your keyboard layout is different, make the appropriate choice from the location list in the left pane of the screen, and then choose from among the available layouts for that location in the right pane. If you're not sure you've made the right choice, you can double-check by typing a few words in the text box at the bottom of the window. Once you've done this, click **Forward**. If need be, you can add other keyboard layouts later, after the system is installed.

6. **Prepare disk space**   What you do at this point depends on what you have on your machine. Assuming you have an operating system on the disk already, such as Windows, accept the uppermost option (selected by default). This will reduce the size of your Windows (or other OS) installation to allow for installation of Ubuntu in a new partition. By default, the partitioner will use the minimum amount of space necessary to install Ubuntu, but you will no doubt want a bit more so as to give yourself room to grow and store files. To create a bigger partition for Ubuntu, drag the small space between the two partitions until you come up with a combination that you think will work for you (Figure 2-6). Once done, click the **Forward** button.

    If you have no operating system on your hard disk, or if you intend to eliminate what you currently have and replace it with Ubuntu, you should instead choose the second option, **Guided – use entire disk**, and then, if given a choice, select the main drive onto which you want to install the system. Once your selection is made, click **Forward**.

    Whatever partitioning scheme you choose, once you've clicked the Forward button, a small window will appear reminding you that any changes you've made thus far will now be written to disk.

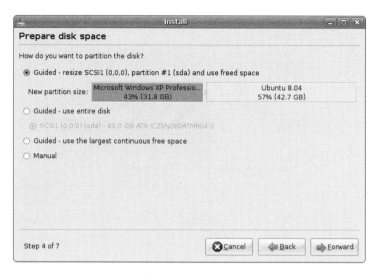

Figure 2-6: Partitioning your hard disk (or not)

7. Click the **Continue** button to continue, keeping in mind that this is the point of no return. After that, wait for the partitioner to do its stuff (depending on the size of your disk and what you've got on it, this could take some time).

8. **Who are you?** On the next page of the installation wizard, you are asked to provide your real name, your login name, and a password. The wizard will automatically generate a name for your computer based on your username (*rg-laptop* in my case), but you are free to change this to something else if you like (I changed mine to *Ubuntu-Acer*). Once all of the fields are filled in, as mine are in Figure 2-7, click **Forward**.

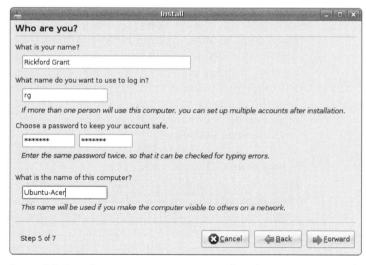

Figure 2-7: Providing your username, password, and computer name in the installation wizard

9. **Migrate Documents and Settings**   If your machine already has another operating system on it and you are setting up a dual-boot system, the installer will scan your hard disk to try to find certain settings, folders, and documents that it can transfer over to your new Ubuntu system environment. In the window like the one shown in Figure 2-8, just check the boxes next to the items you want to transfer, and then click **Forward**.

Figure 2-8: The Ubuntu installer helps you carry things over from your Windows partition.

10. **Ready to install**   The final page of the wizard (Figure 2-9) lists the details of your soon-to-be installed system and hard disk partition setup, along with a point-of-no-return warning. You've come this far, so you might as well go for it, even though there's no turning back. Click **Install**.

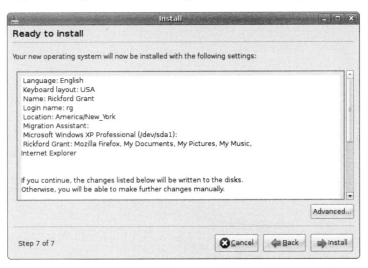

Figure 2-9: Ready to install—the final page of the installation wizard

The partitioner will then do whatever writing to disk it must in order to finish the partitioning process, after which the installation itself will seamlessly begin, without any additional input necessary from you or anyone else. The progress of the installation will be indicated in progress windows so that you don't have to fret (and so you'll know how much more time you have left to veg in front of the TV).

11. **Installation complete**   When you've come to the end of the first phase of the installation, you will be notified in a new window. You are given the option of either continuing to use the live CD or restarting the machine and running Ubuntu directly from your hard disk. Well, you didn't go through all of this just to keep using the live CD, so let's go for the second option by clicking the **Restart now** button, removing the live CD from your drive when it is automatically ejected, and pressing ENTER when prompted on screen to do so. Your machine will then restart.

After that . . . well, that's basically it. You now have Ubuntu installed on your machine. Congratulations. After a few moments, you will see the login screen, so to find out what to do then, go on to the next chapter. See you there. Aloha.

3

A NEW PLACE TO CALL HOME

Getting to Know the Desktop

Now Ubuntu is up and running, and you are ready and raring to go. If you are running Ubuntu from your hard disk, you will first see the login screen that will appear each and every time you boot up (Figure 3-1). There's no need to keep the login screen waiting, so type your username, and press ENTER. After that, you will be prompted for your user password in the same screen, so type it, and press ENTER again. Within moments, you will be face to face with your desktop in Ubuntu.

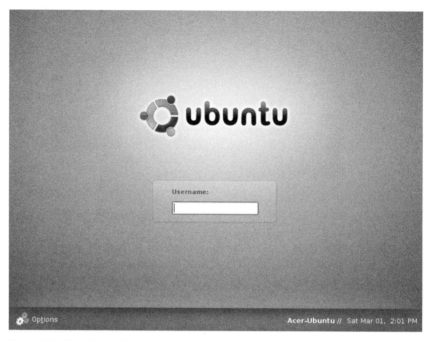

Figure 3-1: The Ubuntu login screen

Welcome to the GNOME Desktop

Ubuntu's implementation of the GNOME desktop is shown in Figure 3-2, and as you can see, it isn't all that different from what you might be used to in a Windows or Mac OS 9 environment, other than the fact that it has task-bars, or *panels*, at both the top and the bottom of the screen. There are also no desktop icons, except when running a live session from the Desktop CD, in which case you'll see a launcher to run the installation wizard (labeled Install). All in all, it is a very uncluttered place to be, and despite its super-ficial similarities to other OS desktop environments, things in the GNOME are different enough to be interesting.

The main elements of the GNOME desktop are the panels at the top and bottom of the screen and the icons that appear upon those panels. The desktop itself, although empty at startup, does see its share of action, but I'll come to that later. For now, I'll focus on the two panels.

The Top Panel

Of the two GNOME Panels on your desktop, the top panel is basically where all the action is. As you can see, there are three menus and a few icons at the left end of the panel, and a number of odds and ends at the other end (Figure 3-3). So that you understand what each of the panel items does, I will now briefly describe each of them, moving from left to right, as seems to be the fashion these days.

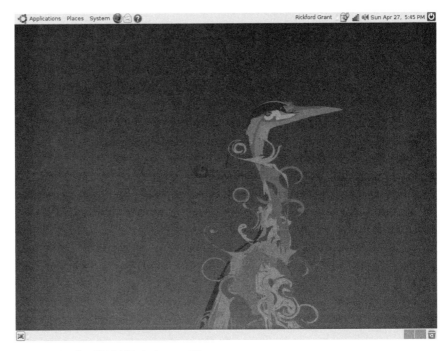

Figure 3-2: The GNOME desktop in Ubuntu

The Left End

At the far left of the top panel, you will find a set of three menus. These provide access to most of what your system has to offer in terms of applications, locations, and utilities. These include:

Applications menu   The access point to the majority of your applications, a software manager, and some system tools.

Places menu   Your system navigator, from which you can access your home folder, browse your computer's filesystem and connected networks, and search for files on your hard disk.

System menu   The access point for your system preferences, software installer, and administration tools. This is also the place to go when you want to shut down or log out of your system.

Figure 3-3: The left and right sides of the top GNOME Panel

Immediately to the right of the three menus are a set of three launchers. When these icons are clicked, they launch the following applications:

Firefox Your web browser

Evolution Mail The very popular Linux email program, scheduler, and task manager

Help Access to the Ubuntu help files installed on your hard disk

The Right End

At the right side of the top panel are a series of icons that perform a variety of functions. Some of these are indicators, while some are applets that allow you to perform certain functions. These consist of:

Fast User Switch Applet Shows you the name of the current user and allows you to quickly switch to other user accounts you have set up on your machine.

Update Notification Tool Tells you when there are system or application updates and allows you to download and install the updates. Only appears when updates are available.

Bluetooth Manager As the name implies. Only appears on machines with Bluetooth capabilities.

Network Manager Applet Lets you see your network status and configure your network devices. When used with a wireless network connection, indicates the wireless signal's strength and allows you to switch between wireless networks easily.

Volume Control A volume controller. Duh.

Calendar/Clock Date and time, as always, but now with weather information and other cool features.

Quit Brings you to the logout screen, from which you can log out, shut down, restart, or switch users.

The Bottom Panel

The bottom panel, as you can see in Figure 3-4, is a much simpler affair, containing only the four items I will now briefly describe.

Show Desktop A button that minimizes all open windows and allows you to see your desktop when it is obscured from view.

Window List A list of windows or applications you have open, which is very similar to what happens in the Windows taskbar.

Workspace Switcher   An application that allows you to switch between virtual desktops. (I'll talk about this more in "Virtual Desktops" on page 45.)

Trash   There is nothing mysterious about Trash . . . other than its rather Mac OS X–ish location on the panel.

Figure 3-4: The bottom GNOME Panel

Project 3A: Customizing the GNOME Panel

The GNOME Panel is not a static thing. You can add *launchers* (respectively known as *program shortcuts* or *aliases* to Windows and Mac users), utilities, and even amusements to make it do almost anything you want it to—within limits, of course. In the various stages of this project, you will customize your panel to get some hands-on experience working with it and to make things more convenient for you as you make your way through the rest of this book. You are, of course, free to change any of the customizations I ask you to make (though you won't have a say in the matter if you're working in a live session from the desktop CD, as you won't be able to save your settings).

Each of the following subprojects is very simple. Most are only three-step, point-and-click procedures that you should be able to handle without any difficulty.

3A-1: Adding Utility Buttons to the Panel

The GNOME Panel allows you to add a number of utility applications, known as *applets*. Each of these has some specific function, such as tracking your stocks, telling you the weather, or performing some particular system-related function. To start out, let's add a clearly useful utility to the top panel: the Force Quit button. The Force Quit button lets you quickly and easily deal with non-responding windows.

Yes, it does happen on occasion: A window suddenly refuses to do anything. Regardless of what you want it to do or what it is supposed to be doing, it just sits there as if it is on strike (maybe it is). With just one click of the Force Quit button, your cursor becomes a powerful surgical instrument that will kill the window you click. You definitely don't want to be without this button, so here's how to add it to the panel:

1. Right-click any open space on the top panel.

2. From the popup menu, select **Add to Panel**, after which the Add to Panel window will appear.

3. In that window, click **Force Quit** once to highlight it, as I've done in Figure 3-5. Click the **Add** button, and then click **Close** to finish the job.

Figure 3-5: Adding launchers and utility applets to the GNOME Panel

To reinforce what you've just learned how to do, let's add another utility to the panel: the Run Application panel applet. Once you start installing applications in Ubuntu, you will find that some of those applications do not automatically install program launchers in your Applications menu. This means that you have to open a Terminal window and type a command every time you want to run such programs, which can get old rather fast. The Run Application panel applet is one way around this problem.

To add the Run Application applet to the panel, just follow the same steps you used in adding the Force Quit button; but this time in step 3, highlight **Run Application** in the Add Launcher window instead of Force Quit.

NOTE *If you later decide not to keep the Run Application panel applet on the panel, or if you just prefer keyboard shortcuts to pointing and clicking, it is worth noting that you can also bring up the applet by pressing ALT-F2.*

3A-2: Adding Amusing Applets to the Panel

The GNOME Panel not only allows you to add very functional utilities, but it allows you to add quite seemingly useless amusements as well. In this part of the project, we will be adding two such amusements: Eyes and a little fish called Wanda.

At first glance, Wanda does little more than bat her tail around and spurt out a bubble or two. However, if you click on her, a window pops up in which Wanda will spew out quotes and offbeat one-liners.

To get a glimpse of Wanda in action, limited though that action may be, the steps are essentially the same as those in Project 3A-1 on page 35, but I'll run through them one more time:

1. Right-click any open space on the top panel.
2. From the popup menu, select **Add to Panel**, after which the Add to Panel window will appear.
3. In that window, click **Fish** once to highlight it, click the **Add** button, and then click **Close**.

Wanda will now appear on your panel, so go ahead and give her a click to see what she has to say.

Now you can add Eyes, which is a pair of eyes that follows your mouse cursor around as it moves about your desktop. Follow the same procedure, but click **Eyes** instead of Fish in step 3.

3A-3: Adding a Program Launcher to the Panel

Now let's move on to something a bit more practical—adding program launchers to the panel. While it is very easy to run an application by navigating through the Applications menu, there are no doubt some applications that you will be using frequently enough to want easy access to them. OpenOffice.org Word Processor (commonly known as *Writer*) is probably one of those.

Method 1

There are a number of different ways to add a launcher to the panel, but let's start with the most conventional. To add a panel launcher for OpenOffice.org Writer, follow these steps:

1. Right-click any open space within the top panel.
2. Select **Add to Panel** in the popup menu to bring up the Add to Panel window.
3. In that window, select **Application Launcher**, and click the **Forward** button that then appears.
4. A new screen will then appear, showing the contents of the Application menu (Figure 3-6). Click the small arrow next to **Office** to expand that menu, and then scroll down and click **OpenOffice.org Word Processor** to highlight it.
5. Click the **Add** button, and then click **Close** to complete the process.

Figure 3-6: Adding an application launcher to the GNOME Panel

Method 2

There is another way to add program launchers to the panel, and it is actually a tad quicker. As an example, we'll add a launcher for the OpenOffice.org spreadsheet program, Calc. Here are the steps:

1. Go to the Applications menu, and navigate your way to and right-click **Office ▸ OpenOffice.org Spreadsheet**.

2. In the popup menu that then appears, select (that's the usual ol' left-click this time) **Add this launcher to panel** (Figure 3-7). The Spreadsheet launcher will then appear in the panel.

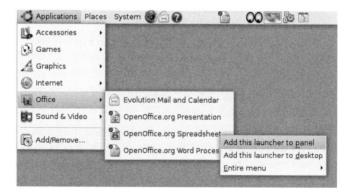

Figure 3-7: Another way to add application launchers to the panel

Method 3

Now that you've learned two ways to add application launchers to the panel, I might as well let you in on a third, even easier method. Just open a menu, select the item you want to add to the panel, and then drag it there. Well, it can't get much easier than that, eh?

3A-4: Changing Panel Launcher Icons

You may feel that your two new program launchers are somewhat plain, and therefore, it is rather difficult to distinguish one from the other. Fortunately, you can change the icon for any launcher quite easily. To learn how to do it, let's address our immediate concerns with the two OpenOffice.org launchers. Here's what we need to do:

1. Right-click the first program launcher you added (the word processor), and select **Properties** from the popup menu.

2. In the Launcher Properties window, click the **OpenOffice.org Word Processor** icon, which will bring up a Browse icons window.

3. In that window, click the **Browse** button to bring up the Browse window.

4. At the top of that window, click the **icons** button. In the right pane, double-click the **hicolor** folder, double-click the **48x48** folder within the hicolor folder, and then select the **apps** folder within the 48x48 folder by clicking it once.

5. When you've finished all that folder clicking, click the **Open** button.

6. You will be back at the Browse icons window, which now displays a different set of icons than you started with. Scroll down in that window until you find **openofficeorg24-writer.png**, and then click it once (Figure 3-8).

Figure 3-8: Selecting a new panel launcher icon

7. Click the **OK** button in that window, which will close it.

8. You will then be back at the Launcher Properties window, which should now look like that in Figure 3-9. If so, click **Close**.

Figure 3-9: A Launcher Properties window

Once you have completed the transformation, follow essentially the same steps for the word processor launcher, but this time around you should select **openofficeorg24-calc.png** as the icon in step 3.

3A-5: Adding a Drawer to the Panel

One of the features I quite like about the GNOME Panel is the drawer. The *drawer* is a little applet that saves on panel space by letting you add drop-down panels, in which you can place launchers that you do not have room to place elsewhere. These drawers are also handy locations to place launchers for applications that you must normally run by typing a command in a Terminal window or via the Launch Application window, such as those you compile yourself from source code or that are run via scripts. You'll learn how to do this in Chapter 9. Of course, you can put anything you want in a drawer, including frequently used files or even whole menus.

Adding a drawer to your panel is very easy, and is basically the same procedure that you used to add the Force Kill button to the panel. Here is all you need to do:

1. Right-click any open space on the top panel.

2. From the popup menu, select **Add to Panel**, after which the Add to Panel window will appear.

3. In that window, click **Drawer** once to highlight it, and then click the **Add** button. Close the window by, quite logically, clicking **Close**.

3A-6: Adding Program Launchers to the Drawer

The drawer you've just added is, of course, empty at this stage, so let's put it to good use by adding launchers for three useful, yet less glamorous, system utilities. These are System Monitor, which allows you to view your computer's running applications and processes, memory and CPU usage, and storage device usage; Terminal, in which you can type and execute commands (slightly geeky, I admit, but very useful); and Synaptic Package Manager, which you can use to download and install applications.

Here's what you need to do:

1. Right-click the **drawer** applet in the panel, and select **Add to Drawer** in the popup menu.

2. In the Add to Drawer window that then appears (and looks and behaves exactly the same as the Add to Panel window), select **Application Launcher**, and then click the **Forward** button that appears.

3. In the next screen, click the small arrow next to **Accessories**, scroll down and click **Terminal** to select it, and then click the **Add** button. The Terminal launcher will now be loaded into the drawer.

4. Next, scroll way down and click the small arrow next to **Administration**.

5. Scroll down within that category until you find **Synaptic Package Manager**, click it to select, and then click **Add**.

6. Finally, add a launcher for the System Monitor by scrolling up to the **System Tools** category, clicking **System Monitor**, and then clicking **Add**. You can now close the Add to Drawer window.

The three launchers should now be loaded in the drawer, so click the drawer to sneak a peek. Yours should look the same as mine in Figure 3-10.

Figure 3-10: Launchers in a GNOME Panel drawer

3A-7: Adding the Entire Contents of a Menu to the Panel

If you find that you use the applications in a particular submenu of your Applications, Places, or System menus a lot, you can opt to add the entire menu to the panel as either a menu or as a drawer in a manner similar to the one you used in Project 3A-3's "Method 2" on page 38. To learn how to do this, let's add the Games submenu to the panel as a menu, and the Sound & Video submenu as a drawer. Here is what you need to do:

1. Add the Games menu to the panel by going to **Applications ▸ Games** and then right-clicking any of the launchers within that submenu.

2. In the popup menu that appears, select **Entire menu ▸ Add this as menu to panel**.

3. Add the Sound & Video submenu to the panel as a drawer by going to **Applications ▸ Sound & Video** and then right-clicking any of the launchers you find there.

4. In the popup menu, select **Entire menu ▸ Add this as drawer to panel**.

You should now have two new launchers on your panel with icons matching those found in the Applications menu next to the relevant items. Click each of these new panel entries to see how they work.

3A-8: Moving Things Around on the Panel

Well, now we've added all we are going to be adding to the panel. It may seem a little messy up there right now, so let's do a bit of housekeeping by moving things around. We will try to group things together somewhat thematically so as to make them easier to deal with.

Fortunately, you can move panel launchers quite easily by right-clicking the launcher in question, selecting Move from the popup menu, and then dragging the launcher to the spot you want to place it. Once the launcher is where you want it to be, click the launcher once, and it will stay there.

To get some practice with this moving business, let's move the launchers, menus, and drawers you added by placing them in the following order, from left to right: Applications, Places, System, Firefox, Mail, Help, OpenOffice.org Writer, OpenOffice.org Calc, Sound & Video, Games, Drawer. Place the remaining launchers at the right end of the panel, to the left of the Fast User Switch Applet, in the following left-to-right order: Eyes, Wanda, Force Quit. Finally, place the Run Application panel applet by itself, midway between the two clusters of launchers. When you've made all your changes, your panel should look pretty much like mine in Figure 3-11.

Figure 3-11: The GNOME Panel with the new launchers

More Panel Fun

In addition to the basic customization you did in Project 3A on page 35, you can do a lot more to change the look and feel of your panel. Of course, you can remove any of your launchers, drawers, or menus by right-clicking the item in question and then selecting **Remove From Panel** in the popup menu, but there are still more options. Most of these are available by right-clicking any open space in the panel and then selecting **Properties**, which will bring up the Panel Properties window.

From this window you can change the position of the panel, alter its size, change its color, or make it transparent—very cool. You can also set the panel so that it will automatically disappear when you are not using it and have it reappear when you bring your mouse cursor into the area where the panel normally resides. Don't feel afraid to play around and give things a try—that's half the fun!

Project 3B: Manipulating Menus

Now that you have learned about some of the cool and useful things you can do with your panel, let's now move on to the topic of menus. A very nice feature of GNOME is that it allows you to edit its menus. You can add launchers, remove items, move items, and even change the icons that appear within the menus. All in all, you have a lot of control over things, but for this project, we'll limit our work to two of these areas: changing icons and moving menu items.

3B-1: Changing Icons Within Menus

As you no doubt recall, one of the problems with the OpenOffice.org Writer and Calc launchers we added to the panel was that they shared rather similar icons. If you go to **Applications ▸ Office**, you will see that the icons for the various OpenOffice.org modules, although not the same, are also a bit similar. To remedy this state of affairs, we will change these icons to the same set we used for the two panel launchers in Project 3A-4. In this case, just follow these steps:

1. Right-click the **Applications** menu and select **Edit Menus**, or go to the **System** menu and select **Preferences ▸ Main Menu**.

2. In the menu editor window that then appears, click **Office** in the left pane. The contents of that menu will then appear in the right pane.

3. In the right pane of the window, right-click **OpenOffice.org Word Processor**, and then select **Properties** in the popup menu. A Launcher Properties window will then appear.

4. In that window, click the **Icon** button. Using the method described in Project 3A-4 on page 39, navigate to /usr/share/icons/hicolor/48x48 in the Browse icons window that then appears.

5. Select the **apps** folder by clicking it once. You can make it easier to add icons for the other OpenOffice.org modules by creating a link to the apps folder; just drag it to the lower portion of the left pane in the same window. Your window should then look like mine in Figure 3-12. Assuming it does, from now on you will be able to navigate directly to this folder by clicking that icon in the left pane.

Figure 3-12: Adding a folder to your list of places

6. Click the **Open** button, which will return you to the Browse icons window.

7. In that window, scroll down to and click **openofficeorg24-writer.png**, and then click **OK**.

8. The new icon should now appear in the Launcher Properties window, though there is sometimes a slight delay. When it does appear, click **Close**, and you will be able to see the change in the menu editor window.

9. Repeat the process for each of the other OpenOffice.org icons, being sure to select the appropriate icons for each of the OpenOffice.org modules (openofficeorg24-impress for the Presentation module, for example). Once you're done, leave the menu editor window open to continue work on Project 3B-2.

3B-2: Changing the Order of Icons Within Menus

While we still have everything open to the Office menu, let's deal with what I consider to be another problem: the order of the items in the menu. It just doesn't make sense to me to have what is arguably the most commonly used office application, your word processor, way down there at the bottom of the menu.

Remedying this situation is easy. Just click the **OpenOffice.org Word Processor** icon in the right pane of the menu editor window. Then click the

Move Up button on the right side of the window as many times as necessary until the Word Processor icon is right there at the top of the list.

While we're being logical and all, why not make things even better by getting the Evolution launcher out of the Office menu, too. After all, there's already a launcher in the Internet menu, which seems a far more natural place for it to be. If you agree and want to hide this instance of Evolution, just uncheck the box next to its name. The name of that entry should then switch to italic typeface, indicating that the item in question will not be visible in the actual drop-down menu. Once you're done, your menu editor window should look something like mine in Figure 3-13. If all seems fine to you, click **Close** and then go to **Applications ▸ Office** to check out the results.

Figure 3-13: Managing menus with the menu editor

Virtual Desktops

It is now time to discuss a rather convenient feature of Linux: *virtual desktops.* While the virtual desktop feature has only recently made its way into Mac OS X and Windows, it has been a Linux feature for years (yes, it started here, folks). But rather than babble on about what this virtual desktop business is and what it can do for you, it is probably best to have you learn about it by giving you some hands-on experience.

In your GNOME Panel, click the **Wanda**, **OpenOffice.org Writer**, and **Firefox** launchers. You will then have three windows open in your present desktop, or workspace. Now look at the Workspace Switcher to the right of the bottom panel. There should be two boxes, with the one on the left (your present workspace) in brown. If you click the other, grayed-out box, all your open windows will suddenly disappear.

Actually, nothing has really disappeared—you are just viewing a new desktop. All your other windows are still open and running in the previous desktop. In this second desktop you can open something else: Go to the **Applications** menu, and select **Games ▶ AisleRiot Solitaire**. The AisleRiot Solitaire card game will soon appear.

You now have windows open in two different desktops, and you can switch back and forth between them. To do so, just go to the Workspace Switcher in your panel and click the first grayed box, which will take you to your original desktop. Once you've done that, the box for the workspace you were just in will gray, and you can then click that one to go back to your game desktop.

As you can imagine, this feature has some potential benefits for you, in addition to helping you avoid clutter. Just imagine that you are at work typing some long document in OpenOffice.org Writer. Eventually, you get tired and decide to goof off a bit by playing a game, such as Mines, for a while. To do this, you switch to another desktop where you open and play the game. A bit later, when you notice your boss making the rounds of the office, you simply switch back to the first desktop so that you look busy when he walks by and asks, "Keeping yourself busy, Boaz?"

Phew!

By the way, you can also switch between virtual desktops by simultaneously pressing and holding CTRL-ALT and then pressing your left and right cursor keys to move to your targeted desktop.

Moving Running Applications Between Virtual Desktops

So what happens if, let's say, you are running OpenOffice.org Writer in one workspace and the GIMP in another, but suddenly think that it would be handy to have them both running in the same workspace? Do you quit the GIMP and start it up again in the other desktop? Fortunately, things are much simpler than that, and there are actually two ways to get the job done.

The first of these ways is to right-click the title bar of the window you want to move, and then select **Move to Workspace Left** or **Move to Workspace Right**. If you've changed the Workspace Switcher preferences so that you have four or more workspaces (right-click the switcher, and select Preferences), you'll be able to select Move to Another Workspace and then select the workspace you want to move the window to by number: Workspace 1, Workspace 2, and so on.

If you prefer keeping your hands more on your keyboard than on your mouse, you can also move a window from workspace to workspace by using hotkeys. With the window you want to move active (on top of the pile, so to speak), press and hold SHIFT-CTRL-ALT, and then use the left and right cursor keys to move the window to the desired desktop.

Wanda Revisited—GNOME Easter Eggs

Well, now that we've finished with our work in this chapter, it's time to goof around a bit by revisiting our precocious piscean pal, Wanda. Knowing what you now do about Wanda the Fish, you might find it odd for me to start talking about her again, but Wanda has a few more tricks beneath her fins. In fact, she is a good means by which to introduce two of GNOME's most famous Easter eggs. *Easter eggs*, in case you don't know, are hidden snippets of code that programmers seem to love to sneak into their programs. They are usually pretty useless things, but they can be found in all operating systems, numerous applications, and even on DVDs (to find out more about those, go to www.dvdeastereggs.com).

A good example of an Easter egg is my first encounter with one on my first Mac, an ancient Mac SE with a whopping 2MB of RAM. On that machine, you could bring up an image (or was it a slideshow?) of the Mac SE development team by pressing the seldom used debug key on the side of the machine and then typing G 41D89A. Pretty cool, I guess, but I would never ever have stumbled upon it had I not read about it in some magazine.

As my example shows, accessing these Easter eggs usually requires some unusual maneuvers, ones that you would never perform in the normal course of things. To see a Wanda-related Easter egg in action, click the **Run Application** button you just added to the panel, type **gegls from outer space** in the Command box, and then click **Run**. You will then see an odd little game of the Space Invaders genre, shown in Figure 3-14, in which Wanda defends our beloved planet from . . . well, gegls, I guess.

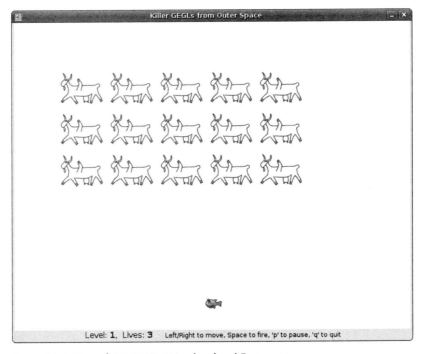

Figure 3-14: One of GNOME's Wanda-related Easter eggs

To try out the other Wanda Easter egg, open the Run Application panel applet again, but this time type `free the fish`, and then click **Run**. Wanda will now appear swimming around your desktop. If you then click directly on her, she will swim away and out of the picture . . . but she'll be back.

To put an end to Wanda's comings and goings, you will need to restart the GNOME Panel. There several rather inelegant ways of going about this, but for now we'll do it by opening the Run Application panel applet again, typing `killall gnome-panel`, and then clicking **Run**. Your panels will disappear for a second or two but will shortly reappear. Wanda, however, will be gone.

Shutting Down

Now that you know your desktop environment so well, you may feel like calling it a day and shutting down your machine. To do so, just go to the **System** menu and select **Quit**, or click the **Quit** button at the far-right corner of the top Panel. Your screen will darken, and then a small window (Figure 3-15) will appear with seven choices to choose from: Log Out, Lock Screen, Switch User, Suspend, Hibernate, Restart, and Shut Down (Hibernate is not an option when running a live session from the Desktop CD). Click **Shut Down**, and the shutdown process will begin. If, however, nothing seems to happen within a few seconds of clicking **OK**, press CTRL-ALT-BACKSPACE in unison, which will bring you to the login screen you saw at the beginning of the chapter (Figure 3-1). Once there, click **Shut Down** at the bottom of the screen. This will bring up a small window asking you if you are sure you want to shut down. Just click **OK**, and shutdown will commence.

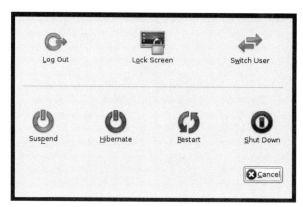

Figure 3-15: GNOME's logout window

The actual shutdown will take a few seconds as the system closes its various services. When it is all done, the system should power down your computer as well, in which case you are done. On a few machines, however, the system cannot power down your machine. You will know if this is so in your case because all screen activity will come to an end. If you get to that point and nothing else happens for 15 seconds or so, then just power down the machine manually by pressing the power button. It is completely safe to do so at that point.

4

MORE THAN WEBBED FEET

The Internet, Linux Style

These days, average home computer users spend more time surfing the Web and writing email messages than doing just about anything else. Even if you're not much of a surfer, there are still numerous other applications that aren't really Internet applications per se but that still make use of the Internet in some way, such as gathering song and album information when you rip audio CDs to create MP3 files. Having a computer that isn't hooked up to the Internet is like buying a new Maserati and then refusing to take it out of the garage.

Of course, how you connect to the Internet depends on your hardware and provider. There are a number of possibilities in this area, including high-speed local area networks (LANs), cable modems, and ADSL connections from phone companies. Most computers also have an internal 56Kb/s modem or can be connected to external dial-up modems for slower connections over regular phone lines. Depending on what you've got, setting things up on your system should prove a cinch in the case of LAN connections and any others that make use of your Ethernet port (such as cable modems), possibly a bit more work in the case of wireless connections, and sometimes a bit of a challenge when it comes to the ol' dial-up connections. In this chapter, you will learn how to set up these connections and learn a bit about what Linux has to offer in terms of the most commonly used Internet applications—your web browser and email client.

Setting Up a High-Speed Connection

If you have a high-speed Internet connection from your cable television company, or if you are connected to the Internet by a LAN at your office, you are really in luck, because these setups are probably the easiest to deal with. Most likely, all you have to do is connect the Ethernet cable from the wall (if you are using a LAN) or from your cable modem to the port of the network card on your machine. If you're using a wireless router, then the Ethernet cable will connect to the wide area network (WAN) port of your wireless router from the wall or modem. After that, once you start up your machine, you should be ready to go without any further settings to fool with.

If you like, you can see if you're connected by opening Firefox (click your Firefox launcher in the top menu, right next to the System menu), and then once it starts up, trying to navigate to a common site, such as www.yahoo.com. If the site comes up, you know you're all set.

If you have a problem getting online, and you are trying to connect via a LAN or cable modem, you could try to release and restore your connection by right-clicking the Network Manager applet in the top panel, unchecking the box next to the words *Enable Networking* in the popup menu, waiting a few seconds, and then checking the *Enable Networking* box in the popup menu again. If that doesn't work, try restarting your machine while physically connected to your Internet source. If the lack of connectivity persists, it is possible that your network card is not supported by Linux. This is relatively rare, but fortunately, easily remedied (by replacing it).

The problem could also be that your network or service provider does not automatically assign addresses via Dynamic Host Configuration Protocol (DHCP). *DHCP* is a means by which your Internet provider can automatically (dynamically) provide your system with the configuration information it needs in order to connect to the Internet. If your provider does not utilize DHCP, you will have to get the necessary information about settings from the network administrator or service provider and enter the settings yourself.

Setting Up a Cable or Ethernet Connection for Providers Not Utilizing DHCP

To input your cable or Ethernet settings yourself, first get the settings you need from your network administrator or Internet provider, and then perform the following steps:

1. From the **System** menu, select **Administration ▸ Network**.
2. The Network Settings window will now appear but will be mostly grayed out, meaning that you cannot alter the settings within it. Click the **Unlock** button to change this.

3. You will be prompted for your password at this point, so type it (that would simply be your user password), and click **Authenticate**.

NOTE *If you do not provide your password and click the Authenticate button soon after being asked for it, you will receive an error message saying that the system was unable to authenticate. If this happens, close the authentication window, and click the Unlock button again.*

4. You will now be able to alter the settings found within the Network Settings window (shown in Figure 4-1). Select **Wired connection** by clicking it once. Once you're done, click the **Properties** button.

Figure 4-1: The Network Settings window

5. In the Properties window that appears, uncheck the box next to the words *Enable roaming mode*. Change the Configuration selection to **Static IP address**.

6. Enter the information from your Internet provider or network administrator in the three text boxes shown in Figure 4-2. Once you've entered the settings, click the **OK** button.

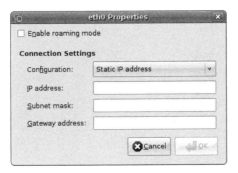

Figure 4-2: Manually inputting network IP settings

7. Your system will then try to connect to the Internet using the settings you have provided. Once the connection is made, you can close the Network Settings window and surf to your heart's content.

NOTE   *If you are wondering what Internet protocol (IP) and domain name service (DNS) are all about, you can simply think of them in this way: The DNS translates the easy-to-remember URLs that you have come to know, such as www.google.com, into numerical, or IP, addresses that the Internet can understand. The address http://www.google.com thus becomes http://209.85.165.99. You can type the numerical version into your browser later to see for yourself.*

Setting Up a Wireless Connection

Laptops have made the computer a more versatile tool. With the right wireless hardware, you can now surf the Web just about anywhere you can catch a wave, so to speak. Whether you happen to be at your breakfast table, on your backyard deck, in the library of your university, or at your local Starbucks, Port City Java, or Dunkin' Donuts, you can now go online without having to physically hook up your computer to anything. Fortunately, the process of setting up wireless networking in Ubuntu is quite easy—little different than what you just read in "Setting Up a High-Speed Connection" on page 50. In fact, as I just mentioned, chances are that everything will just work from the get-go.

Hardware

If you lead a solely wired existence or are just inexperienced in this particular area, there are a few things worth knowing. To get started, you need to have the right hardware. If you just want to go wireless outside of the home, then all you need is a wireless network interface card (NIC). These are often built in to modern laptops, while for others they are usually add-ons in the form of cards that pop into the PCMCIA slot on the side of your computer (as seen on the right of Figure 4-3).

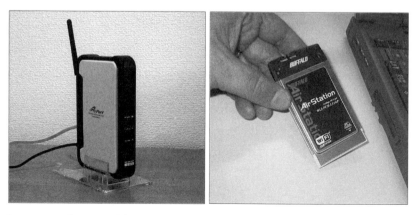

Figure 4-3: All you need for a WiFi setup—an access point and a network interface card

There are, however, also some NICs that plug into one of your machine's USB ports or, in the case of desktop models, one of its PCI slots. While support for NICs of this type has improved through the last couple of years, there are still gaps, and some can be rather tricky to deal with. If you're looking for a sure thing, Centrino IPW-2100 and IPW-2200 cards are definitely supported by Ubuntu. As for NICs of the built-in or PC card variety, you will find support much better, but even then you have to make sure, or at least hope, that the card you are using is Linux compatible. No matter what NIC you are wondering about, the easiest way to find out whether or not it will work is to just try it out. The Linux kernel now comes with several wireless drivers built in, and Ubuntu updates often provide new ones, so if you use a card that is compatible with one of those drivers, things will be smooth sailing. If things don't seem to work, check Ubuntu's list of supported cards (https://help.ubuntu.com/community/WifiDocs/WirelessCardsSupported) or check the Ubuntu forums to find a driver that is compatible or to see if anyone has experience with your particular card.

If you want to set up a wireless system in your home or office, then you will also need to get a wireless access point (WAP), shown on the left of Figure 4-3. Fortunately, Linux compatibility is not really much of an issue in this department, because the access point doesn't physically interface with your computer, and the settings are handled via your web browser.

You should be aware, however, that there are a few WAPs that require you to use Internet Explorer to handle their setup chores. Although it is possible to get Internet Explorer up and running in Linux via Wine, you can't be 100 percent sure that it will work. That said, unless you have a Windows machine somewhere else in your house or office on which to handle such chores, it is probably a good idea to steer clear of WAPs of this kind.

Activating Your Wireless Card

Setting up a Linux-compatible wireless PC card is actually relatively simple. First connect your WAP to your Internet source, and then turn on the WAP. Once it is up and running, plug your wireless NIC into the PCMCIA slot on your laptop, unless, of course, your NIC is built in, in which case you can forgo this step. Any LEDs on the external card will most likely light up at this time.

If your WAP was on when you booted up your computer, and your wireless card was in place during bootup, you probably don't need to do much else to access the Internet. Just follow these steps:

1. Click the **Network Manager** applet to reveal a drop-down menu showing the wireless signals that are present in your vicinity and the strength of each signal (Figure 4-4).

2. From that menu, select the signal for your WAP (or any other wave you are entitled to latch onto) by clicking it.

3. Your system will then try to connect to the Internet, and once a connection is made, the Network Manager applet icon will morph into a small signal-strength indicator. Pretty handy.

NOTE *Some WAPs employ an added level of security in the form of Wired Equivalent Privacy (WEP) or, more recently (and more securely), a WPA (Wi-Fi Protected Access) key. If the WAP to which you are trying to connect requires such a key, a window will appear prompting you to enter it. If you don't happen to know the key, then chances are you are not supposed to be making the connection in the first place. Naughty, naughty.*

Figure 4-4: The Network Manager applet shows you available wireless networks and their signal strengths.

If it turns out that you were not successful in making your wireless connection (the system will tell you if that's the case), there are a few possibilities beyond the annoying non-compatible-card scenario. First of all, double-check to make sure your card is actually physically turned on. I know that sounds dumb, but I have been guilty of this oversight myself on numerous occasions.

Another possibility is that your network does not utilize DHCP, in which case you will have to manually input your connection settings as provided by your network administrator or service provider. Armed with that information, simply follow the steps listed earlier in "Setting Up a Cable or Ethernet Connection for Providers Not Utilizing DHCP" on page 50. Just be sure to click **Wireless connection** instead of Wired connection in step 3.

Releasing and Renewing Your Wireless Connection

There will be times when you want to turn your wireless card off, such as when you use your laptop on an airplane, or when you just want to flush the IP address in your network settings (*release*) and update the settings with the IP address of a new network (*renew*), as you might when moving your laptop from one wireless hotspot to another without rebooting your computer.

This last point might seem a bit mysterious to you, so I will explain things briefly. When you boot up your computer, your wireless card (NIC) performs a scan of available networks (WAPs) in order to see which one it can connect to. Once it finds a network, it gathers an IP address from that network via

DHCP in order to allow you to access the Internet. Utilizing release and renew allows you to change WAPs without having to reboot your computer or when your machine, for whatever reason, just can't seem to make the change on its own.

To perform a quick and easy release/renew operation, click the **Network Manager** applet once to reveal the list of available wireless networks (i.e., signals). In that list, click the network to which you are connected. Within a second or two, you will be disconnected, and almost immediately after that, your system will try to get you connected again. Wow.

Okay, so how do you turn off your wireless card, particularly if you don't have a physical way to do it? Just right-click the **Network Manager** applet, and then deselect **Enable Wireless**. All quite simple.

Oh, and if you want to turn that card back on again, just get back to that menu, and select **Enable Wireless** again.

Setting Up a Dial-Up Connection

Although much of the world is moving to high-speed Internet connections, many of you may still be using dial-up Internet connections, which means that you need to have a traditional dial-up modem to reach beyond your box to the outside world. In case you broadband surf-gods have forgotten, modems are those wonderful machines that whistle, chime, screech, and spit whenever you dial up your Internet provider. I suppose you could think of them as noisy telephones in need of a good burp.

The good news is that setting up your dial-up connection is a simple process that much resembles what I've covered thus far for other connection types. Now here comes the bad news—in the world of Linux, very few internal modems are supported. The main reason behind this compatibility problem is that most built-in modems are software dependent, and the software they depend on is part of, or designed for, Windows. Such modems are thus called *Winmodems.*

Of course, the Linux community has been working on ways to deal with these Winmodem beasts so that they will work with Linux systems. Though support for the wide variety of Winmodem models out there is still rather spotty, things are better than before, so you might just luck out. My advice is to hold off on the wondering and worrying and just give your modem a try to see if it works. If it does, then you're all set. If it doesn't, well, then you've got some options open to you, but at least you haven't done any damage to your system.

With all that intro-babble out of the way, let's get down to the steps for setting up your dial-up connection. First, get the setting information you need from your Internet provider. Most providers gear their operations to Windows and often Mac users, and very few offer Linux support, other than NeanderTech and a few others. Still, there is no technical reason for your Linux system not to work via their setup, so just nag and push them until they give you the information you want. After that, make sure your modem is connected to a live telephone connection—for example, the phone jack in your wall—and then do the following:

1. Go to the **System** menu and select **Administration ▸ Network**, after which the Network Settings window will appear.

2. In that window, click **Unlock**, after which another window will appear asking for your password.

3. Provide your password, and then click **Authenticate**.

4. Back in the Network Settings window, click **Point to point connection** to select it, and then click the **Properties** button.

5. When the Properties window appears, check the box next to the words *Enable this connection.*

6. In the Internet service provider data section of that window, type the dial-up connection phone number as given by your provider, and the dial prefix, if necessary, to dial out of your current phone system (some offices require that you first dial 9, for example, to make a call out of the office).

7. Type your username and password, as given by your provider, in the boxes in the Account data section of the window.

8. Click the **Modem** tab, and then select either **Tones** or **Pulses** in the Dial Type section of the window, depending on the type of dialing scheme you have for your telephone service. Most are tone dialers these days, so you can choose that if you're not sure. You can generally figure it out yourself by paying attention to the sounds made when you dial a call. If you hear a series of different tones—almost a melody that you can recognize—then you have tone dialing.

9. Select **Off** or **Low**, **Medium**, or **High** in the Volume section of that tab, depending on whether or not you want to hear your modem doing its dialing. While testing things out, it is a good idea to select **Low**, **Medium**, or **High** so that you can hear what is (or is not) happening.

10. Now you have to try to figure out where your system thinks your modem is connected by testing out the various options in the box labeled *Modem port.* Start out with /dev/modem, and if that doesn't work after going through steps 9 and 10, try out the others one by one before finally opting for more dramatic measures.

11. Once your modem port has been found (or you've chosen one on your own), click the **Options** tab, and then check the box next to the words *Set modem as default route to Internet.* Once you're done, click the **OK** button.

12. In the Network Settings window, be sure to check the box next to the words *Point to point connection* before closing the window.

Once the steps are completed and assuming your modem and system are in loving compatibility, you should then hear your modem begin its dialing, spitting, and churning sequence as it makes the connection with your provider. Once it does, you can go on and start your browsing, emailing, or whatever else it is you do online.

What to Do If Your Modem Isn't Compatible

What I've just described is pretty much a best-case scenario. What happens, however, if your modem and Ubuntu do not see eye to eye? Well, there are a few options. My first, more radical suggestion, is to dump those extra movie channels from your cable service (nothing all that great on them anyway) and pay for cable Internet service instead. If that is not an option, then you have two ways to go. One is to try to geek around with your modem to see if you can get it to work. This is a slightly more complicated process, but there are instructions at https://help.ubuntu.com/community/DialupModemHowto. If you are faint of heart or a novice user, you may find what the process entails to be a bit more than you're willing to deal with.

The simpler, although costlier, way to get your modem to work is to change your modem—in this case, changing to a true hardware modem. *Hardware modems*, in case you are not familiar with the term, are modems that are not software dependent and thus work with whatever system you happen to use with them. You can think of them as telephones without a handset.

Such modems come in two forms: internal and external. As for the internals, the USRobotics models 56K V.92 Performance Pro Modem (internal slot) and 56 PC Card Modem (PC card slot, for laptops) are true hardware modems that are easily available and are said to work. You can check out the USRobotics site (www.usr.com) for more information on these models, though checking the Ubuntu forums for suggestions is always a good idea.

External Dial-Up Modems

Perhaps the safest of all solutions is to buy an external serial modem. An external modem sits in a box outside your computer, and it connects to the serial port in the back of the computer, which is usually the only connector with little prongs in it (see Figure 4-5). Because the modem doesn't use your operating system to operate, it does not tie up system resources while it's busy, which may result in a possible pickup in computer speed.

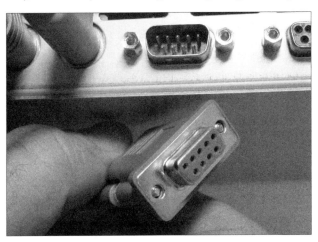

Figure 4-5: Serial port and connector

Most external serial modems should work with your system, or at least that is what most people will tell you. If you are worried and are looking for a sure thing, Zoom Telephonics (www.zoom.com) makes an external serial modem that is compatible with Linux, and they say so right on their website. The USRobotics 56K V.92 External Faxmodem is also said to work, though I haven't tried out this model myself.

If you find another model that you think will do the trick, before you commit to it by slapping down the cash, do a Yahoo! or Google search with that modem's make and model number, along with the word *linux*, and see what search results you get. Of course, you can also try out one of the Linux forums and ask about the modem make and model there. There are a lot of people in the same boat, so you are sure to get plenty of opinions and advice.

Firefox: Your Internet Browser

Now that you are connected to the Internet, you no doubt want to get down to some cyberspace discovery and exploration, and the most commonly used means of doing that is with a web browser. The default web browser in your Ubuntu system is Firefox, which is enjoying increasing popularity in not only the Linux world, but in the Windows and Mac worlds as well. Chances are you are already a Firefox user, but if you are not, then you needn't worry—things work more or less the same in all browsers. That being the case, you should be able to use Firefox's basic features without any instruction. Of course, there are some features that do distinguish Firefox from its competition, so I will mention those.

Controlling Browser Window Clutter with Tabs

Usually when you click a link on a web page, the new page opens in the same window. On some pages, links are coded so that the new page opens in a new, separate window, or maybe you occasionally opt for opening a link in a new window by right-clicking the link and then selecting the Open Link in New Window option. This can be very useful; however, once you have more than a few browser windows open, it gets sort of hard to find what you're looking for in all those open windows. It can also slow things down a bit.

This is where Firefox's tab feature comes in handy. To see how it works, try it out yourself right here and now. Open your Firefox browser by clicking the launcher on the top GNOME Panel (or going to **Applications ▸ Internet ▸ Firefox Web Browser**); then Google the word *nyckelharpa* using Firefox's handy search box, which is at the top-right corner of the browser window (see Figure 4-6). By default, Firefox will perform searches for keywords entered in the search box using Google. You can, if you like, select other search engines by clicking the G icon in the search box and then making your selection. Amazon.com, eBay, and Yahoo! are available, to name a few, and you can even add others. For now, however, let's stick to Google for our present search, by typing `nyckelharpa` in that search box. Once you've finished typing, press the ENTER key, after which a page of Google results should appear in the main pain of the Firefox window.

Figure 4-6: Performing a Google
search from the Firefox search box

The top result should be the American Nyckelharpa Association, and you are now going to open that page in a new tab, rather than in the same or a new window. To do that, right-click the link, and in the popup menu that appears, select **Open Link in New Tab**. You can, if you prefer, make things a tad easier and dispense with the popup menu selection step by simply clicking the link with both mouse buttons simultaneously or by holding down the CTRL key as you click the link. Either way, the new page will appear in a new tab, while your original page of search results remains, ready and waiting in the other tab (see Figure 4-7). I am pretty confident in saying that, once you get used to this feature, you will wonder how you ever got along without it.

Figure 4-7: A link opened in a new tab in Firefox

Other Firefox Features: Popup Manager

Firefox has a number of other useful features. One is its Popup Manager, which suppresses those annoying popup windows that often appear when you access a new web page. You can enable or disable this feature from the Preferences window (**Edit ▸ Preferences**) by clicking the **Content** icon in the top pane of that window and then checking or unchecking the box next to the words *Block pop-up windows.* You can also permit certain sites to provide popup windows (some popups are not only useful, but necessary for the correct functioning of a site) by clicking the **Exceptions** button to the right of that *Block pop-up windows* entry and inputting the URL for the site in question.

Project 4A: Installing Firefox Extensions

One of the coolest things about Firefox is that it allows you to further expand its functionality by adding various extensions. These extensions include all sort of things; many are quite functional, while others are just plain fun and goofy. They range from blog-writing tools to image viewers. For this project, however, we will be installing a blog editor called ScribeFire (Figure 4-8) that allows you to write entries, log in to your blog, and upload your new addition. All of this is available at the click of a button from an icon in the bottom-right corner of the window.

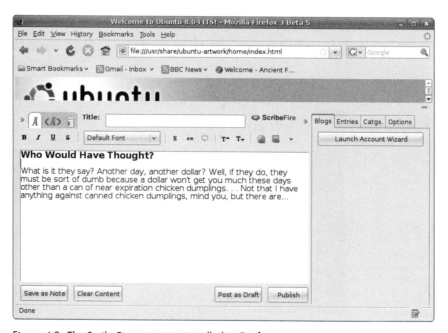

Figure 4-8: The ScribeFire extension installed in Firefox

4A-1: Downloading and Installing the ScribeFire Extension

To get started with the process of installing any Firefox extension, you have to first, quite logically, find and download one. To do this, go to the Firefox **Tools** menu, and select **Add-ons**. The Add-ons window will then appear, showing you the extensions, themes, and plugins you already have installed. To add the ScribeFire extension, click the **Get Add-ons** button in the pane at the top of the window, after which Firefox will make some download recommendations that you can accept or ignore.

As you can see in Figure 4-9, ScribeFire just happens to be Firefox's recommendation at the time the screenshot was taken. Chances are, however, that it won't still be when you open the Add-ons window. If that is the case, just do a search for *scribefire* in the Search All Add-ons box. Once you find it, click the **Add to Firefox** button.

Figure 4-9: Adding extensions in Firefox

A Software Installation window like the one shown in Figure 4-10 will then appear. Just click the **Install Now** button in that window after it becomes active (only about a four-second wait) to start the installation.

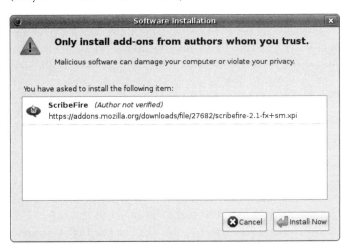

Figure 4-10: Firefox gives you a pre-installation warning.

Once the installation process is complete, a message will appear in the Add-ons window telling you to restart Firefox. To do this, click the **Restart Firefox** button in the bottom-right corner of that warning message (Figure 4-11).

4A-2: Setting Up the ScribeFire Extension

When Firefox first starts up after you've installed the ScribeFire extension, you will see a small icon in the lower-right corner of the window. Just click that icon, and ScribeFire will appear as a resizable pane in the lower half of your current Firefox window.

Figure 4-11: A message appears telling you to restart Firefox after the installation is complete.

Project 4B: Installing the Flash Plugin

While installing any of Firefox's available extensions can be cool, there are certain near-essentials that can be added in the form of *plugins*, although perhaps I am splitting hairs a bit in terms of the difference between the two. The most frequently used browser plugin for any system is Adobe's Flash Player. Flash provides websites with all sorts of exciting multimedia effects and capabilities, and as a result, it is utilized in an ever-increasing number of sites. In fact, chances are you've probably seen numerous Flash-enhanced pages without even being aware of it. For example, if you've ever watched a video on YouTube, you've enjoyed the wonders of Flash.

How do you get the Flash Player plugin? Well, the easiest way is to simply find a page that uses Flash, and install the plugin from there—the site will sense that you don't have the plugin and guide you through the installation. If you're not sure how to go about things, just follow these steps:

1. First of all, find a site that uses Flash. If you don't know of one off hand, try YouTube (www.youtube.com), which is what I will be using in these examples.

2. Once you have arrived at YouTube, click any video link you see.

3. On the page that opens, you will not see the video playback panel that you normally find, but you will see a message telling you that you don't have the right Flash Player (Figure 4-12). Do *not* click the link that says *Get the latest Flash player*. Instead, click the **Install Missing Plugins** button directly below the Bookmarks Toolbar.

4. A Plugin Finder Service window will now appear showing the plugin you are about to install. Make sure that Adobe Flash Player is selected, and then click **Next**.

5. From that point on, just agree to anything you are asked to agree to until the installation is complete.

Figure 4-12: Viewing a YouTube page without the Flash Player plugin installed

After that, go back to the page you had originally been viewing, and you'll be able to see the YouTube video that eluded you only moments before (Figure 4-13).

Figure 4-13: A Flash page after installation of the Flash Player plugin

Email with Evolution

Evolution is the default email program in Ubuntu, and it could probably best be described as a better-groomed, spunkier clone of Microsoft Outlook (see Figure 4-14). It allows you to send and receive mail, make appointments, and keep a list of tasks. It can also filter junk mail, which is a necessity these days, and even synchronize with your PalmPilot, if you still have one of those. Also, if such things are important to you, it is a much more handsome program to look at than Outlook.

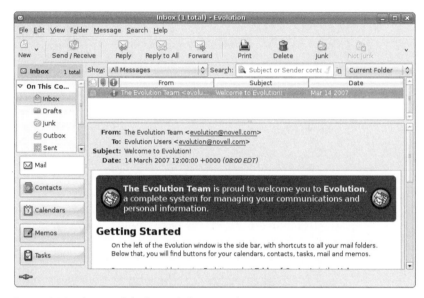

Figure 4-14: Ubuntu's default email client—Evolution

To use Evolution, just click the email launcher on the top panel or go to the **Applications** menu and select **Internet ▶ Evolution Mail**. When you first run Evolution, you will be greeted by a setup wizard, so have the account details you received from your Internet service provider handy. These should consist of your POP host address for receiving mail, your SMTP host address for sending mail, and your mail password, which is very often different from your Internet logon password. Your mail password is not actually entered during the various wizard steps, so check the checkbox next to the words *Remember password* when filling in the POP details. When you first connect to your mail server, you will be prompted for your mail password, so you can type it at that time, and you won't have to deal with it again.

An Email Alternative: Thunderbird

Evolution is, without a doubt, the most popular email software in the Linux world, but despite its obvious attractions and popularity, I have to say that I don't much like it to the extent that others do, and I can't quite put a finger on the reason why. I just prefer the more straightforward Thunderbird for my email chores. In contrast to the multifunctional Evolution, Thunderbird

(Figure 4-15) is a more mail-oriented program that is very straightforward to use, yet includes most of the most important email functions you've come to expect, such as junk mail filters. In fact, it is remarkably similar to Outlook Express in terms of appearance and handling. It also lacks the quirkiness that always seems to squirrel its way into Evolution in some form or another. The fact that Thunderbird is also available in both Mac and Windows versions means that you may already be familiar with it, or prepared to deal with it if you find it in use on another system you happen to be using.

Figure 4-15: The Thunderbird email client

Thunderbird does not come bundled with Ubuntu, so if you would like to try it out, you will have to download it and install it yourself. Now that you have set up your machine to connect to the Internet, however, you can easily do this after going over the contents of Chapter 5 (okay, so I'm jumping the gun a bit again). Just do a Synaptic search for *thunderbird*, and then mark **thunderbird** for installation. Once it is installed, you can then run it from the **Applications** menu by selecting **Internet ▸ Mozilla Thunderbird Mail/News**.

As I mentioned, both Evolution and Thunderbird are equally capable and possess essentially the same features in terms of mail handling. The difference is primarily a look-and-feel matter. Why not try both Evolution and Thunderbird and see which you like better?

By the way, if you find that you prefer Thunderbird to Evolution, you can add a panel launcher for it so as to make things easier on yourself when you want to run the program. Just go to **Applications ▸ Internet ▸ Mozilla Thunderbird Mail/News**, right-click that entry, and then in the popup menu that appears, select **Add this launcher to panel**. You can then remove the Evolution launcher, if you are so inclined.

Other Internet Applications

What I've covered thus far in terms of Internet applications is just the tip of the iceberg (might as well use that worn-out phrase before there aren't any icebergs left, right?). Ubuntu also comes with a couple of other Internet applications that you might want to consider. These include the Instant Messenger client called Pidgin (**Applications ▸ Internet ▸ Pidgin Internet Messenger**), which allows you to do use any one of your MSN/Windows Instant Messenger, Google Talk, Yahoo! Messenger, AOL Instant Messenger (AIM), ICQ, Gadu-Gadu, GroupWise, IRC, or Jabber accounts . . . or all of them simultaneously. If you want to give Internet telephony a try, Ekiga Softphone (**Applications ▸ Internet ▸ Ekiga Softphone**) also comes bundled with your distribution, so you need not despair.

There are still more Internet applications that you might want to consider downloading and installing after you've completed Chapter 5, including Thunderbird, which I've already mentioned in this chapter. If this all sounds enticing, get those fingers of yours flipping—the mother lode awaits!

5

ROUNDING OUT THE BIRD

Downloading, Installing, and Updating Programs the Easy Way

One of the handiest things about Ubuntu is that it is equipped with a very simple-to-use application installation mechanism. The engine, using the term loosely, behind this is a mechanism called Advanced Package Tool (APT), which allows you to easily download, install, update, and remove software packaged in DEB archives, or *packages*.

APT is a rather foolproof way of installing programs; nothing will go missing, since it automatically downloads and installs any files that the main application you are installing requires to run. Tracking down such files, called *dependencies*, proves to be a significant headache for most Linux users. The painful quest of finding and then installing this file or that, as well as any dependencies that those files themselves might have, has led to the missing dependency problem being referred to as *dependency hell*. APT makes that pretty much a thing of the past.

So where does APT find all these files and applications? Well, the packages that APT searches for, downloads, and installs are located in a set of specific online repositories. These *repositories* are basically online servers in which a great number of applications, support files, and more are stored for use with your particular system. All of the files that originally came bundled with your system, including the system (kernel) itself and updates, when available, are stored there.

The one thing about APT that some people, especially beginners, might consider a problem is that it is a command-driven application. This means that you control it via commands in a command Terminal. Fortunately, Ubuntu has a number of different graphical front ends for APT that allow you to bypass the command line and make everything about as easy as you could hope it would be. In this chapter we will be focusing on three of these front ends.

Project 5A: Installing Applications via GNOME App Install

By far, the easiest to use of the APT front ends is GNOME App Install. Being the most graphically satisfying of the front ends, it is especially useful when it comes to browsing for cool or handy applications.

To get a feel for GNOME App Install, go to the **Applications** menu and select **Add/Remove**. The Add/Remove Applications window will open for the first time in a grayed-out state while it checks the online repositories to make sure it has the most up-to-date list of what is available. Once done, it will look pretty much like what is shown in Figure 5-1.

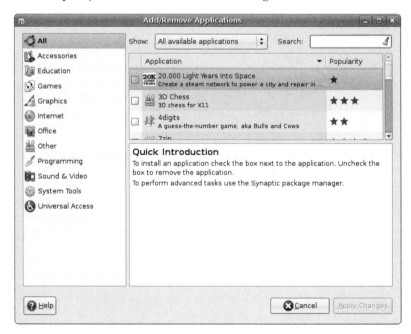

Figure 5-1: GNOME App Install

As you can see, items in GNOME App Install are categorized pretty much in the same manner as in the Ubuntu Applications menu itself. If you click any of the category icons in the left pane of the window, you will see a list of all the items available for that category in the top-right pane—installed items are checked, while those that are not installed are unchecked. Not surprisingly, you will find that the checked items within each category mirror those in the relevant submenu of the Applications menu.

5A-1: Selecting Applications for Installation

GNOME App Install can install multiple applications simultaneously, so to give it a whirl, we'll try installing a troika of applications that might be of interest to you. Before getting down to selecting the applications, however, be sure to select **All available applications** in the menu button next to the word *Show*. Doing this will enable you to view everything that is available to you in the online Ubuntu repositories.

Now that all there is to be seen can indeed be seen, let's start by selecting the very cool and decidedly useful address book application Rubrica (shown in Figure 5-2). To select Rubrica, just click the **Office** category in the left pane of the Add/Remove Applications window, scroll down the list of available applications in the top-right pane, and check the box next to the words *Rubrica Addressbook*. A small window will appear posing the question: *Enable the installation of community maintained software?* Click **Enable** to proceed.

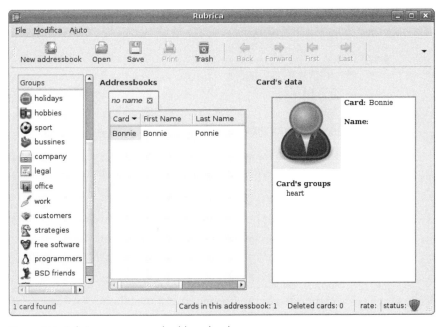

Figure 5-2: Rubrica—a very cool address book

Let's also select the handy audio application SoundConverter (not to be confused with soundKonverter) that converts audio files from one format to another—MP3 to Ogg Vorbis, for example (you'll learn more about SoundConverter in Chapter 16). To select it for installation, click the **Sound & Video** category in the left pane of the window, scroll down in the top-right pane, and check the box next to the words *Sound Converter* (not *soundKonverter*).

Finally, let's add a useful utility by the name of *Sysinfo* (Figure 5-3), which is a system profiler that can tell you all sorts of things about your machine and system. Just click **System Tools** in the left pane, and then check the box next to *Sysinfo* to add it to the installation queue.

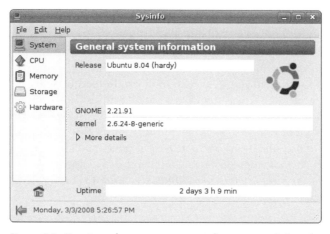

Figure 5-3: Keeping tabs on your system information with Sysinfo

NOTE   *Be careful not to uncheck the boxes next to any of the already checked applications listed in GNOME App Install. Doing so will result in their being removed once you go on to Project 5A-2.*

5A-2: Downloading and Installing Selected Applications

Once you've made your selections, click the **Apply Changes** button at the bottom of the Add/Remove Applications window. A new window, like that in Figure 5-4, will appear, showing what you are about to install. Click **Apply** in that window, after which you will be prompted for your password because you will be installing the software in write-protected territory (more on that topic in Chapter 6). That said, go ahead and type your user password, and click **OK**. A window (Figure 5-5) will then appear showing you what will be installed, what will be removed (nothing in this case), and what will be left unchanged. Click **Apply** in that window. GNOME App Install (APT, actually) will then begin the download and installation process, showing its progress via progress windows.

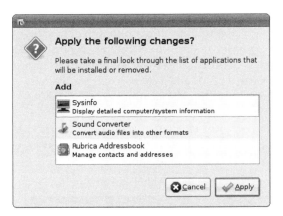

Figure 5-4: GNOME App Install tells you what it is
about to install.

When the installation is done, GNOME App Install will update its database
to reflect the status of the newly installed apps, after which a window somewhat like the one you saw at the beginning of the installation process (see
Figure 5-4) will appear. Click **Close**; GNOME App Install will close and you'll
be ready to run your new applications.

Figure 5-5: Another warning window lets you know what is
about to happen to your system.

You can run the applications you've installed by going to the Applications menu and then looking in the submenu that matches the category in which each application was located within GNOME App Install. That would be Office for Rubrica, Sound & Video for SoundConverter (which you'll learn more about in Chapter 16), and System Tools for Sysinfo.

As you can see, installing applications via GNOME App Install is quite simple, and if you paid heed to my warning, you also know how easy it is to uninstall applications. Just check the target app and click **Apply Changes** to install; uncheck the target app and click **Apply Changes** to remove. Can't get much easier than that, you have to admit.

Project 5B: Installing Applications via Synaptic

As I mentioned, Ubuntu comes with a number of graphical front ends for APT. We have already covered the simple, though arguably more attractive, GNOME App Install; and now we will discuss the main application handling workhorse, Synaptic.

To get a look at Synaptic, go to the **System** menu, and select **Administration ▶ Synaptic Package Manager** (or just use the launcher you added to the Drawer on the Panel in Chapter 3). Like GNOME App Install, Synaptic installs things in your system in areas that are write protected. Unlike GNOME App Install, however, you will be prompted for your password in a separate window before Synaptic actually appears, rather than after you've made your software selections. Type your user password when prompted to do so, and click **OK**. Synaptic, shown in Figure 5-6, will soon appear.

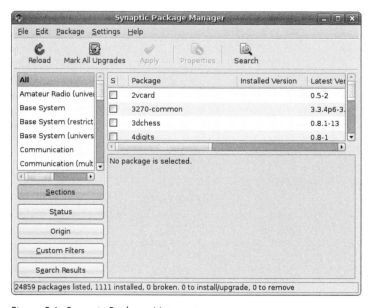

Figure 5-6: Synaptic Package Manager

Although the Synaptic interface may seem rather simple at first glance, it is a very powerful program. It not only allows you to search for, download, and install applications, but it also allows you to find and install the less glamorous, but equally important, libraries and support files that you might need for use with other applications that come bundled with Ubuntu (such as MP3 support), or those you install by other means. You can also use Synaptic to find other things such as fonts, foreign language localization files, and less common utilities, and to update the software you have installed on your system when such updates are available.

Of course, if you don't know what you're looking for, you can browse through the packages available via Synaptic by clicking the **Sections** button at the bottom-left corner of the window, selecting a category of interest in the pane above that, and then clicking the name of a specific package in the top-right pane, after which a description of that package will appear in the pane below.

Installing Frozen-Bubble

Let's get a feel for Synaptic by installing a popular Linux game called Frozen-Bubble. What you will be doing is basically the standard method you would use to search for and install any package via Synaptic, so it is a process well worth remembering. Here are the steps:

1. Each time you take Synaptic out for a spin, it is a good idea to first click the **Reload** button so as to make sure that Synaptic is aware of the most recent files available on the online repositories.

2. Once the database update is complete, click the **Search** button in the main Synaptic window.

3. A Find window will appear. Be sure that **Description and Name** is selected in the Look in menu (to provide a more forgiving search), type `frozen` in the Search box, and then click the **Search** button.

4. After a short period of time, a list of results will appear in the upper-right pane. Look for **frozen-bubble**, and click it once to select it. A description of that file will then appear in the bottom-right pane.

5. Once you've read the description and are sure you want to install the package selected, click the box at the left end of that same entry, and then select **Mark for Installation** in the popup menu that appears.

6. A window will then appear telling you that other packages will also need to be marked for installation (these would be the dependencies we mentioned earlier). Click the **Mark** button.

7. You are now ready to roll, so just click the **Apply** button in the main Synaptic window, after which yet another window (Summary) will appear, telling you what is going to be installed, what is going to be changed, and what is going to be left alone (Figure 5-7).

Figure 5-7: Synaptic lets you know what additional packages will be installed.

8. Click **Apply** in that Summary window, after which Synaptic will begin the installation process, showing you its progress in a separate window.

9. When the installation is complete, a new window like that in Figure 5-8 will appear to let you know. Click **Close** in that final window, and then wait until Synaptic snaps out of its temporary state of grayness, which signals the complete end of the installation process.

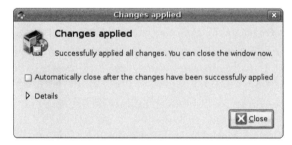

Figure 5-8: Synaptic lets you know when it's done doing its thing.

You can now run Frozen-Bubble (Figure 5-9) by going to the Applications menu and selecting **Games ▶ Frozen-Bubble**.

Figure 5-9: Frozen-Bubble

A Little More Practice with Synaptic

If you happen to have an ATI or NVIDIA graphics card, there is another
project you will very likely want to perform with Synaptic before calling it a
computing day—installing EnvyNG. EnvyNG, shown in Figure 5-10, checks
to see if your computer has an ATI or NVIDIA graphics card, and if it does,
EnvyNG downloads and installs the appropriate driver. This is a very handy
improvement over the somewhat squirrelly way you had to go about such
things in the past. To get it, just do a search for *envyng,* and then mark
envyng-gtk for installation. Once installed, you can run it from **Applications ▸
System Tools ▸ EnvyNG**.

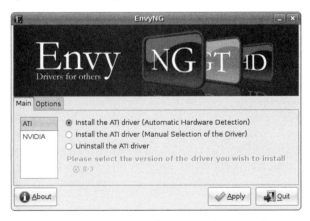

Figure 5-10: Finding and installing ATI and NVIDIA drivers
made easy with EnvyNG

Removing Applications via Synaptic

To remove applications installed from a DEB package via Synaptic, GNOME App Install, or any other means, search for the application you wish to remove either by clicking the **Search** button and typing the name of the application you wish to remove, or by clicking the **Status** button in the bottom-left corner of the Synaptic window, clicking **Installed** in the pane above that, and then scrolling through the list of installed packages that then appears in the top-right pane. Once you find the application in that list, right-click its name, and select **Mark for Complete Removal** to remove the application and any setting or configuration files for that application. When the window that tells you what is going to be axed appears, check through it carefully so as to make sure you aren't inadvertently uninstalling something you would mourn the loss of—like your whole desktop environment, for instance. Assuming everything looks okay, click the **Mark** button, after which the process will be the same as that for installing applications.

Upgrading Applications via Synaptic

As I mentioned, you can also use Synaptic to upgrade applications installed in your system. To do this, click the **Status** button in the bottom-right corner of the Synaptic window. In the pane above that button, then click the entry **Installed (upgradable)**, after which a list of the installed applications with available upgrades will appear in the upper-right pane. Right-click any application listed there that you would like to upgrade, and select **Mark for Upgrade** in the popup menu that then appears. Repeat the right-click procedure for any other application you want to upgrade, then click the **Apply** button. The procedure from then on out will be the same as that for installing packages.

Performing System Upgrades via Update Manager

The third graphical front end for APT that we'll cover here is called Update Manager, and it is used for updating your system. It is probably a good idea to save yourself some time by first checking for available updates via Update Manager before updating individual packages via Synaptic.

To get started, go to the **System** menu, select **Administration ▸ Update Manager**, and make sure that Synaptic and GNOME App Install are both closed (you can't run two APT front ends at the same time). Once the Update Manager window (Figure 5-11) appears, click the **Check** button to make sure the database is as up to date as possible. You will then be prompted for your password, so give what is asked for, and after a short while a list of all of the available updates will appear in the Update Manager window.

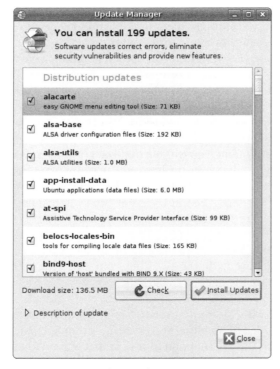

Figure 5-11: Upgrading packages en masse via
Update Manager

In that window, a list of all of the available updates will appear. You can
scroll through that list and uncheck the box for any application you don't want
to upgrade, but if you don't really know what you're doing, you had better
just leave it as is. Either way, once you're ready, click the **Install Updates**
button. The updates will then be downloaded and installed, with the progress
shown in the same types of windows you saw when using Synaptic and
GNOME App Install. Once the installation is complete, you will be notified
in a separate window. Click **Close** in that window, and then do the same in
the Software Updates window. Depending on what you installed, another
notification icon may appear telling you that you will have to restart your
system in order for changes to take effect. If so, it is best to be obedient and
reboot.

If an Update Ruins Your Day . . . or System

Now, I don't want to worry you too much, but one thing about massive
system updates is that afterward, sometimes things just go all screwy, leaving
you with all sorts of regrets and a mouthful of expletives just waiting to be
uttered and, hopefully, deleted. This is a fact of life no matter what operating
system you are using. It can happen in Windows, it can happen in Mac OS,

and it can happen in Linux. Therefore, it is always a good idea to wait a bit before installing a seemingly major update and to check the user forums first to see if there are any disaster stories out there.

If you go ahead only to find that your system won't start up again, don't worry. All is not lost. In fact, nothing is lost . . . most likely. Just start up your machine again. If you have a dual boot system, you will arrive at the GRUB boot menu, just like always. If you're not a dual-booter, you'll have to get to this menu by pressing ESC as soon as you're prompted to do so just a few moments after starting the machine.

In the GRUB menu, you will see that you seem to have more than one Ubuntu system installed on your hard disk, which is true to some extent. For a short-term fix, you can take advantage of this quasi-fact by traveling back in time to the core system (the Linux kernel) that you had in place before your ill-fated upgrade. Just use your arrow keys to select a kernel that ends in a number lower than the highest (2.6.24-28 rather than 2.6.24-91, for example), press ENTER, and *voilá*, you are back to the system you have come to know and love. You'll have to do this each time you start up your machine, but at least you will have the chance to back up your valuable files before doing some research and trying again later.

Hopefully, with all this disaster and recovery talk, I haven't scared you away from the idea of updating your system. After all, chances are great that nothing like this will ever happen to you. Still, it is good to know that if things do go awry, there is no need for panic. You've got backup.

6

A TIDY NEST

File and Disk Handling in Ubuntu

 No matter which operating system you are using, you have to deal with files. Some people are very organized, placing every file in a logically named folder as soon as that file is saved for the very first time. Then there are people like me, who save everything to the desktop until it is so full of junk that they can no longer make out the wallpaper, and only at that point do they start organizing in earnest (if placing all of those files in a single folder called March17Cleanup can be called organizing). Ah.

Of course, files not only get stored on your hard disk, but they are also copied to and from CDs, DVDs, external hard disks, flash drives, and other storage media and devices. They are also often saved in archives, which are then compressed to reduce their spatial footprint, making them easier to send via email or to fit onto spatially challenged removable storage media.

With that intro, you may have already guessed that in this chapter I will be dealing with file handling in Ubuntu, particularly in relation to the Nautilus File Manager, which is at the heart of GNOME's file-handling capabilities.

Nautilus: Your File Manager

As I mentioned, the program that creates the file viewing and organizing interface in your system is called Nautilus, and it comes as part of the GNOME desktop environment. You may not have thought of an operating system's file manager as a program before, but in fact, that is what it is. (The Windows file manager is called Windows Explorer.) To have a look at Nautilus, just go to the **Places** menu, and select **Home Folder**.

When Nautilus opens up to your home folder (shown in Figure 6-1), you will find that you can store your files thematically: Documents, Music, Pictures, Public, Templates, and Videos. There is also another folder, titled Desktop, which, if double-clicked, will show everything you have stored on your desktop (a lot in my case; most likely nothing in yours). There is also another folder, called Examples, which contains sample files that give you an idea of what Ubuntu has in store for you, along with a video of Nelson Mandela discussing ubuntu (the concept, not the distribution).

You can create additional folders and, of course, files to your heart's content, so this preconfigured state of affairs is sure to change once you get down to really using your system. In fact, you will be making some changes in Chapter 7, which will make everything look a bit more lived in.

Figure 6-1: The contents of your home folder as viewed in a Nautilus window

The Side Pane

Nautilus has a lot of interesting features that deserve mention, and the most obvious of these is the side pane, which appears at the left side of the window. The side pane allows you to view a variety of information via selectable views. You can make your choices by clicking the drop-down menu at the top of the side pane (Figure 6-2).

Figure 6-2: Selecting views
for the Nautilus side pane

The default view in Ubuntu is Places, which is a sort of quick navigation tool. In Places you will find icons representing various data-storage locations available to your system, such as your home folder, desktop, full filesystem, any network shares you are connected to (more on that in a moment), and any removable storage media or devices you have in or connected to your system. Double-clicking any of these icons will show the contents of that location in the right panel of the Nautilus window.

There are, of course, other views, such as Tree, which provides you with an expandable hierarchal view of your filesystem, and History, which shows you where in your filesystem you have been most recently, much in the way the history function works in a web browser. There are still other views for you to choose from, a couple of which you will work with in Chapter 7.

Now You See It; Now You Don't

The side pane is a rather handy feature, but there may well be times when you would prefer to have more space to view the contents of your window and thus want to get rid of the pane temporarily. You can do this quite easily by clicking the little orange close button in the upper-right corner of the pane or by going to the **View** menu of a Nautilus window and then deselecting **Side Pane**. The check mark next to that entry will then disappear, as will the side pane. To get it back, just return to the **View** menu, and select **Side Pane** again. The check mark will then reappear, as will the side pane itself.

There is another way to hide the side pane that many people seem to stumble upon accidentally, usually resulting in a bit of unnecessary panic. If you look at the gray border at the right side of the side pane, you will notice that there is a small ribbed section in the center (see Figure 6-3). Dragging this ribbed section allows you to resize the width of the pane. What most folks don't realize straight off, however, is that simply clicking that ribbed section acts as a toggle to hide or show the side pane. When the pane is hidden in this way, the ribbed section still appears at the left border of the window, which is not true when the pane is hidden in one of the ways mentioned earlier.

So there it is—the side pane's little secret. No, it's not a particularly interesting secret, but one that should not only provide you with an added layer of convenience, but also some peace of mind.

Figure 6-3: Another way of showing and hiding the Nautilus side pane

File Handling in Nautilus

Since Nautilus is primarily a file manager, it only makes sense to get down to the business of using it at that level. Of course, most folks who use computers today are already familiar with the basics of drag-and-drop and a few other means of creating folders and copying, cutting, and moving files. But for those who are unfamiliar with one way or another of performing these essential procedures, I thought it best to spell it all out. If you find this all a bit redundant, please bear with me for the good of the masses.

Creating, Naming, and Renaming Folders

Creating a folder is a simple enough task, and there are two ways of going about it. The easiest (in my opinion) is to right-click any empty space within a Nautilus window, and select **Create Folder** in the popup menu that appears. If you prefer using menus to right-clicking empty space, you can instead start things rolling by going to the Nautilus **File** menu, and selecting **Create Folder**.

Regardless of where you made your Create Folder selection, a new folder with the name *untitled folder* will appear in the Nautilus window. The name box of the folder will be highlighted and surrounded with a black box, which means that you can immediately give that folder a name by simply typing one—nothing to click or do other than that. Press ENTER or click any open space in the Nautilus window to complete the job.

If you later decide that the name you gave your folder needs some tweaking or even a complete revision, you can rename it by right-clicking it and selecting **Rename** in the popup menu. Alternatively, you can click the folder once to highlight it, and then select **Edit ▸ Rename**. After that, you can type the new name for the folder and then press ENTER or click any open space in the Nautilus window to seal the deal.

Moving Files and Folders

Perhaps the easiest of all file manipulations you can perform in Nautilus is moving a file by means of drag-and-drop. I am pretty sure that anybody who has wielded a mouse is familiar with that particular move. There is another way of moving files and folders, however: cut and paste.

The easiest way of doing this is to right-click the file (or folder) you want to move, and then select **Cut** from the popup menu (**Edit ▸ Cut** will also do the trick). At this point, it will seem as if nothing has happened, as the file will still be there, so don't worry. After that, right-click any open space in the folder to which you wish to move the file, and then select **Paste** in the popup menu. The file will then disappear from its original location and appear in its new one.

Can you use key combinations to do this, you ask? Sure. Simply follow the directions I just gave, but use CTRL-X to cut and CTRL-V to paste.

Copying Files and Folders

Based on the instructions I just gave, you can pretty well imagine the methods for copying files and folders, as they are essentially a variation on the same theme. Just right-click the file you want to copy, select **Copy** from the popup menu, right-click any open space within the target location, and then select **Paste**. Keystroke-wise, that would be CTRL-C to copy and, as before, CTRL-V to paste.

It is also possible to copy folders and files via the wonders of drag-and-drop, though this involves more hands than required for a simple drag-and-drop move; fortunately, the two you have will do nicely. Just press and hold the CTRL key while you drag the file or folder you want to copy to the target location. Be sure to release the mouse button and then the CTRL key (releasing in the opposite order will not work), and you will find a copy of the file in its new location.

Navigating in Nautilus

Navigating through your various folders and subfolders in Nautilus is quite straightforward. In fact, all is conceptually pretty much the same as what you are accustomed to in Windows and Mac OS. You can simply move into and out of folders through a combination of double-clicking folders and clicking the Back, Forward, and Up buttons.

Tabbed Browsing in Nautilus

In addition to the hierarchal view option provided in the side pane, there is another handy feature that can make your navigation chores even easier: Nautilus's tabbed browsing feature. These tabs (they look like buttons, actually) appear in the navigation bar for each folder you opened on the way to the one you are currently viewing.

Say, for example, that you have a folder called gooseberries inside a folder called Dalarna inside a folder called SwedeStuff inside a folder called NordicStuff, which itself is in your home folder. As you click your way to that gooseberries folder, starting with a double-click on the NordicStuff folder, Nautilus will display a tab for that folder . . . and any folder opened before it. Take a look at Figure 6-4 to see what I mean.

Figure 6-4: Tabbed navigation in Nautilus

As you can see, there is a tab button for each of the folders within the path from your home folder (mine, in this case) to your target: gooseberries. So what, right? Well, say you want to go back to the NordicStuff folder to open a file in which there's some text that you want to copy and then paste into a doc within the gooseberries folder. Sounds like a minor pain, right?

Well, rather than goof around with the Back button, you can instead simply click the NordicStuff tab button, and the contents of that folder will be there before you. Need to go back to gooseberries? Just click the gooseberries tab button. Back to SwedeStuff, you say? Just click the SwedeStuff tab button. All quite *fantastisk*!

Spelling It Out—Typing File Paths in Nautilus

If you prefer typing to clicking, you will be happy to know that you can navigate to a folder by typing its path. Just click the toggle button to the left of the tabs or go to the **Go** menu, and select **Location**. (Keyboard shortcut lovers can just press CTRL-L.) A search box will then appear in the location bar (Figure 6-5) showing the current location, which, in the case of my berried example, would be /home/rg/NordicStuff/SwedeStuff/Dalarna/gooseberries. You can type the path to your target folder in that box, and then press ENTER, after which the contents of the target folder will appear below in the main pane of the Nautilus window.

Figure 6-5: Typing the path to your target folder

Bookmarks Within Nautilus

With all this clicking away to deeply buried subfolders, it is worth mentioning another very handy feature of Nautilus: bookmarks. Yes, Nautilus lets you bookmark folders to which you have navigated. While you are no doubt familiar with creating bookmarks for web pages that you frequent, you may be wondering why on earth you would want to create bookmarks within your filesystem.

Well, imagine that you have a folder that you need to use often, but it is even more buried away than my gooseberries folder in the previous section. Getting there would take an excessive number of mouse clicks, and all that clicking is bound to eventually give you a bad case of carpal tunnel syndrome. While that is great for your HMO, it is most decidedly not good for you. Instead of maiming yourself, you could click your way to that folder once, and then, in the **Bookmarks** menu of the Nautilus window, select **Add Bookmark**. After that, whenever you want to get back to that buried folder, you can just click the **Bookmarks** menu, and the folder will be right there waiting for you in the drop-down list.

Another handy thing about Nautilus bookmarks is that they also appear in Save As dialog boxes, such as when you save an OpenOffice.org document or download a file via Firefox. To use them in any such Save As dialog box, just click the **Save in folder** button, and you will find your bookmarks.

Understanding the Linux Filesystem

With all that path typing, navigating, and bookmarking you've just been learning, you should pretty much be able to figure out how to get from here to there in your home folder. Still, it is probably a good idea to know where your home folder actually is in the scheme of things, just in case you manage to get yourself really lost someday. To understand this, you should have a basic understanding of the Linux filesystem which, as you will find, is a bit different from what you were accustomed to in your previous operating system.

Unlike Windows, the Linux filesystem all stems from a single point called *root* and is represented by a solitary forward slash (/). Your own user account folder is located within a subfolder of root called *home*. This is represented as /home, or to put it into words, the home folder within root. If your user account were to have the same name as mine, rg, the path to that folder would be /home/rg, or the rg folder within home within root. Whatever the name of your user account or the names of any other accounts you have on your machine happen to be, just remember that when you are lost, your folder, and those for all the other folks with user accounts on your machine, are located within the home folder. If you're a more graphically oriented person, the map in Figure 6-6 should help you out.

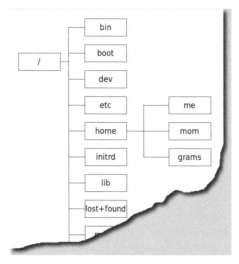

Figure 6-6: The location of your users' folders within the Linux filesystem

What's in All Those Other Folders?

Needless to say, there is more to the Linux filesystem than the root, home, and user account folders. There are several other directories at the same level as home, though for the most part, you really shouldn't be directly mucking around with them unless you know what you're doing. Fortunately, most of these folders are write protected, so you should be fairly well protected from yourself. Still, it is natural to be curious about what those other folders are there for, since . . . well, they're there. So, to satisfy your curiosity a bit, I'll do a little explaining.

In Ubuntu there are four folders that contain most of the applications on your system. The essential elements of your system are located in /sbin. Other elements that need to be there, though they may not be used, such as commands and the like, are located in /bin. Most of the applications that you actually think of as applications and use in a hands-on way are located in /usr. Finally, there are some add-on applications, such as RealPlayer, that install themselves into /opt.

Three other top-level folders that might be of interest to you are /etc, /lib, and /media. The first of these, /etc, is the location of all the configuration files on your system. The second, /lib, is the home of all of the libraries that are required by your system or applications installed on it. These libraries are the Linux equivalent of a Windows .dll file. Finally, /media is where the contents of your various attached external media (such as USB drives and CDs) appear when present.

There are other top-level folders, but their purposes are a bit less straight-forward for the average Linux newbie and, to be honest, probably not all that interesting to you at this stage of the game. Anyway, as I mentioned before, there is no reason for you to be mucking around with any of these folders for the time being, as the items located within them can be accessed in different, and much safer, ways.

Using Nautilus as a Network Browser

Another handy Nautilus feature is its ability to function as a network browser. You can, for example, see what networks and shares are available to you on your home or office network by double-clicking **Network Servers** in the side pane of the Nautilus window or by going to the **Places** menu in the GNOME Panel and selecting **Network**. You can do the same from within a Nautilus window by going to its **Go** menu and selecting **Network**. Icons for any networks or computers on that network would then appear in the Nautilus window. From that window, you can then double-click your way to a share that you have permission to access, such as the Shared Documents folder of a Windows machine or the public folders of a Mac. By the way, in case you are wondering what a share is, I'll clear that up for you. Basically, a *network share* is a location on a computer, such as a folder, where other users on a network can access and save files. The Shared Documents folder on a Windows system is a good example. Other users on a network can copy files from and (usually) write files to the Shared Documents folder, whereas they cannot access any other part of the filesystem on that host machine.

If the share you are trying to open requires a username and password, you will be asked for those in a new window. Note that in this case, the username and password you need to enter are those for the machine to which you are trying to connect—not the ones you're using in Ubuntu (unless the usernames and/or passwords happen to be the same, of course). You can then copy files to and from that share as if it were a folder on your own hard disk.

In some cases, especially when trying to access shares on a Mac running OS X, the double-click method will not work. You will not be able to access any share on a particular machine, even if an icon for that machine appears in the Nautilus window. In such cases, double-click the icon for the machine you are tying to access, and then once open (to an empty window), go to the **Go** menu, and select **Location**. A text box will appear in the location bar (just like in Figure 6-5) with the location of the machine you are trying to access already listed.

To that location, add a forward slash (/) followed by the username used on the target machine. For example, if the target machine is called cowboycats, and the username is mewtoyou, the location would be `smb://cowboycats/mewtoyou`. You can also narrow things down to a particular folder on the machine, as long as you know the path to that folder, by adding to the path you've already typed, `smb://cowboycats/mewtoyou/Documents`, for example. If you prefer, you can type `smb://` and your Mac's IP address, which consists of a set of four numbers separated by periods. In the case of one of my machines, I would type `smb://192.168.0.100`.

In case you don't know, you can find a Mac's IP address by going to the Mac's System Preferences, clicking **Sharing**, and then clicking **Windows Sharing**. The address should appear immediately below the service selection pane.

NOTE   *In case you are wondering, the* smb *at the head of that path stands for* server message block, *but to make things easier (and perhaps more useful in terms of your memory) you can just think of it as being short for* Samba, *which is software used by Unix-based systems (such as Linux and Mac OS X) in order to interact with Windows networks.*

Once you've made your way to the folder you wish to browse on the networked machine you've connected to, it might be a good idea to use the bookmark function in Nautilus to bookmark that open share window. You can then easily access that share in the future by choosing the share's name in the Nautilus Bookmarks menu. Pretty cool, if I do say so myself.

Using Nautilus as an FTP Client

Nautilus not only allows you to browse and mount shares on local networks, but it can also act as an FTP client, say for instance when you want to change the files for your website on a remote server. To do this, go to the Connect to Server window (**File ▶ Connect to Server**), and then select **FTP (with login)** for Service type. Then type the information provided by your website host, and click the **Connect** button. An FTP Network Share icon will then appear on the desktop and in the side pane. Double-click that icon, type your password (for that account—not the one for your Ubuntu system, unless it happens to be the same) when prompted to do so, and then you will be able to view and add to the files you have there.

File and Folder Permissions Within Nautilus

As you make your way in the world of Ubuntu, you will find that occasionally you'll come across files or folders which are in some way locked, either in terms of your being able to read them, being able to alter them, or both. These readability and alterability states of being are referred to as *permissions.*

Now you may be (legitimately) wondering what the point of this permissions business is, so in order to help you understand, I will give you some examples of how it can be useful. Let's say that you have some files that you don't want your spouse or kids to see—some bad poetry or a Christmas shopping list, for example. By denying read permission to those files, or to a folder containing those files, no one would be able to sneak a peek unless they were savvy at changing permissions and had the permissions necessary to change permissions for those files or folders.

As another example, imagine you have a file that you have worked many hours on and have finally completed. To alleviate fears that you might accidentally ruin that file in some way, you could deny yourself write permissions. By doing this, you wouldn't be able to save any changes you make to that file. You would be given the Save As option, but if you wanted to change the file itself, you would have to change the permissions. When you place such restrictions on a file or folder, a lock emblem appears on the icon for it, as shown in Figure 6-7.

Stay Out Palster   DO NOT TOUCH.txt

Figure 6-7: Nautilus tells you when permissions restrict your freedom of movement.

Changing File and Folder Permissions in Nautilus

To change file or folder permissions in Nautilus, just right-click the file or folder in question, and then select **Properties** from the popup menu. Once the Properties window opens, click the **Permissions** tab, and you will see who the owner of the file or folder is and what you and others are allowed or not allowed to do with it. As you can see in Figure 6-8, the options for folders and files are slightly different.

You might find this permissions business a bit confusing, but it is really quite simple to understand. Permissions can be granted or denied to the *owner* of the file or folder (you), to a specified *group*, or to *others* (everybody else). Traditionally, these permissions are referred to as follows:

Read   Permission to view the contents of a file or folder

Write   Permission to alter the contents of a file or folder

Execute   Permission to run a program or script

Nautilus has tried to spell things out a bit more, as you can see in Figure 6-8. In general, however, you needn't worry all that much about setting permissions for your own files, as you are really the only one who has access to your user account. One possible exception you might run into is when you transfer files from CD to your hard disk. In this case, the files will be write protected, meaning that you cannot alter the files until you change the permissions for them. You can change the permissions of such files in order to allow yourself to alter them by going to the **Owner** section of the Properties window and selecting **Read and write** in the menu next to the word *Access* (for files) or **Create and delete files** in the menu next to the words *File access* (for folders). Once you are done, click the **Close** button, and you'll be on your way.

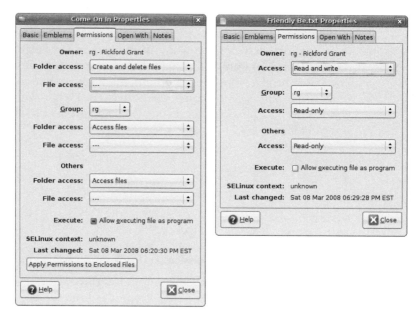

Figure 6-8: Changing permissions in a Nautilus Properties window for files and folders

Keeping Your Home Folder Private

Another exception to my you-don't-need-to-worry-about-permissions claim, and a potentially important one at that, is the state of permissions for your home folder, particularly when other people have user accounts on your machine. In Ubuntu, when someone logs in to their own account on your computer, they can click their way to your user folder and view its contents.

To remedy this situation—and thus protect the sanctity of your home folder, the privacy of its contents, and the peace of mind of its owner (you)—you can change the permissions of your home folder. Here's what you need to do:

1. Open up a Nautilus window, and then double-click **File System** in the side pane. The contents of your entire hard disk will then appear in the right pane of the Nautilus window.

2. Look for and then double-click the folder named **home**. When the contents of the home folder you just clicked appear in the right pane, there should only be one folder there—your own folder, which will have the same name as your own username. For example, mine, as I mentioned earlier, is named rg.

3. Right-click your folder, and then select **Properties** in the popup menu.

4. In the *username* Properties window (mine says *rg Properties*), click the **Permissions** tab.

5. In the Permissions tab, go down to the Group and Others sections, and select **None** in the drop-down menus next to the words *Folder access*. Be sure to do this in both the Group and Others sections. When you're done, your window should look like mine in Figure 6-9. If so, click **Close**.

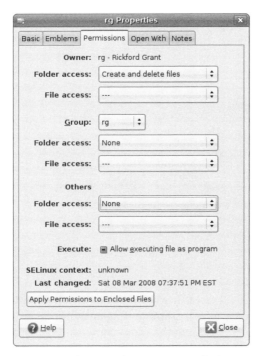

Figure 6-9: Changing the permissions of a home folder for privacy

Reading Data CDs and DVDs

Dealing with data CDs and DVDs in Ubuntu is quite simple, as everything is automatic. To read a CD or DVD with data on it, rather than music or video, place the disk in your drive, and a CD or DVD icon (they look the same) will automatically appear on the desktop and, if you have a Nautilus window open, in the side pane. You can double-click either of those icons, after which the disk's contents will appear in Nautilus. After that, you can copy files from the CD or DVD to your hard disk using standard drag-and-drop or copy-and-paste procedures.

When you want to remove the CD or DVD, just right-click the desktop icon for that disk or the icon for that disk in the side pane, and then select **Eject** in the popup menu. The disk will then be ejected automatically.

Burning Data CDs and DVDs

Burning data CDs and DVDs in GNOME is extremely easy. All you have to do is place a blank CD-R (CD-Recordable) or DVD (DVD-RW, DVD-R, and DVD+RW are all supported by Ubuntu) in your drive, making sure to select a media format supported by your drive, and Nautilus's CD/DVD Creator window will then appear, which as you no doubt notice looks pretty similar to other Nautilus windows, save for the brown band below the location bar and the Write to Disc button (Figure 6-10).

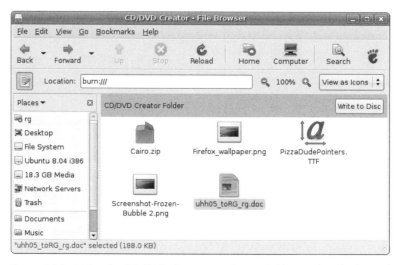

Figure 6-10: A Nautilus CD/DVD Creator window with files ready to be burned to disk

Once the CD/DVD Creator window is open, copying the files you want to burn to disk is pretty much a simple drag-and-drop maneuver. Just open a new Nautilus window, and drag the files you want to burn to disk from that window over to the CD/DVD Creator window. If you prefer to do things in a decidedly Windows-esque fashion, you can select the files you want to transfer to disk by clicking each file once, holding down the CTRL key while doing so, for multiple selections. If you want to select multiple consecutive files, you can click the first file in the group, press and hold SHIFT, and then click the last file in the group, automatically selecting all the files in between. Once you've made your selections, release the CTRL or SHIFT key, right-click any of the highlighted files, and select **Copy** in the popup menu. After that, go back to the CD/DVD Creator window, right-click any open space, and then select **Paste** in the popup menu.

It is probably worth mentioning that the files you copy to the CD/DVD Creator window are not actually copied. Instead, what you see in the Creator window are essentially aliases pointing to the original files in their original locations. Thus, if you move one of the files from its original location before burning the contents of the CD/DVD Creator window to disk, a window will appear asking you if you want to "skip unreadable file." The file is unreadable only in that it isn't there when the CD/DVD Creator looks for it. This is not problematic, because all you have to do is click **Skip**, but it is something worth being aware of.

Once you have copied all of the files you want to burn to disk, click the **Write to Disc** button, after which a window (shown in Figure 6-11) will appear, telling you, among other things, how many megabytes of files you have selected to write to disk. In this window, you can give your disk a title and adjust the speed at which your disk will be burned (slower speed = fewer chances for errors), though you can just as well accept the defaults.

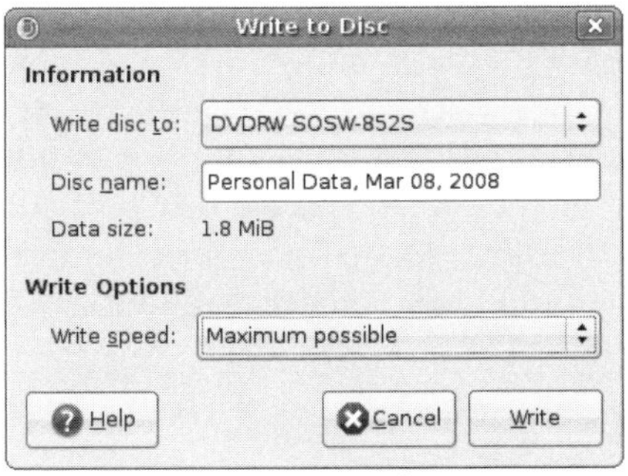

Figure 6-11: Setting options before burning a CD or DVD

Once you are ready to burn the disk, just click the **Write** button, and the CD/DVD Creator will do its work. In some cases a warning window will appear telling you that some of your files may not be suitably named for Windows compatibility. Just click **OK** if you come face to face with such a window, unless you do intend to transfer the files to a Windows system, in which case, you had better go back and rename the files according to Windows naming conventions before you get down to the actual burning. In particular, avoid special characters and diacritics (such as umlauts and accents), and do not use the following characters, which are reserved for Windows system functions: / : ? * " < > |.

Once the burning gets under way, its progress will be shown in a new window, and then when the job is done, you will be asked what you would like to do next. Assuming you are done with your disk burning for the day, click **Eject**, and then click **Close**.

In case you are wondering, the disks you burn in Linux *will* be readable in other operating systems.

Dealing with CD-RW Disks

CD-RW disks are pretty much like CD-R disks except that they can be erased and then written to again. They are also quite a bit more expensive than CD-R disks and, generally, cannot handle faster burning speeds.

Using CD-RW disks is much like working with CD-R disks. If the disk is blank, there is no difference in the process at all, which makes things quite simple. And, if the CD-RW disk already has data on it that you wish to replace with something else, the process is only slightly different.

One of these differences is that Nautilus will treat your CD-RW disk as a regular data disk rather than a blank one. This means that when you pop your disk into the drive, a regular Nautilus window will automatically open, rather than a CD/DVD Creator window.

To write to the disk, you will need to manually switch from the Nautilus window to a CD Creator window, which is easily done by selecting **CD/DVD Creator** in the **Go** menu of the Nautilus window opened for that disk. Once you've done this, the window will become a CD/DVD Creator window. Now drag the files you want to burn to CD to that window, and, once you are ready to burn, click the **Write to Disc** button.

As is the case with regular CD-R disks or DVDs, a Write to Disc window will appear. When you click the **Write** button in that window with a used CD-RW disk in the drive, however, a slight difference occurs. At this point, a new window like that in Figure 6-12 will appear telling you that the disk seems to have files already written on it. Click the **Erase Disc** button in that window, and the CD/DVD Creator will erase the files already on the CD-RW and replace them with the new ones that you dragged to the CD/DVD Creator window. Not bad at all, eh?

Figure 6-12: Erasing a CD-RW disk with Nautilus

Burning ISO Images to Disk

When you download Ubuntu or other Linux distributions from the Internet, you usually download them in the form of one or more disk images, which are commonly referred to as ISOs because such files end in the .iso extension. An *ISO* is an image of a CD's file contents, which means that it is the CD minus the media itself. To put it another way, if CDs had souls, the ISO would be the soul of a CD; take away the CD's metal and plastic, and the remaining data would be an ISO.

As it is impossible to download a physical CD over the Internet, the bodiless ISOs are the next best thing. For example, to get a working copy of Ubuntu from the Web, you need to download an ISO, which you then burn onto a blank CD in order to give the images their bodies back, so to speak. In the process you create the working installation disk that you need to install Ubuntu.

Fortunately, burning an ISO to disk is a pretty simple chore. Just open a Nautilus window, and locate the icon for the ISO file you want to burn to disk. Right-click the ISO file, and in the popup menu that appears, select **Write to Disc**. Once you do this, the Write to Disc window will appear; just click the **Write** button, and you'll be on your way.

Creating Your Own ISO Images

While on the topic of ISOs, it is good to know that you can create ISOs of your own. Of course, you're probably not going about creating your own Linux distros, but you might come up with a set of files that you need to repeatedly burn to disk now or in the future. To create your own ISO, follow the normal process for creating a data CD, but when the Write to Disc window (Figure 6-12) appears, select **File image** in the drop-down menu next to the words *Write disc to*. After that, click **Write**, which will bring up a new window asking for a filename for your new disk image. Give it a name, click **OK**, and in a very short time, you will have an ISO of your own creation.

Burning Multisession CDs

If you are coming from the Windows environment, you are no doubt familiar with multisession CDs. These are CDs on which data is added one session at a time. For example, you burn a few files to disk today, add a few more to the disk tomorrow and a few more files the day after that. Each time you burn additional files to the same disk, you are adding a session, which explains the name *multisession*. If that explanation seems a bit obtuse, you can basically think of them working like floppy disks (albeit with considerably more storage capacity). Unfortunately, Nautilus cannot (yet) deal very well with multisession disks, so to work with them, you will need to use a different disk-burning application. Fortunately, Ubuntu now comes bundled with such an application—Brasero, which can also be used for all of your other disk-burning chores.

You can run Brasero from the **Applications** menu by selecting **Sound & Video ▸ Brasero Disc Burning**.

When you run Brasero, a window appears asking if you want to make Brasero your default disk-burning software. Until you know what method of burning disks appeals to you, click **No**. In the main Brasero window that then opens, click the **Data project** button. You may once again be asked if you want to make Brasero your default disk-burning software. Click **No** for now.

To burn the first session to CD, drag the files you want to burn to disk from the navigation panes at the left side of the window to the project pane on the right side (Figure 6-13), or select files in the left pane, and then click the **Add** button to add them to the right pane.

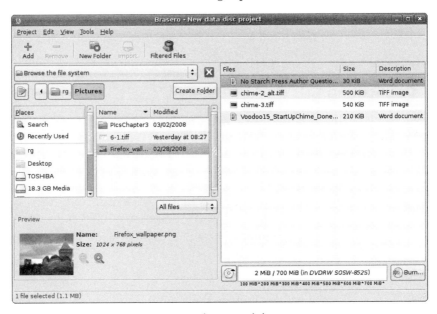

Figure 6-13: Using Brasero to create multisession disks

When you have all the files in place that you want to burn, click the **Burn** button at the bottom-right corner of the screen. A new window, Disc burning setup, will appear. In that window, check the box next to the words *Leave the disc open to add other files later.* (This is the step that sets up a multisession disk.) Once you've done that, give your disk a name, insert a blank disk in the drive, close any Nautilus CD/DVD Creator–related windows that appear, and click **Burn**. The burning process will begin. Brasero will eject the disk when the burn is complete.

Burning Subsequent Sessions

Adding a new session to a multisession disk in Brasero is very similar to the process used for creating the initial session. Here's what you do:

1. Run Brasero, and click the **Data project** button. (If Brasero is already up and running and you have files from a previous session listed in the right pane, go to the **Edit** menu, and select **Empty Project** to clear the right pane.)

2. Insert your multisession disk into the drive, and when the drive stops spinning and you've gotten any Nautilus windows for that disk out of the way, click the **Import** button, after which the contents of your previous session will appear in the right pane of the Brasero window.

3. Add files to the previous session, using either of the methods you used when creating the original session (drag-and-drop or select-and-click-**Add**).

4. When you've added the files you want, click **Burn**. The process from then on out is exactly the same as it was for the first session. To add files in subsequent sessions, just follow the process outlined above yet again.

Duplicating CDs and DVDs

Now that you are familiar with Brasero, this is as a good a time as any to introduce another of its features: CD/DVD duplication. To duplicate a disk, place the disk in the drive, start up Brasero, and then click the **Disc copy** button. In the window that then appears (Figure 6-14), click the **Copy** button.

Brasero will begin copying your disk, and when it is done doing that, it will eject the disk and ask you to insert a blank one. A few seconds after you insert the blank disk, Brasero will automatically start writing to it. When the process is complete, Brasero will eject the disk. You can then quit Brasero.

USB Storage Devices

No chapter dealing with file handling and storage would be complete without touching upon the topic of USB storage devices, so that is exactly where I will now turn. Unless you have been under a digital rock for the past few years, you are no doubt well familiar with USB devices. Your printer is

CD/DVD copy options

Select source drive to copy

DVDRW SOSW-852S

Type:	CD-R
Size:	629.4 MB free
Contents:	data tracks
Status:	data can be appended to the medium

Select a drive to write to

DVDRW SOSW-852S   Properties

**The drive that holds the source media will also be
the one used to record.**

*A new recordable media will be required once the one
currently loaded has been copied.*

Number of copies 1

Cancel   Copy

Figure 6-14: Using Brasero to duplicate disks

very likely a USB device, as is your scanner. And although your digital camera is not a USB device in the traditional sense, chances are that every time you connect it to your computer in order to transfer photos, you are doing so via a USB connector.

Among the most popular USB devices out there are those for file storage. These include external hard disks, flash memory card readers, and the tiny, finger-sized devices known as *flash drives* (Figure 6-15). Flash drives are especially popular today, and deservedly so: they are quite inexpensive; extremely handy when you need to transfer fairly large, but not gigantic, amounts of data from computer to computer (from work to home, for example); and pretty safe in terms of cross-platform (including Linux) compatibility.

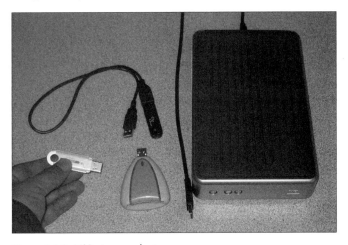

Figure 6-15: USB storage devices

Putting USB Storage Devices to Work

Let's start with some good news here by pointing out that working with USB storage devices is really easy. Just plug the device into one of the USB ports on your computer. The LED on the device will do a bit of blinking as the system reads what's on it, and after that, a disk icon for that device will appear on your desktop. A few moments later, a Nautilus window will open, revealing the contents of the device. An icon for the USB device will also appear in the side pane of the Nautilus window. You can then copy files to and from the device using the drag-and-drop or copy-and-paste procedures I mentioned earlier in this chapter.

Once you are done and wish to remove the device, right-click its desktop icon, and select **Unmount Volume** in the popup menu. You can also right-click the icon in the Nautilus side pane, in which case you would select **Unmount** in the popup menu. If there is any data that needs to be written to the device, the system will start writing and tell you so in a message at the bottom-right corner of the screen (shown at left in Figure 6-16). Another message will appear in the same location when the writing process is complete, telling you that it is safe to remove the drive from the USB port (Figure 6-16, right).

Figure 6-16: Ubuntu lets you know what is happening with your USB drives.

Working with Bluetooth Devices

While we're on the topic of file handling, it is probably a good time to learn how to work with Bluetooth devices. As I mentioned in Chapter 3, if you have a Bluetooth adapter in your machine, either built in or plugged into a USB port, a Bluetooth icon will appear in the right half of the GNOME upper panel.

Browsing Devices

To browse another Bluetooth device to which you have access, right-click the Bluetooth icon in the top panel, and select **Browse Device**. A window like the one in Figure 6-17 will then appear. Select the device you wish to browse and click **Connect**. A window will appear in the target device asking for a passkey. Pick four easy numbers, and type them. A window will then appear on your Ubuntu desktop asking you to type the same passkey. Click **Enter passkey**, after which another window will appear in which you actually type the key. Once you type it, click **OK**. The device will then appear in the side pane of a Nautilus window, and its contents, if viewable, will appear to the right.

Figure 6-17: Searching and selecting nearby Bluetooth devices in Ubuntu

Sending Files by Bluetooth

To send a file by Bluetooth from your computer to another Bluetooth-capable device, right-click the Bluetooth panel icon, and select **Send File**. A window will then appear in which you can navigate to the target file. Once you have made your selection, click **Open**. The Select Device window will then appear. Select the recipient machine, and click **Connect**. Your machine will then begin transferring the file. If the recipient machine is set up to seek permission first before accepting a Bluetooth file transfer, you or the recipient will have to perform the appropriate action on the recipient machine before the transfer can be completed.

Receiving Files by Bluetooth

In order to receive files by via Bluetooth from another Bluetooth-capable device, you have to first set up your device to allow such transfers. To do this, right-click the Bluetooth panel icon, and select **Preferences**. In the Bluetooth Preferences window, click the **General** tab, and then check the top box in that tab, next to the words *Receive files from remote devices*. Your machine will then automatically receive files sent to it via Bluetooth and save them to the desktop.

Project 6: Creating and Extracting Compressed Files

Since I have been talking about file storage, it seems only fitting to wrap things up in this chapter by teaching you how to create and extract compressed files. In the Windows world, these are generally referred to as Zip files, while in the Linux world, *tarball* is the operative name. The Linux name, in case you're wondering, comes from the application that is used to create the archive for such files, Tar.

Anyway, to get some of the hands-on stuff down, we'll be creating a Windows/Linux/Mac–friendly Zip file, and then extracting it. We can get down to business by opening a Nautilus window and creating a couple of dummy files to work with. You can do this by going to the Nautilus **File** menu and selecting **Create Document ▶ Empty File**. A new file will appear in the Nautilus window, with its name highlighted. You can now just type a name for the file, such as the one I'm using: *dogwood*. Now repeat the process to create a second file. I'll be calling that one *violet*. Use something equally evocative for yours.

Now that we have two files to work with, let's start creating the compressed archive by following these steps:

1. Select the two files either by clicking your mouse to the side of the files, and then dragging the cursor (with the mouse button still pressed) over both files until they are highlighted, or by holding down the CTRL key and clicking on each file individually.

2. Once both files are highlighted, right-click either one, and select **Create Archive** from the popup menu.

3. In the Create Archive window that then appears, type **blossoms** in the Archive text box, and then select **.zip** from the drop-down menu button to the right of that. Once everything looks like what I've set up in Figure 6-18, click the **Create** button, after which a compressed archive of your two files (blossoms.zip) will appear in your home folder.

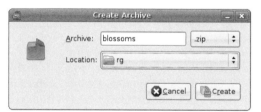

Figure 6-18: Creating a compressed archive

Now that you know how to put things together, let's get back to work and learn the equally simple task of ripping it all apart—well, okay, *extracting* it.

1. Drag the original dogwood and violet files to the Trash to get them out of the way.

2. Double-click the **blossoms.zip** file you've just created. A window showing the contents of the file will then appear (Figure 6-19).

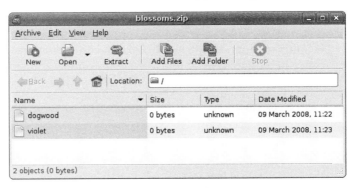

Figure 6-19: Extracting a compressed archive

3. In that window, click the **Extract** button, after which another window, Extract, will appear.

4. Click the **Extract** button in that window, and within a second (two at the most), you will find two new copies of dogwood and violet in your home folder.

Now you've created and extracted a compressed archive, which is in this case a Zip file. You can also create a compressed tarball in the future by following the same procedure (hopefully with real rather than dummy files), but when it's time to select an archive type, select **.tar.gz** instead of .zip. Other than that single step, it is the same creation and extraction process.

7

DRESSING UP THE BIRD

Customizing the Look and Feel of Your System

Before entering the world of Linux, I had used just about every desktop operating system around. Despite the differences among them all, however, one thing that I eventually suffered from in each case was a kind of visual boredom. I suppose you might call it GUI fatigue. It wasn't that I was tired of using a graphical interface; it was just that I couldn't help but get sick of looking at the same old icons, window borders, and color schemes. Of course, there were some changes that could be made, but it just wasn't possible to get around the basic look and feel without add-ons that demanded a price in terms of performance.

One of the features of Linux that pleased me to no end, and continues to do so, is that users can drastically change the look of things. I don't mean just the icons and backgrounds, but everything, including the actual window borders and controls. Add to that the variety of graphical desktop environments and window managers available for Linux, and you have a totally customizable system. Is it any wonder that there are so many more Linux desktop screenshots out there on the Web than for any other system? If you don't believe me, just have a look at a site dedicated to Linux screenshots, www.lynucs.org, and click the **Screenshots** link.

You may not be as fickle as I am in terms of the look and feel of your system, but you can learn to use and enjoy all the graphical customization power that Linux offers you as you work through this chapter.

Project 7A: Creating a New User Account

If you are reluctant to alter the look of your present setup, you can create a new user account and experiment with making the changes in this chapter when logged in to the new account. If you opt to go this route, your regular home environment will remain untouched because look-and-feel customizations that are performed in one user account do not affect other user accounts. When you are all done with the project, you can then simply delete the new user account. Either way, it's up to you.

To set up a new user account, follow these steps:

1. Go to the **System** menu, and select **Administration ▶ Users and Groups**.

2. Once the Users Settings window appears, click **Unlock**.

3. A new window will appear telling you that someone is trying to mess with your system. No need to worry because that someone is you, so type your password, and then click **Authenticate**. The buttons in the Users Settings window will now be active.

4. Click the **Add User** button, which will bring up a New User Account window.

5. In that window, type a new username: **graphika**. In the Real name field, you can type whatever you like; I used *Graphics Lover* in the example.

6. In the Profile section, give yourself the ability to install software and perform other administrative tasks in the new account by selecting **Administrator** in the drop-down menu.

NOTE   *Normally, the privilege to install software and perform other system-wide changes (Administrator) is not selected by default on new user accounts, since you probably don't want your kids, workmates, or anyone else with his or her own user account on your computer installing all sorts of weird stuff and screwing up your system settings.*

7. Skip over the Contact Information section of the window, and in the Password section, type an easy-to-remember user password in the two password boxes; in this case, the same one you're using for your present account will probably be easiest to deal with since the graphika account is your account, too. Your window should now look more or less like the one in Figure 7-1.

Figure 7-1: Creating a new user account

8. If everything looks fine and dandy, click **OK** to close the window and get back to the Users Settings window, which will now list your new user account right below your current one (see Figure 7-2).

Figure 7-2: The new user account displayed in the Users Settings window

Logging In to Your New Account

To use this new account, go to the **System** menu and select **Quit** (or just click the **Logout** button at the far-right corner of the top panel). When the logout window appears, click **Log Out**. After a few seconds, you will be back at the login screen. Type your new username in that window, and then press ENTER. After that type the new password for the account, and press ENTER again. You will soon be at the desktop for your new user account.

Switching Users

It's worth knowing that there is another way to switch users other than simply logging out of one account and into another. This alternative approach is logically referred to as *switching users*. Switching users differs from the logout/login approach, in that you remain logged in to your original account while you log in to your other account (or while someone else with an account on your computer logs in to theirs). Going this route keeps all of the windows or applications you have open. These windows will not appear in the account you are switching to, but they will be there, conveniently waiting for you, when you switch back to the account from whence you came.

This is a good way to proceed if you plan to be switching back and forth between your two accounts. It is also a good approach when, say, your child needs to log in to his or her account for a moment to do a quick email check, burn a CD to play on the way to the beach, or print a file for school. When your child is done, you can quickly get back to what you were doing before without having to reopen files, web pages, or whatever else you happened to be dealing with at the time of the switch.

You can switch users quite easily by clicking your username in the top GNOME Panel (the Fast User Switch Applet) and selecting the user account you wish to switch to in the drop-down menu that appears. Once the selection is made, your screen will darken for a second or two until you are delivered to the login screen, where you need only type the password for the account you selected, followed by a press of the ENTER key. (Do not type the username as you would during a normal login.) After that, you will be at the desktop of the selected user account.

To get back to your original user account after going the switch-user route, just click the username from which you came and, after a few seconds of darkness, a window will appear in which you must type the user password of the account you are returning to. Type your password, click **Unlock**, and you will be back at your original desktop, with everything as it was when you last saw it, open windows and all. Pretty cool.

Logging In to Another Account in a Separate Window

If switching back and forth between accounts seems like too much of a hassle to you, there is yet another, almost surreal, alternative—logging in to another account in a separate window while still in your regular user account.

This being-two-places-at-the-same-time approach requires a little bit of work up front, but it provides a lot of convenience in the long run, not only when going through Project 7B on page 108, but also whenever one of those "Hey 'rents, can I check my email for a second?" moments arises. To set things up so that you can do this, you need to install, set up, and use an application called Xnest. Here are the steps:

1. Run Synaptic, do a search for *xnest*, and install it.

2. Once Xnest is installed, close Synaptic, right-click the **Applications** menu, and select **Edit Menus** in the popup menu.

3. When the menu editor window appears, click **System Tools** in the left pane, and then check the box next to the words *New Login in a Window* in the right pane.

4. Click **Close** to finish.

After performing these steps, you can log in to your new account by going to the **Applications** menu and selecting **System Tools ▸ New Login in a Window**. An Xnest window will appear, and after a few seconds, the Ubuntu login screen will appear within that window (Figure 7-3). In that screen, type your new username (*graphika*, or whatever name you chose) and password as you would during any other login. Your new desktop will soon appear in the Xnest window.

When you are done with your Xnest session, click the **Logout** button at the far right of the top panel within the Xnest window, and then click **Log Out** in the set of choices that appears. The Xnest window will automatically close after you have been logged out of that session.

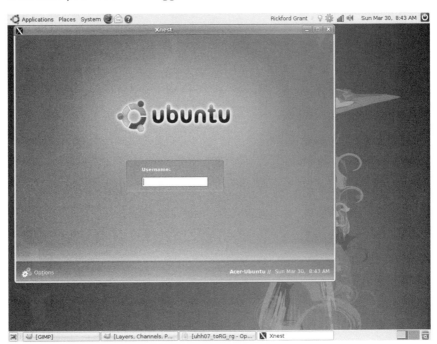

Figure 7-3: Using Xnest to log in to another account while still in your own

Project 7B: Customizing Your Desktop Environment

Whichever user account you've decided to play with, you are now ready for action. By the time we get to the end of the process, you will have created a much wilder, and, depending on how you look at things, gaudier desktop environment than you've ever seen before. All of this is in good fun, of course, and when you are done, you should be able to completely and confidently customize things the way you want on your own. So let's go.

7B-1: Adding Emblems to Folders

One of the coolest things about Nautilus is that it allows you to add little folder-top icons called *emblems*. These emblems can graphically remind you what each folder is for, and they're not only for folders—you can add them to any folder or file. The look of these emblems also changes when you change your desktop themes, so you're in for more visual excitement later on in this chapter. For now, however, let's learn how to use them by adding one to the Documents folder. Just right-click the folder, and then select **Properties** in the popup menu. When the Properties window appears, click the **Emblems** tab and scroll down until you see the emblem called *documents* (Figure 7-4). Click the checkbox next to it, and then click the **Close** button. The emblem should now appear on your folder.

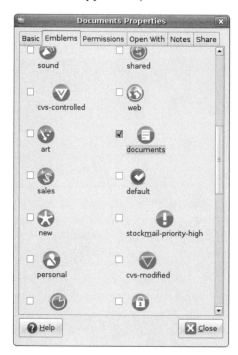

Figure 7-4: Choosing emblems for your folders

Now, for additional practice, try adding the **sound** emblem to your Music folder. Just use the same steps as before, and substitute the appropriate items and entries.

7B-2: Setting Window Backgrounds (and Emblems Again)

Once you've added those two emblems, your folders should look a bit spunkier (and we'll make those emblems look spunkier still further along in the chapter). Nevertheless, the background of the Nautilus window is still white. You need not stand for that if you don't want to; you can change it as well. To do so, just go to your home window, click the **Edit** menu, and select **Backgrounds and Emblems**. The Backgrounds and Emblems window will then appear (see Figure 7-5).

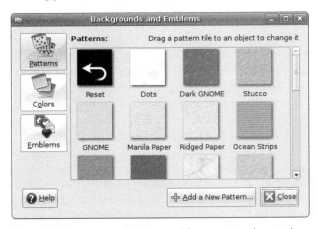

Figure 7-5: Choosing a background for your Nautilus window

From this window, you can drag any pattern into your home window, or into any other Nautilus window for that matter, and the pattern will then become the background for all your Nautilus windows. So, for experience's sake, scroll down to find the pattern swatch called **Manila Paper**, and then drag it to the white space in the main pane of your home window. Once you've done that, the previously white window area will look like the wallpaper in a lawyer's office. Very nice, if you like that sort of thing. You can change it to a different background in the same way, of course, or you can go back to the default white by dragging the **Reset** swatch into the window.

NOTE   *If you prefer to use an image of your own for the Nautilus window background, you can also do so quite easily. Just locate the image in a new Nautilus window, click it with both the left and right mouse buttons (or just the middle mouse button, if you have a three-button mouse), and then drag the image to any open space within the target window. When you release the buttons, select **Set as Background** in the popup menu that then appears.*

In addition to the buttons for pattern and color swatches, there is a third button in the Backgrounds and Emblems window called Emblems. Clicking the Emblems button reveals all of the emblems you saw in Project 7B-1 on page 108, thus providing you with another way to add emblems to your folders. This method is far handier when adding emblems to several folders or files in the same go.

To see how this works, click the **Emblems** button. Then drag the **camera** emblem onto your Pictures folder and the **people** emblem onto your Public folder. The selected emblems will then immediately appear on those folders.

7B-3: Dolling Up the Side Pane (and Emblems Yet Again)

Now let's change the look of the Nautilus side pane. Keeping the Backgrounds and Emblems window open (if you already closed it, open it again), click the **Places** menu button in the Nautilus side pane, and select **Information**.

You can add a different background pattern to the side pane now as well, but for practice let's add a color instead. To do this, click the **Colors** button in the Backgrounds and Emblems window. The window will now be filled with swatches of color. Drag the **Grapefruit** swatch to your side pane, and it will turn from gray to, of all things, grapefruit (albeit a very dark and unusually colored grapefruit). You can also create a two-color gradation effect by adding yet another color. Drag the **Mango** swatch to the very bottom of the side pane (but still within the pane), and you should have a grapefruit-to-mango, top-to-bottom gradation within the pane. Of course, if you are not pleased with this tropical color set, you can get back to your original default gray panel by dragging the **Reset** swatch onto the area. When you're done, you can close the Backgrounds and Emblems window.

The side pane of your Nautilus window provides yet a third way to work with emblems. But before I let you in on this third, and last, way, let's add another folder to your home folder. Create a folder and name it Finances, which you can use to store files dealing with your relative worth in the modern scheme of things.

After you've created the new folder, go to the side pane, click the **Information** drop-down menu, and select **Emblems**. A list of emblems will appear within the side pane. Select the **money** emblem, and drag it onto your Finances folder. Next, select the **draft** emblem, and drag it onto your Templates folder. Finally, drag the **multimedia** emblem onto your Videos folder. Your window should now look like that in Figure 7-6.

Once you are done, go back to the drop-down menu and select **Information** to get everything back to relative normalcy again.

Even if it's not your cup of tea, you have to admit that your Nautilus window is definitely more colorful now. You can, of course, change it to look however you want it to, but I'll ask you to hold off on that a little while longer, because you are going to be doing a some more playing around with it shortly.

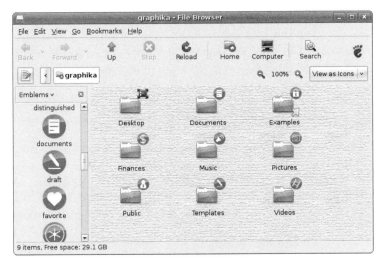

Figure 7-6: Selecting emblems from the Nautilus side pane

7B-4: Changing the Desktop Background

Now that your home folder window is all gussied up (or gaudied up, depending on your aesthetic sense of things), you may feel that your desktop looks rather drab in comparison.

Changing the desktop background (often called *wallpaper*) is easily achieved by right-clicking any open space on the desktop and selecting **Change Desktop Background** in the popup menu. This will bring up the Appearance Preferences window, opened to the Background tab (see Figure 7-7).

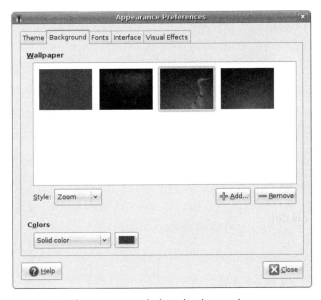

Figure 7-7: Changing your desktop background

Installing Additional Wallpapers

As you can see, the default wallpaper in Ubuntu is called Ubuntu, but other than that there really isn't much for you to choose from. To remedy the situation, you need to provide some images of your own. These could be photos from a digital camera, works of art you created on your computer, or just about anything you want to put there. In this case, however, you are going to venture out onto the Web to get and then install some wallpaper. A number of sites provide free desktop wallpaper, such as those for automobile manufacturers, singers, television shows, and so on.

Two sites specifically geared toward Linux users are www.kde-look.org and http://art.gnome.org, but you can get wallpaper from wherever you like. If you want to follow along using the same bigger-than-life-Tux wallpaper that I use here, go directly to the wallpaper image by pointing your web browser to www.taiabati.com/linux/OLDindex.php, scrolling down the page a tad to the second TUX section, and then clicking the download button next to the image size that best matches your screen. When the picture appears in the browser window, right-click it, and then select **Save Image As**. In the Save Image window, give it an easy-to-remember name (*wall_TUX-2_1024x768.jpg* may be exact, but it might prove a bit much to deal with after a while) or use the one I gave it, *mightyTux.jpg*, and click **Save**. If you prefer, you can download any wallpaper you like from wherever you like, as long as it is in a supported format, such as BMP, PNG, or JPEG. It's all up to you.

Once you've downloaded your wallpaper, place it in your Pictures folder. You may want to create a Wallpapers subfolder to keep things better organized, but that's up to you. After that, you can install the new image by going to the **Background** tab in the Appearance Preferences window and clicking the **Add** button. In the Add Wallpaper window that then appears, navigate to your new wallpaper, click it once to highlight it, and then click **Open**. The wallpaper will then appear highlighted in the Appearance Preferences window and will soon thereafter appear on the desktop itself (Figure 7-8). Once it does, click **Close** to complete the process.

Wallpaper from Internet to Desktop—Quick and Easy

It is also possible to almost automatically set an image from the Web as your desktop wallpaper by right-clicking that image within your web browser and then selecting **Set As Desktop Background**. A small window will then appear, in which you can preview what the download will look like on screen (Figure 7-9). You can also adjust the position (tiled or centered, for example) and background color for your desktop in this window. Once you're done making adjustments, click the **Set Desktop Background** button. The image will then appear on your Desktop, while the image file itself will be saved to your download location (your home folder, by default) with the title *Firefox_wallpaper.png*.

Figure 7-8: The newly wallpapered desktop

Figure 7-9: Selecting web page images as
desktop wallpapers

Hiding the Bottom Panel

By the way, you may have noticed that you can barely see the panel at the
bottom of the screen in Figure 7-8. This is because the panel obscured
the bottom of the new wallpaper, which irritated me. I went to the Panel
Properties window by right-clicking some empty space in the bottom panel
and selecting **Properties** in the popup menu. In the Panel Properties window,
I clicked the checkbox next to the word **Autohide** and then clicked **Close**.
The autohide function works just like it does in Windows or Mac OS X—the
panel stays out of view until you move your mouse into the general vicinity of

where it should be. You can make the same change if you like, but that is an aesthetic matter that I will leave up to you. Ah, the sweet taste of artistic freedom.

7B-5: Downloading and Installing the Art Manager (GNOME Art)

Searching the Internet for wallpaper to install can in itself be a rather fun adventure, but sometimes it can also feel like quite a chore. Fortunately for you, me, and all involved in such things, there is an even easier way: the Art Manager. The Art Manager, also known as GNOME Art, is a handy application that searches the art.gnome.org site, and downloads a list, with thumbnails, of all the wallpapers that are available there. It can also do this for the various window borders, controls, and icon theme sets that you can use in the following parts of this project. Using the thumbnailed lists, you can easily download and install whatever you want—all without ever placing a cursor in your web browser. Needless to say, the Art Manager is decidedly cool!

Unfortunately, the Art Manager is not installed by default; however, after having gone through Chapter 5, you know how easy it is to download and install applications like the Art Manager. All you have to do is run Synaptic, do a search for *gnome-art*, and then install it.

You can then run Art Manager by selecting **System ▸ Preferences ▸ Art Manager**. The GNOME Art window will then appear with absolutely nothing in it. To put it to use, and relieve that emptiness, go to the **Art** menu, and select **Backgrounds ▸ GNOME**. (You can select **All** instead of GNOME if you like, but it will take longer to download the list of available wallpapers.)

Once your selection is made, the Art Manager will begin downloading a list of all that is available for you at http://art.gnome.org. It may seem like nothing is happening for a minute or so, but that is normal; just hang in there. When it's done, you will see a list of thumbnails for you to choose from (Figure 7-10).

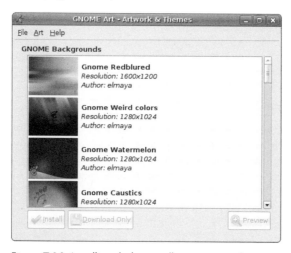

Figure 7-10: Installing desktop wallpapers using the Art Manager

You can now install wallpaper by scrolling down until you find one that suits your fancy, clicking it once to highlight it, and then clicking the **Install** button. Art Manager will then download and install it. After that, just open the Appearance Preferences window, and choose the wallpaper you just downloaded as your desktop wallpaper. As I said before, Art Manager is a very handy tool to have, especially since you'll be using it more soon within this project.

7B-6: Changing Window Borders, Controls, and Icon Sets

Now we get to my favorite part of this journey through the world of digital cosmetic surgery—changing the way window borders and controls look in GNOME. Let's set about doing just that.

The procedure is really quite easy. Go to the **System** menu, and select **Preferences ▶ Appearance**. The Appearance Preferences window will open to the Theme tab, showing you a list of the themes that are installed on your system (see Figure 7-11). The default theme in Hardy Heron is called Human-Murrine, but, as you can see, there are several others.

Figure 7-11: Selecting a theme in GNOME

To get the hang of things, have a look at each of the themes listed by clicking them one by one. The changes will take effect immediately. Just clicking a theme will change your window borders, controls, and even, if you take a peek in your home folder, the icons. This is especially noticeable when you click Crux or Glider.

Each theme consists of a window border, a set of controls, and a collection of icons. This being the case, it is possible to mix and match these elements on your own. For example, let's say that you like the look and color of the quasi-industrial controls in Crux, but you prefer the window icons in Mist and the borders in Human. Well, you needn't despair, because you can create a custom theme consisting of these three different elements.

To create your own mix-and-match theme, just click the **Customize** button in the Theme tab of the Appearance Preferences window. A new window will open, in which you will find five tabs: Controls, Colors, Window Border, Icons, and Pointer (Figure 7-12). From within each of these tabs you can select the components you prefer. For now, let's first click the **Controls** tab and select **Crux**. Then click the **Window Border** tab and select **Human**. Finally, click the **Icons** tab and select **Mist**.

Figure 7-12: Creating a custom theme in Ubuntu

Now keep the Customize Theme window open, but open your home folder and take a look at what you've done. Hmm . . . not bad. But, perhaps you don't really like the look of those Human window borders all that much. To find something that suits you better, click the **Window Border** tab again, go down the list, and click each entry until you see something you do like (Metabox seems to do the trick for me), and select that. Better? Now that you are satisfied, you can click the **Close** button.

You will now be back at the Appearance Preferences window, where you will notice your new theme listed with the name *Custom*. If you want to save this new combination for later use, click the **Save As** button. Doing so will open a dialog box in which you can name your theme and write a brief comment about it. So, name your theme, write a comment if you like, and then click **Save**. Your new theme will now appear in alphabetical order within the theme list under the name you chose.

Once that's all done, your home folder window should look like that in Figure 7-13 (and take a look at your panel and Applications menu while you're at it). Ah, très cool!

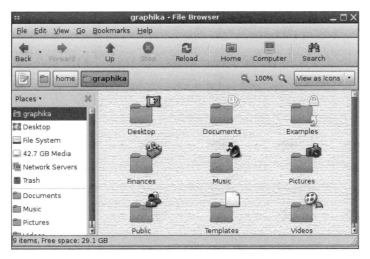

Figure 7-13: Changing the look of your system windows

7B-7: Installing Additional Window Borders, Controls, and Icons

If you are excited about this customization thing but you're not satisfied with the theme choices included with the system, you can download and install still other window borders, controls, and icons. To show you how to do this, I will walk you through creating a faux Mac theme, which will look fairly similar to the standard Aqua theme of Mac OS X, as you can see in Figure 7-14.

Figure 7-14: An Aqua-fied Ubuntu desktop

Getting and Installing the Files You'll Need

To get the files you'll need to do this, take the Art Manager for another ride. Once it is up and running, go to the **Art** menu, and select **Backgrounds ▸ Other**. Once the list of available wallpapers appears in the Art Manager window, scroll down until you find one called **Real shoot**, install it by clicking the **Install** button, and then select and apply it in the Background tab of the Appearance Preferences window.

NOTE *If Art Manager does not automatically start downloading a list of available files when you make a selection from the Art menu, just restart Art Manager and try again.*

Next get a set of matching application control widgets and window borders by going back to the Art Manager **Art** menu and selecting **Desktop Themes ▸ Application**. When the list is downloaded, look for a file called **Yattacier 3**, and install it. In the Appearance Preferences window that then appears, select **Yattacier 3** in the list within the Theme tab.

To round things up, let's add some new icons to the mix by going back to the Art Manager, heading to the **Art** menu, and selecting **Desktop Themes ▸ Icon**. Once the list is downloaded, look for and install **Snow-Apple**. After that it's basically a repeat of the previous step, but this time around, click the **Icons** tab in the Customize Theme window, and then select **Snow Apple**.

Finishing Touches

Well, things are certainly sort of Mac-ish now, but there is even more we can do to emphasize the effect. First, open the Preferences window for your bottom panel by right-clicking the area to the far right of Trash and selecting **Properties** in the popup menu. In the **General** tab of that window, uncheck **Expand**, and then increase the size of the panel to around 54 pixels. When you're done, click **Close**, and then start adding launchers for the applications you use most.

NOTE *If you'd like an even more OS X–ish Dock, try out Avant Window Navigator, which is available via Synaptic (search for* avant-window-navigator*). You must have Visual Effects turned on in the Visual Effects tab of the Appearance Preferences window in order to use it.*

Once you're done, go to the top menu, and remove the three icons next to the System menu. After that, add a Window Selector applet, so that you have some way to navigate through your open windows. You might also want to change the background in your home folder, since the warm tones presently there no longer match your new cooler configuration.

The transformation is now complete, but you can also add trash can and computer icons to your desktop by going on to Project 7C, after which, your desktop should look something like mine back in Figure 7-14. You can stick with your new OS X–ish theme, or switch to something else. For consistency's sake, I will switch back to the default theme now. By the way, if you do decide to keep the faux-Aqua theme, remember to click the **Save Theme** button in the Appearance Preferences window and give the theme a name.

As you are already aware, unlike Windows, Mac OS X, or other Linux distributions, Ubuntu has a completely empty desktop upon installation. A lot of people advocate this approach because it discourages the permanent use of the desktop as a location to store files and program launchers. After all, as the argument goes, you don't place your trash can or file cabinet on the desktop in your office, do you?

All such logic aside, there are still many people who prefer to have their trash can, hard disk, and home folder on their desktops, thank you very much. If you are one of them, as I am, here's what you need to do:

1. Press ALT-F2 to bring up the Run Application window. This keyboard shortcut is the equivalent of clicking the Run Application panel applet that you placed on the panel in your original user account.

2. Run the GNOME Configuration Editor by typing `gconf-editor` in that window and then pressing ENTER.

3. When the Configuration Editor window appears, click the small arrow next to *apps*, scroll down to *nautilus*, and click the small arrow next to that.

4. Click **desktop** in that expanded nautilus section, after which the options for that item will appear in the right pane of the window (Figure 7-15).

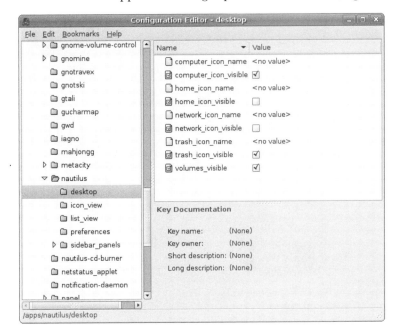

Figure 7-15: The Configuration Editor

5. Check the boxes next to the items you would like to appear on the desktop. You have four unchecked choices to choose from: computer_icon_visible (like My Computer in Windows), documents_icon_visible (to create a link to your Documents folder, if you have one), home_icon_visible (for quick access to your home folder), and trash_icon_visible (for you-know-what).

6. When you're done, close the Configuration Editor.

Stretching Desktop Icons

A relatively new and cool feature in the GNOME desktop is stretchable icons. This allows you to make individual desktop icons any size you want, which can be not only aesthetically pleasing but also quite functional. For example, you could stretch one of your most commonly used launchers to make it easy to locate, or you could stretch the thumbnail of a photo file so that it appears as desktop art (see Figure 7-16).

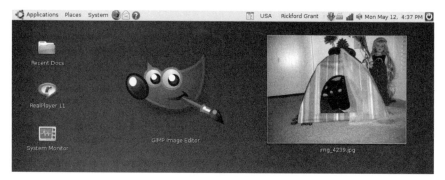

Figure 7-16: Desktop icons can be stretched to any size you want.

To stretch a desktop icon, right-click the icon, and select **Stretch icon** in the popup menu. Four blue squares will appear at each of the corners surrounding the icon (as shown in Figure 7-17). Just click and drag any of those squares until the icon is the size you want. Once you are done stretching, click anywhere on the desktop, after which the squares will disappear.

Figure 7-17: Stretching a desktop icon

You may have noticed while working with the Art Manager that there is a menu selection (**Art ▶ Other Themes**) for something called Login Manager. The Login Manager is your login screen, also known as a *greeter*—the screen where you type your username and user password when you first log in to your system. The Login Manager is another thing that you can customize, but be forewarned that any changes you make will be system-wide, not just for you; whatever Login Manager theme you install and choose will be the Login Manager theme that everyone else with user accounts will see when they use the machine. Of course, if you are the only one using your machine, this point is moot.

7D-1: Downloading a Login Manager Theme

In order to try customizing the Login Manager, run the Art Manger, and select **Art ▶ Other Themes ▶ Login Manager**. Once you've done this, browse through the various themes in the list, and choose one or two that you want; I give you free rein on this one, but I'll be choosing the theme called ManzanaTux to complete the faux-Mac theme, in case you want to follow along exactly.

Unlike your other experiences with the Art Manager up to now, Login Manager themes can only be downloaded, leaving you to do the installation yourself. That being the case, once you've made your selection, click the **Download Only** button. Once the download is complete, you will find the file in archive form, with a tar.gz ending, in your home folder, or any other folder you decided to save it to. You do not need to extract, or *untar*, the archived file.

NOTE   *If you have any trouble installing greeters via Art Manager, go to http://art.gnome .org, click the Login Manager link on that page, and then download a greeter directly.*

7D-2: Installing Your New Login Manager Theme

Once you've downloaded a theme or two of your liking, you need to open the Login Window Preferences window. To do this, go to the **System** menu, and select **Administration ▶ Login Window**. A dialog box asking for your password will then open. Type the password for the account you are currently using, and click **OK**. The Login Window Preferences window will soon appear (see Figure 7-18). Click the **Local** tab in that window to see a thumbnailed list of the greeters available.

Figure 7-18: Customizing the Login Manager

You can add the greeters you just downloaded to this list by dragging the files directly to the list. A small window will then appear, asking if you're sure that you want to install the file you've just dragged to the list, and since you do want to install the file, click **Install**.

To select the greeter you wish to use, just click the round button next to its name in the list in the Login Window Preferences window, and then click the **Close** button. Of course, to see your greeter in action, you will have to log out first so you can log back in, but you needn't restart or shut down the machine. You can then see your new greeter when the login screen appears (Figure 7-19), though yours may well be different.

Project 7E: Changing Your Splash Screen

Well, now you've changed just about all there is to change system-wide, but there is actually one more item that you can tinker with—the splash screen. This version of Ubuntu doesn't actually have a splash screen, so you may very well be unfamiliar with the term. Basically, it is a small, borderless window that appears in the middle of the screen while GNOME is starting up, right after you log in but before you get to your desktop. It isn't really necessary, but it can look pretty cool and add a touch of personalization to your system.

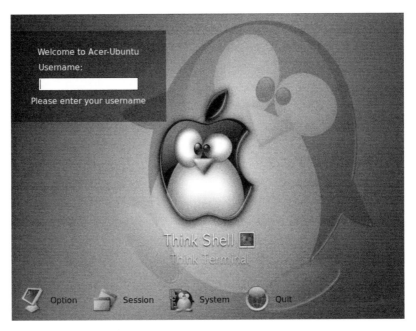

Welcome to Acer-Ubuntu
Username:

Please enter your username

Think Shell
Think Terminal

Option   Session   System   Quit

Figure 7-19: The new login screen

7E-1: Enabling Automatic Login

While the Login Window Preferences window is open, it's as good a time as any to mention an option that may be of interest to you. If you find it a bit of a drag to type your username and password every time you start up your machine, you'll be happy to know that you can bypass the whole login process. If you share your machine with other users, of course, this isn't something you'd want to do because anybody with access to your machine would have access to your user account. I also wouldn't recommend doing this on a laptop, since they are more easily lost or stolen, thus leaving your data at risk to absolute strangers.

To enable automatic login, click the **Security** tab in the Login Window Preferences window, and then click the checkbox at the top of the page next to the words *Enable Automatic Login*. After that, click the arrow on the right side of the drop-down menu next to the word *User*, and select your username from the list. Once you're done, click the **Close** button. The next time you start up your machine, you will bypass the login screen and be delivered directly to the desktop.

7E-2: Installing Splash Screens

As I mentioned, Ubuntu does not come with any splash screens for you to play with, so in order to make changes, you first need to download and install some splash screens with which to work. This can be done quite easily by opening Art Manager (**System ▸ Preferences ▸ Art Manager**) and following these steps:

1. Go to the **Art** menu, and select **Other Themes ▸ Splash Screen**. Art Manager will then download the available splash screens.
2. Once the download is complete, scroll through the offerings, and select one that suits your fancy by clicking it once.
3. Once your selection has been made, click the **Install** button, after which Art Manager will download and install the file. When it's done, the GNOME Splash Screen Preferences window will appear, showing the newly installed screen.
4. Go back to the Art Manager, and repeat steps 2 and 3 to add a few more screen choices to your repertoire.
5. Once you have installed three or four splash screens, close Art Manager.

7E-3: Selecting and Activating Splash Screens

When you have multiple splash screens installed on your system, you can select and then activate them via the GNOME Splash Screen Preferences window (Figure 7-20), which should already be open. When it isn't, you can bring it up by going to the **System** menu and selecting **Preferences ▸ Splash Screen**.

Figure 7-20: Choosing a new login screen

When the window first opens, all of the installed screens will be grayed out, and thus cannot be selected. In order to select and activate a particular splash screen, first check the box next to the words *Show splash screen on startup.* The thumbnails for the installed screens should now be selectable, so make your selection by clicking the splash screen of your choice once and clicking the **Activate** button. You will then see your splash screen in action when you next log in to your system.

Choosing a Screensaver

Screensavers used to be a must-have (and must-use) item for computer users who wanted to prevent damage (burn-in) to their monitors. Video display technology, however, has now advanced to the point where screensavers are no longer completely necessary. Nevertheless, screensavers are cool to look at, and one very nice thing about Ubuntu is that it comes with an unusually extensive collection of screensaver modules—nearly 200 of them! There are so many that you are sure to find at least a few you like. Right out of the box, the screensaver is set up to merely blank your screen after 10 minutes, but you can choose to have the various screensaver modules switch randomly, changing every few minutes, or you can opt for a single module that you especially like. You can change these settings by going to your **System** menu and selecting **Preferences ▸ Screensaver**, after which the Screensaver Preferences window (Figure 7-21) will appear.

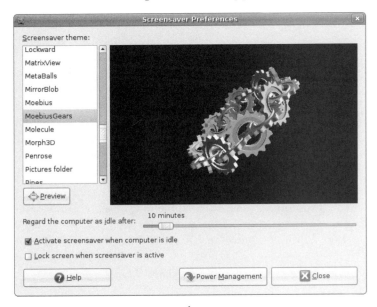

Figure 7-21: Setting screensaver preferences

Screenshots

Now that you know how to make your Ubuntu desktop look a bit more like your own, you might want to share or record the results of your artistic endeavors, and taking screenshots is the way to do just that. The easiest way to go about this is by going to the **Applications** menu and selecting **Accessories ▸ Take Screenshot**.

The Screenshot application, shown in Figure 7-22, will appear. In this window you can decide whether you want to take an image of the whole screen or of a selected window. You can also apply a delay before the screenshot is taken to give yourself some wiggle time. You can even add effects to your window shots, such as a drop shadow.

Figure 7-22: Taking a screenshot in Ubuntu

Once the screenshot has been taken, a window, like the one in Figure 7-23, will appear. In that window, you can name the image and decide where to save it.

Figure 7-23: Saving a screenshot in Ubuntu

If you prefer, it is also possible to take screenshots via key combinations. To take a shot of the entire screen, just press the PRINT SCREEN key. To take a shot of a single window, press ALT-PRINT SCREEN.

Why Don't My Window Screenshots Have Borders?

If you try taking screenshots of single window, you may find that the window borders refuse to appear no matter what you do. This is not a problem with the screenshot mechanism, but rather a side effect of your system's visual effects engine, Compiz. Compiz not only provides the cool drop shadows for the Panel and windows, but it is also responsible for the way windows drop out of nowhere to open and shrink and then appear to vaporize as they close.

NOTE   *Compiz isn't enabled on some incompatible graphic cards, so if you don't know what I am referring to here, you may well have such a card.*

Now that you know what the root of the problem is, you also know the possible solutions for taking single-window screenshots with window borders. One is to use the GIMP for your screenshot-taking chores (discussed in Chapter 14) or to shut off Compiz. To do the latter, just go to the **System** menu and select **Preferences ▶ Appearance**. When the Appearance Preferences window appears, click the **Visual Effects** tab, and once in that tab, select **None** (Figure 7-24). The change should take place almost immediately, and once it does you can close the Appearance Preferences window.

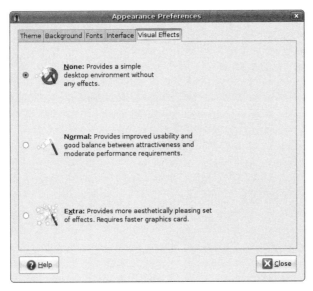

Figure 7-24: Turning off visual effects in order to capture window borders in screenshots

Visual Effects

Having learned how to customize your system using the more traditional tools at your disposal, it's time to let loose and have some fun with some of the newest customization tools the Linux world has to offer. In fact, if you read the section immediately preceding this one ("Why Don't My Window Screenshots Have Borders?" on page 126), then you are already aware of Ubuntu's new visual effects engine, Compiz, which provides all sorts of wild and interesting visual effects for your desktop.

As noted earlier, Compiz will only be automatically enabled at startup if you have a graphics card that supports its basic set of features. An easy way to tell if Compiz has kicked in on your machine is to open any window (your home folder, for example), and then check to see if that window has a drop shadow. If it does, Compiz is at work.

The effects that are active by default are really the tip of the iceberg. Depending on the capabilities of your graphics card, you will get the drop shadows and a few other bells and whistles, such as cooler window-opening transitions, but that may be just about it . . . on the surface, at any rate. If you have a faster graphics card, you can kick the effects up a notch by going to the **System** menu, selecting **Preferences ▶ Apperance**, clicking the **Visual Effects** tab of the Preferences window, and finally, selecting **Extra** in that tab. I should warn you not to be freaked out at first when you try to move your windows and they start wiggling like jelly—that's one of the additional effects (*Wobbly Windows*). Hmmm.

Whatever the hardware capabilities of your system, if you really want to take control of all that Compiz has to offer, it is worth your while to install the CompizConfig Settings Manager (Figure 7-25), which you can get via Synaptic (search for and install *compizconfig-settings-manager*). Once it's installed, you can run it from **System ▸ Preferences ▸ Advanced Desktop Effects Settings**.

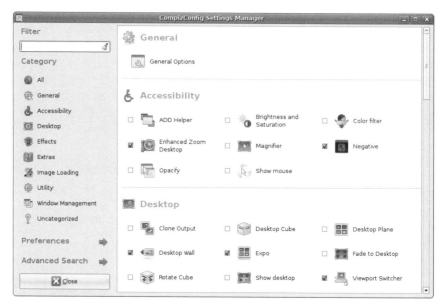

Figure 7-25: Taking control of Compiz's special effects

Once the Settings Manager is installed, you can see everything Compiz is capable of doing and pick and choose from those features as you see fit. While most of what Compiz has to offer is essentially eye-candy (which is what this chapter is all about, after all), there are some functional utilities and extras. A favorite of mine is the Annotate tool, which allows you to write all over your screen while doing presentations, brainstorming, or just flipping out (shown in Figure 7-26).

Enabling Individual Compiz Features

Activating the Annotate tool is essentially the same process used when activating any other Compiz feature: Locate the feature and enable it by checking the box next to its name. In order to figure out how to actually use the feature, click the name of the feature itself, which will bring up a tab showing the settings, including, when appropriate, the keystrokes needed to initiate the feature (Figure 7-27).

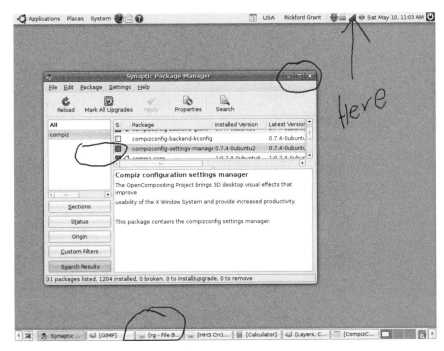

Figure 7-26: Compiz's Annotate tool in action

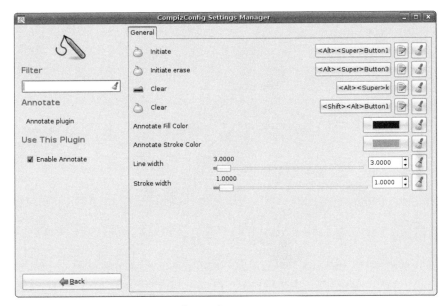

Figure 7-27: Almost every Compiz feature has its own settings.

You can also edit the various keystroke combinations by clicking the button upon which the current keystroke combination is shown and then making your new choices in the Edit window that appears (Figure 7-28). When you're done with the settings for an individual feature, click the **Back** button in the lower-left corner of the Settings Manager window to go back to the main screen.

Figure 7-28: Changing the keystroke combination used to initiate a Compiz feature

8

SIMPLE KITTEN WAYS

Getting to Know the Linux Terminal and Command Line

Many people shy away from Linux because they envision it as a system for compu-geeks, an environment in which you do everything the hard way—by command line. In this era of graphical interfaces, the idea of typing commands to get things done seems a dreadful throwback to the days of DOS, and that puts many people off—especially those who remember what it was like in the "old days."

This reaction is fair enough, but it is not really an accurate reflection of the reality of the Linux world. After all, most Linux users today utilize some sort of graphical interface. They can, and often do, achieve all that they hope to achieve through drop-down menus and mouse clicks alone. Many are able to survive quite happily without ever once opening their Terminal. The same could be true of you.

Be that as it may, there is still much to be said for the power and convenience of the command line. The fact that the command line can now be utilized within a graphical environment also makes it much less forbidding. The Terminal is just a tiny text-based island in a sea of graphical bodies (see Figure 8-1). Using the command line can be as pain-free as anything else you do on your system, and it can actually provide you with a little fun if you are willing to give it a try.

Figure 8-1: Putting the Terminal in perspective

Unfortunately, many guides to using the command line are written by hard-core command-line junkies, whose enthusiasm for what they see as a really good thing inadvertently makes what they write seem even more off-putting to the recent Linux immigrant or wannabe.

For your sake, I will try to curb my own enthusiasm so as not to scare you right back to Chapter 5 and the more comfortable world of Synaptic. I will also try to help you keep things in perspective by teaching you, whenever possible, to use the command line as a complement to the various graphical tools that you have at your disposal, rather than presenting it as the sole way of going about things. Of course, I am not going to cover every possible angle in this regard—just enough to give you some exposure and experience and, hopefully, make you feel at least a little more at ease with the command line. Who knows; could you actually come to think of using the command line as . . . fun? Well, I won't get too carried away.

Meet the Terminal

The Linux Command Terminal application in your Ubuntu system can be run by going to the **Applications** menu and selecting **Accessories ▸ Terminal**. When the Terminal opens, it will, in all its simplicity, look much like Figure 8-2.

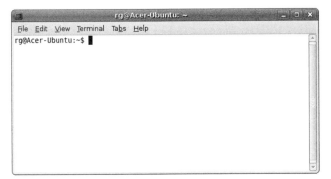

Figure 8-2: The Terminal application

As you can see, all it says is `rg@Acer-Ubuntu:~$`. In this case, the `rg` is my username, `Acer-Ubuntu` is the name I gave my computer during installation, and the tilde (~) signifies that I am in my home folder. If it were to say `~/Music`, for example, it would mean that I am currently in the Music folder within my home folder. Of course, all this will be different in your case, as your username and computer name will be different. If your username is *frog* and your computer's name is *wetrock*, for example, the command line will say `frog@wetrock:~$`. If all this is sounding rather obtuse to you, just think of it this way: *username@computer_name*`:~$` in the Terminal is the equivalent of your home folder in Nautilus.

Typing in the Terminal is straightforward enough; you just type as you usually do. You can also delete and insert letters or phrases by using the DELETE and BACKSPACE keys and the cursor keys. For practice, try the following:

1. Type `I like strawberries so very much`.
2. Change `strawberries` to `cherries` (because cherries are, in fact, so much better). Just use your left cursor key to move the cursor in front of the first *s* in `strawberries`.
3. Tap your DELETE key as many times as necessary to erase the word `strawberries` (uh, that would be 12 times, methinks).
4. Just type `cherries`, and then use your right cursor key to move the cursor back to the end of this meaningful sentence.

Now that you've completed this fascinating bit of typing practice, press the ENTER key. As you will almost immediately see, the Terminal's response to your efforts thus far is merely a dismissive `bash: I: command not found`. Although you've typed a string of text that has meaning to you, it means absolutely nothing to your system. In fact, the system was so shortsighted that it could see nothing other than the first word you typed in the Terminal (I); and because I is not a valid command, the system had no idea what do to with it.

Shells

You may be wondering what this bash business is all about and why it is talking to you. Well, Bash (Bourne Again Shell) is one of the many shells that are used in Linux systems, and it's the one that happens to come with your Ubuntu distro (and most others, for that matter). A *shell* is a program that interprets the commands you type into the Terminal and delivers them, so to speak, to your system so that it can act upon them. I like to think of it as a command-handling subsystem, for which the Terminal acts as a graphical front end. Some scripting languages, as you will find out in Project 8C on page 153, also have their own shells; but other than those few exceptions, you generally need not be unduly concerned with shells other than to know what they are and what people are talking about when referring to them.

Some Goofy, Yet Useful, Fun with the Command Terminal

A rather cool thing about typing in the command Terminal is that it has what you might call short-term memory. Try it out by typing the word **cherry** and then pressing ENTER. Ignoring the command-not-found message, go on and type **vanilla**, and press ENTER. Now type **gelato**, and press ENTER. So far, so dumb, right? Well, not really. Let's type everything we've typed thus far again, but this time let's do it with only one key.

Huh?

Yes, just press the up cursor key once, and what do you see? That's right—the last command you typed appears, which in this case would be gelato. Press the up cursor key again, and the command that you typed before that will appear—vanilla. One more time? Yes, cherry. And one more time for the grand finale . . . I like cherries so very much.

Considering what we have thus far, this may all seem a bit silly, but imagine that you're not typing goofy little words and instead have to deal with considerably longer strings, such as a simple copy command (which you'll learn about later in this chapter) like

```
cp Photos/mypics/stpierre/coastal/onthebeach1_27.jpg /home/frog/
photos_for_mom/stpierre
```

By typing that string, you are copying an image called onthebeach1_27.jpg from the coastal folder to another folder called stpierre. If you wanted to copy another photo in the coastal folder, onthebeach1_16.jpg, for instance, you could simply press the up arrow key once, use the left cursor key and DELETE key to move over to and delete the 27, replace it with **16**, and then use the right arrow key to get back to the end of the command. All in all, it would be much simpler and much faster. It would also help you avoid mistakes in typing. Not so dumb anymore, eh?

Nontoxic Commands

As you now know, all of this typing is easy enough, but in order to actually do something useful with your Terminal, you need to type commands—and there are more of them than you could ever hope or need to know. To get you started, we will begin with some commands that are easy to understand, nontoxic, and completely kitten-friendly.

$ whoami

There is no command as easy, safe, or even as seemingly useless, as whoami. Rather than help those with multiple-personality disorders discover who they are at any given moment, the whoami command simply tells you which user is currently logged in. Try it out by typing **whoami** after the $ and then pressing the ENTER key. Remember that commands are case sensitive.

The Terminal will now tell you the username of the person currently logged in. If you are logged in as frog, you should get frog as the answer to your command.

$ finger

If you enjoyed discovering who you are with the whoami command, then you might enjoy finding out even more about yourself using the finger command. The finger command can be used in a number of ways, but a very simple one is finding out about a particular user. Try this out on yourself by typing **finger** and then your username. In my case, that would be **finger rg**. Once you've typed the command, press ENTER and see what you get. You can see my results in Figure 8-3.

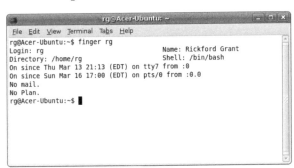

Figure 8-3: Output from the finger command

As you can see, my login name is rg, my real name is Rickford Grant, my home directory is /home/rg, I am using the bash shell for typing my commands, I have been logged on since Thursday March 13 at 21:13 EDT, I've had my Terminal session open since Sunday March 16 at 17:00, and I have no mail or plan. It doesn't tell you my social security number or my mother's maiden name, but it is pretty cool, don't you think?

I mentioned that the results said I had no plan, and you may well be wondering what that is all about, so I'll fill you in. A .plan file is a small file kept in your home folder that other users see when they use the finger command on you. Traditionally, a .plan file contained information about where you were going to be or what you were working on. These days, however, most people use them to leave odd little messages, quotations, or whatever, much as they do in email signatures. Take a look at Figure 8-4 to see what happens after I add a .plan file to my home folder.

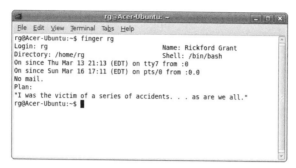

Figure 8-4: Output from the finger command with a plan

You can now see my plan, which is a quotation from Kurt Vonnegut's *The Sirens of Titan* (or Al Stewart's song by the same name, for that matter), though you can put anything you want in your own. You will get the chance to create your own plan file in Project 8A on page 146, so if this all seems fun to you, just hang in there.

Before moving on, I should mention that you can also use the finger command to do a little domestic espionage of sorts. Let's say your child, Chris, has a user account on your machine. Chris, who wants your permission to go to the movies, claims to have been hard at work on the computer all day writing up a report for school. Having your doubts, you could type finger chris to see what the facts actually are. It may be a bit underhanded and rotten, but it works. It also works both ways, so others can check up on you as well. You can give it a try right now by seeing when the last time you logged in to your graphika account was. Just type **finger graphika**, and then press ENTER.

You can even use the finger command to find out facts about people on other systems, providing their network's finger service is active and you know their email address. Typing something like finger *username@hostname*.com would do the trick. Kind of cool, but also kind of spooky, I suppose.

$ pwd

If you know who you are but aren't exactly sure where you are, pwd (print working directory) should come in handy. The pwd command tells you exactly where the Terminal is in your directory tree.

Let's say, for example, that my Terminal is in my personal home directory (which is actually called rg) in the system's home directory (which is actually called home, and which is where all the user account directories are located) when I use the pwd command; I would, after pressing the ENTER key, get /home/rg printed to my Terminal. You should get similar results if you try it out.

NOTE   *The word* print, *in this case, has nothing to do with your printer; it merely means that the response will be printed to, or displayed in, the Terminal.*

$ df

Another safe and easy, but much more useful, command is df (disk file-system). The df command tells you how much disk space you have used, as well as how much space you still have available, on each of the partitions on your various mounted disks. Try it out by typing **df** and then pressing ENTER. Your output should look something like that shown in Figure 8-5 (depending, of course, on the size of your mounted disks and how they are set up).

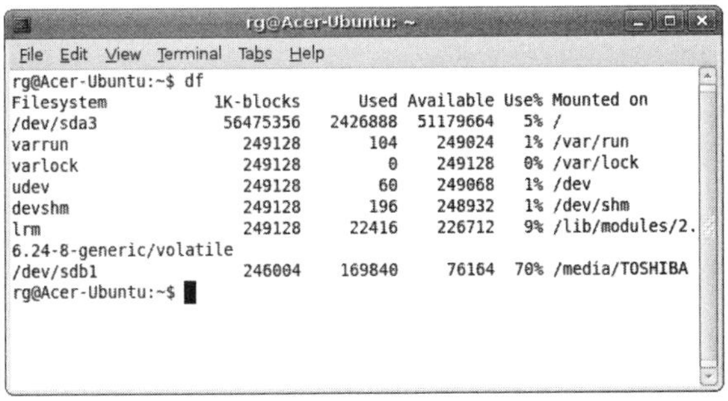

Figure 8-5: Output from the df command

As you will notice, the sizes are given in kilobytes (KB) rather than the gigabytes (GB) and megabytes (MB) you are probably more used to, but there is a way around this. Many commands accept a *flag*, or *option*, to further fine-tune how the command performs. These flags are written directly after the main command and are preceded by a space and a hyphen.

In this case, you can try using the -h (human readable) flag to have your figures come out in the way you are most familiar with. Try this out by typing **df -h** on the command line and pressing ENTER. The output should now appear in a more familiar format (see Figure 8-6).

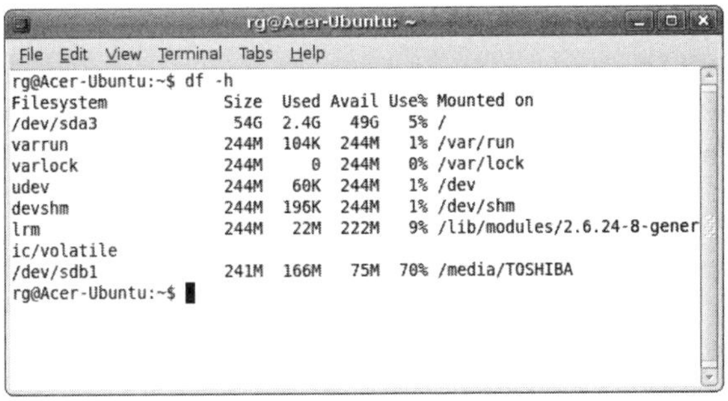

Figure 8-6: Output from the df command with the -h flag

$ ls

Another harmless but handy command is ls (list directory contents). The ls command shows you what is in your current directory. This is the non-graphical equivalent of double-clicking a folder in Nautilus to see what is inside. Try it out by typing **ls** and then pressing the ENTER key.

If you've been following *my* commands so far, your results should list all of the folders in your home directory. You can also use the -R flag to show not only the list of files in the folder, but also what is within the subfolders. Of course, you should have no subfolders in any of the folders you created in Chapter 6, so you can hold off experimenting with this for a while. Instead, try typing `ls -a` to see your invisible, or *hidden*, files.

$ calendar

I'll let you experiment with this one on your own. Just type **calendar**, and press ENTER to see the somewhat interesting results.

$ exit

The exit command is a simple one that allows you to exit the Terminal. Just type **exit**, and press ENTER. The Terminal window will close.

Commands with Some Teeth

The simple commands you have tried so far are all of the safe-and-sane, fire marshal–approved variety; they merely print information to your Terminal. Now you are going to try to get some real tangible results from the commands you use. These commands are also essentially safe and sane if you follow my instructions.

$ mkdir

You have already learned how to create folders by means of menus and your mouse, but you can also do this using the command line. The command is `mkdir` (make directory), and it is easy as pie to use (though I've never been quite sure how pie is easy).

To see how this command works, and to work with the commands that follow, use the `mkdir` command now to create a folder called command_exp (for command experiments). All you have to do is type **mkdir command_exp** in a new Terminal window, and press ENTER. The new folder should appear in your home folder, so go ahead and check to see if it is there by clicking the home icon on your desktop.

Okay, good, *bra, bueno*! Now let's create another new folder within that new folder—a *subfolder*, if you will. We'll call this one sub. So, just type **mkdir command_exp/sub**, and press ENTER. You can now go take a peek and see if the subfolder appears within the command_exp folder, if you like.

$ mv

The next command is the `mv` (move) command, but before we experiment with it, we need to create a dummy file—we need something to move, after all. We can do this by using another command—touch. To make the file, and let's call it expfile.txt, go to the Terminal, type **touch expfile.txt**, and press ENTER. The new file will now appear in your home folder.

To move the file that you've just created, you will use the mv command, of course. Just type mv expfile.txt command_exp/sub (this tells the system which file to move and where to move it to), and press ENTER. The file will now be in your sub folder.

$ cd

Until now, you have been using the command line from your home folder. With the cd command, you can change your Terminal's location to another folder. This is a very handy command that you will be using quite a lot when doing the other projects in this book. To take it out for a spin, let's get inside the command_exp folder by typing cd command_exp and pressing ENTER. If you've done this correctly, the prompt in your Terminal should now read *username@computer_name*:~/command_exp$. If so, you can pat yourself on the back.

While you are there, you might as well try out the ls command with the -R (recursive) flag to see how that works. Just type ls -R, and press ENTER. Your Terminal should now show that you have a subfolder there called sub and a file inside that subfolder called expfile.txt.

That is all you really want to do in there for now, so to get back to your home directory, just type cd, and press ENTER, which will take you back home, so to speak.

For future reference, it is worth noting a couple of other cd command shortcuts. If you are within a subfolder of a subfolder and want to move back a step, so to speak (from /home/rg/peas/pudding to /home/rg/peas, for example), you can do so by typing cd .. (with a space between cd and ..) and pressing ENTER. You can also type cd - (with a space between cd and -) in order to get back to a directory where you were previously (from /home/rg to /home/rg/peas/pudding, for example).

$ cp

Being fickle, as humans are by nature, you might decide that you not only want your expfile.txt file in the sub folder, but that you also want a copy in your home directory, where it was in the first place. To copy expfile.txt, you can use the cp (copy) command.

To do this, the command needs to know where the file you want to copy is, what it is called, and where you want to copy it, which in this case is to your home folder. Normally you would type cp command_exp/sub/expfile .txt /home/*username* to do this, but if you recall my mention of it near the beginning of this chapter, you can abbreviate the /home/*username* portion of the command string to ~/, which means the same thing, and is an important tip to remember, as the tilde is frequently used in online instructions. As reducing wear and tear on the fingers is always a desirable goal, type the following command, and then press ENTER:

```
cp command_exp/sub/expfile.txt ~/
```

Be sure to put a space between the file you are copying and its destination (in this case, between the expfile.txt and ~/).

Once you've done this, you should have two copies of expfile.txt, one in your home folder and one in your sub folder. Go have a look to see the fruit of your endeavors.

$ rm

When you were a kid, you may well have experienced the joy of building a castle out of LEGO bricks and then the even greater joy of tearing the whole thing down (preferably by hurling D cell batteries at it). We will now embark on a similar move. The first tool in this nostalgic endeavor is the rm (remove) command, with which we can trash files.

The rm command, albeit very useful and easy to use, should be used with caution. Once you remove a file with this command, there is no going back—the file will not be placed in the Trash; it is gone for good.

To play it safe, let's try out the rm command by getting rid of that new copy of expfile.txt that we just created in the home folder. The basic rm command structure consists of the command itself, rm, followed by the name of the file that you wish to remove. In this case, you want to remove the file called expfile.txt located in your home folder. Assuming your Terminal shows you to be home, remove the file by typing **rm expfile.txt** followed by a tap on the ol' ENTER key. The file will then be gone, and gone for good.

Now, double your pleasure by getting rid of the version of expfile.txt that is located in the subfolder sub. In this case, you need to specify where the file is because it isn't in the folder that the Terminal is in. Just type **rm command_exp/sub/expfile.txt**, and then press ENTER. Oooh, very cool. Brings ya back, doesn't it?

$ rmdir

You will now continue the fun with the rmdir (remove directory) command, which is a bigger and more powerful version of the rm command.

The rmdir command, like the rm command, should be used with caution. There are no do-overs with rmdir. Once you remove a directory or folder with this command, it is gone for good.

To try this command, you can get rid of that sub folder you created. Type **rmdir command_exp/sub**, and press ENTER. The sub folder should now be gone. Finally, to round out the fun, use the rmdir command once more to get rid of the command_exp folder that we created earlier. You've probably got it down by now, but just in case you haven't, type **rmdir command_exp**, and then press ENTER.

$ chmod

In Chapter 6, you learned how to change file permissions via the Nautilus interface. This is without a doubt the easiest way to go about such things, but you might find times when it is easier to use the command-line approach.

The command for changing file permissions is chmod (change mode). To use it, just type the command followed by the permissions you want to extend to a file, and then the location of the file itself. For example, let's say that you copied a JPEG file, mybirthday.jpg, from a CD to the personal subfolder within the Photos folder on your hard disk, and the file is write protected. To change the file so that you have write permissions (meaning that you can alter the file), you would type the following and then press ENTER:

```
chmod 744 ~/photos/personal/mybirthday.jpg
```

To change the permissions of all the files and subfolders (and all the files within those subfolders) in one fell swoop, you can add the -R (recursive) flag to the chmod command. The command would thus be as follows:

```
chmod -R 744 ~/photos/personal
```

The number *744*, by the way, extends read, write, and execute (run) permissions to you, the owner, but gives read-only rights to everyone else— a pretty safe choice when in doubt. If you want to figure out permission numbers for yourself, it is pretty easy. You are basically dealing with three number positions, each of which has eight numerical possibilities (0–7). The left slot represents permissions for the owner; the center slot represents permissions for the group; and the third slot represents permissions for others. The meanings of the numbers themselves are as follows:

7   Read, write, and execute permissions

6   Read and write permissions

5   Read and execute permissions

4   Read-only permissions

3   Write and execute permissions

2   Write-only permissions

1   Execute-only permissions

0   No permissions

Figure 8-7 points out the meaning of each of these numbers and what each number slot represents. In fact, if you don't mind a bit of simple addition, things are even easier to understand. To start out with, remember that 1 = execute, 2 = write, and 4 = read. Add any of those numbers together, and you get the other permissions combos. For example, 1 (execute) + 4 (read) = 5 (read and execute). As you can see, permissions aren't all that complicated.

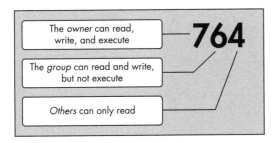

Figure 8-7: The meaning of permissions numbers

Now if you're more of a letters than numbers sort of person, you'll be happy to know that there is another way to change permissions that is probably even easier. In this approach, you only have to deal with two groups of letters and the symbols + and −.

The first group consists of the following:

u   User (owner of the file)

g   Group (specified group of users)

o   Others (anyone who is not the user or a member of the group)

a   All (all of the above)

The second group consists of:

r   Read

w   Write

x   Execute

You might already be able to figure out how this is all going to work, but I'll spell it out just in case your intuition is worn out for the day. Let's say you want to change the permissions of a file (butterhaters.txt, for example) so that all users on your machine can read and write to it. After opening a Terminal window, you can make the change by typing chmod a+rw butterhaters.txt and pressing ENTER.

Oops! Just remembered that you don't want anyone changing the content of the file, eh? Well, to take back the write permissions for that file, you just need to type chmod a-w butterhaters.txt and then press ENTER. As you can see, the + gives permissions, while the - taketh away.

Much simpler, you've got to admit.

$ sudo

When you ran Synaptic back in Chapter 5, you were first asked to input your password before you could run the program. The reason for this, as I mentioned then, is that Synaptic installs the files it downloads in various folders throughout your system, almost all of which are write protected. By supplying your password, you are telling your system that you, as holder of the password, have the right to allow Synaptic to do that.

The command version of that same password-giving process is the sudo command. To perform an operation in a folder that is write protected, you would first type sudo and then the command you want to perform. For example, if you wanted to copy an icon image, let's call it myicon.png, to the globally located and write-protected pixmaps folder (/usr/share/pixmaps), you would type sudo cp myicon.png /usr/share/pixmaps.

After typing a command preceded by the sudo command and pressing ENTER, you will be prompted for your password. Once you type your password and press ENTER again, the command will be executed. I should mention that once you input your password, it will stay in memory for about five minutes. This means that you will not be prompted for your password when using the sudo command again within that time frame.

$ locate

Now that you are familiar with the sudo command, let's take it out for a spin by working with the locate command. The locate command is essentially a command-line alternative to the graphical Search tool found in the Places menu. Using the command is quite easy: Simply type the command followed by a space and the name of the file you are searching for.

Before you can use this command, though, you will need to create a database of filenames for locate to use. This is where using the sudo command, along with yet another command, updatedb, comes into play. Just type **sudo updatedb** and press ENTER. After you type your password when asked to do so, it will seem that nothing is happening for a while, but don't worry. As long as the cursor in your Terminal is blinking, progress is being made, and when your user prompt returns, you will have successfully created the database file. After that, you can go on and use the locate command. Oh, and in the future if you think that the process seems to be taking longer and longer, don't worry—it is. The more files and applications you add to your system, the longer it will take your system to catalog them all.

To take this new command out for a test drive, let's look for the openofficeorg24-writer.png file that we worked with in Chapter 3. Just type the following, and press ENTER:

```
locate openofficeorg24-writer.png
```

Your results should look like those in Figure 8-8.

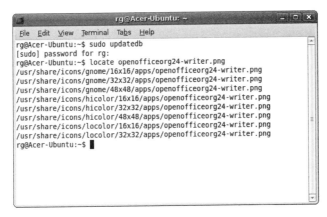

Figure 8-8: The results of a locate search

$ apt-get

To wrap up this section, let's finish with a command that might seem a bit familiar to you: apt-get. Yes, this command is indeed the key to controlling the powerful package download and installation tool, APT, which I covered in Chapter 5. Although it might not be as pleasing to use APT via the command line as it is via Synaptic or Add/Remove Programs, it can come in handy. I'll cover the basics for you here.

Before using the `apt-get` command, be sure to close any APT front ends you might have open, such as Synaptic. As I mentioned before, you can only run one APT tool at a time. Once the coast is clear, you should always start out any operations involving `apt-get` with an update of the APT database so that you will be downloading the newest stuff. To do this, just type the command `sudo apt-get update`.

If you want to install a single package without heading over to Synaptic, you can do so by typing `sudo apt-get install` *package-name*. For example, if you want to download and install the Shufflepuck game clone, Tuxpuck, you would type `sudo apt-get install tuxpuck`. If you eventually get annoyed with Tuxpuck after having lost one too many times, you can uninstall it by typing `sudo apt-get remove tuxpuck`.

Finally, bearing in mind all the warnings offered in Chapter 5, if you want to upgrade your entire system via the command line, you can do so by typing `sudo apt-get dist-upgrade` (but only after doing a `sudo apt-get update` first).

A Couple of Other Biters You'll Be Using Soon

This is as good a place as any to introduce two more commands that you will be called upon to use in this chapter and elsewhere in the book: `ln` and `tar`. You needn't practice with these yet, as you will be using them very soon, but you might as well know what they are all about.

$ ln

The `ln` (link) command is used to create a link file that launches or activates another file located in a separate folder. This is very useful when trying to activate a file that is buried deep in the subfolder of a subfolder of a subfolder somewhere on your hard disk. The command is very often used with the `-s` (symbolic) flag, which provides essentially the same thing as the shortcut you've come to know in Windows, or the alias on the Mac.

The easiest way to use the `ln` command is to first use the `cd` command to change the Terminal's location to the folder where you want to place the link. Then you can type the `ln` command on the command line, followed by the path of the file you wish to link to. For example, let's say that you want to put a link in your home folder for an OpenOffice.org Writer file of your autobiography called myLife.sxw. The file is pretty well buried in a nest of subfolders deep within your home folder: /home/*username*/Documentia/personal/self/autobiography/myLife.sxw. To create the link, you would open a new Terminal window, type the following command string, and then press ENTER:

```
ln -s Documentia/personal/self/autobiography/myLife.sxw
```

Once you are finished, the link will appear in your home folder as an icon matching the original file in appearance, albeit sporting an arrow to signify that it is a link.

$ tar

In Chapter 6 you learned to create and extract archives, or tarballs, but did you know that you can also create and extract tarballs using the command line? The tar command is your key to doing this.

To create an archive, you would simply type tar -cvf, followed by the name the final tarball will be, and then the name of the folder or file you are trying to archive. For example, let's say that you want to create an archive of your photos folder, and you want to call it pics4pals. In this case, you would type the following command, and then press ENTER:

```
tar -cvf pics4pals.tar photos
```

As you no doubt noticed, there are some flags after the tar command in that string. The *c* tells the tar program to *create* a new archive. The *v* tells the program to be *verbose*, or, in other words, to tell you what it is doing in the Terminal as it is doing it. Finally, the *f* tells the program that what follows is the *file information*.

If, after creating the archive, you suddenly remember that there is one more file you want to add to the mix, you can use the -r flag to append the archive. For example, to add a file called cranky.png to the archive, you would type the following and then press ENTER:

```
tar -rvf pics4pals.tar cranky.png
```

Of course, chances are that you will be doing more tarball extracting than creating, so you no doubt want to know how to do that. Fortunately, the process is pretty similar to what you use when creating the tarball. The main difference is in the first flag. Rather than using the tar command with the -c flag, you would instead use it with the -x flag, which tells the tar program to *extract* the specified archive. So if you want to extract a tarball called spicyfood.tar, type the following command, and press ENTER:

```
tar -xvf spicyfood.tar
```

What you have been doing thus far is creating and extracting archives, which are basically just collections of files. They are not, however, compressed. In fact, most tarballs you find will be compressed, and you can tell by the ending *tar.gz*. That *gz* means that the archive was compressed using the gzip program. Extracting a compressed tarball is just as easy as extracting a straight tar archive; all you have to do is add the -z flag, which tells your system to use the gzip program to decompress the archive. For example, if you want to extract a compressed tarball called goosedown.tar.gz, type the following command, and press ENTER:

```
tar -xzvf goosedown.tar.gz
```

Well, now that you know how to decompress and extract a gzipped tarball, you probably want to know how to create one. This is, again, little different than creating the tar archive itself; you would just add the -z tag to tell the program to use gzip to compress the folder. For example, to create a compressed version of your Documentia folder, which we'll call tightdocs.tar.gz, for example, you would type the following, and press ENTER:

```
tar -czvf tightdocs.tar.gz Documentia
```

It's worth mentioning at this point that you may also come across some files compressed with the bzip program. Such files are recognizable by some variation on the .bz file extension. Dealing with these files should pose no problem, as the commands are almost identical to those for gzip. Just substitute -j for -z in the command string.

Compressing and Extracting Compressed Single Files

If you want to compress or decompress a single file, there is no real need to use the tar program at all, since its purpose is to create archives consisting of several files. You can instead use the gzip and gunzip commands directly. For example, to compress a file called matilda.png, you would type gzip matilda.png, and press ENTER. The matilda.png file would then become matilda.jpg.gz. To decompress the file, you would type gunzip matilda.jpg.gz, and press ENTER, after which the matilda.jpg file would be back to normal.

So can you compress an archive you've already created with the tar command? Sure. For example to compress the spicyfood.tar archive we mentioned before, you would type gzip spicyfood.tar, and voilà—you've got yourself a compressed spicyfood.tar.gz archive. Pretty cool, don't you think?

Project 8A: Creating a Plan

Well, now that you have a bit of command experience, it's time to get some practice and put all those commands to good use. In this project we start off easy by creating a .plan file, like I mentioned in the section "$ finger" on page 135. The actual .plan file is a hidden file (as you can see by the period before its name), which contains the plan or message that you add to that file. That message will appear in the output of someone's Terminal when they use the finger command to find out more about you. You may not need such a .plan file, but it is an easy enough way to get started working a bit more with commands and the Terminal itself, so let's give it a try.

To start out, we are going to open the Terminal-based Pico editor to create the .plan file. To do this, open a Terminal window, type **pico .plan** (being sure to put a space between pico and .plan), and press ENTER. Your Terminal should now look a bit different, as you can see in Figure 8-9.

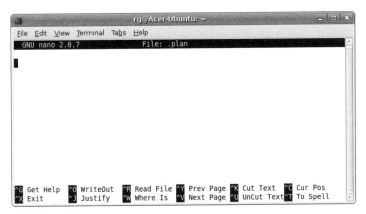

Figure 8-9: The Pico editor

You will now be looking at your new, and totally empty, .plan file within the Pico editor. All you have to do now is type your plan or message. Once you've done that, press CTRL-X to exit the Pico editor, and it will ask you if you want to save your work. You do, so type Y, after which you will be presented with a set of save options. You have already named the file .plan, as you can see near the bottom of the screen, so all you have to do is press ENTER. You will be back at your now-familiar user prompt in the Terminal window.

To wrap things up, you want to change the permission of the new .plan file by typing `chmod 644 .plan` in the Terminal window and then pressing ENTER. The .plan file should now be in your home folder and visible by all, so go on and test your work by typing **finger *username*** and pressing ENTER. The message you entered in your .plan file should now appear in the results in place of the `no Plan` you found there earlier. If you want to change the contents of your .plan file later on, just follow the same steps, and change the text when the .plan appears in the Pico editor.

NOTE   *The name of the .plan file is preceded by a period, which means that it is a hidden file. Thus, if you take a look in your home folder, you will not be able to see the file unless you have checked the box next to the words* Show hidden and backup files *in the Nautilus Preferences window.*

Project 8B: More Command Practice with pyWings

Now let's get some more experience behind the Terminal by installing a simple, and admittedly kind of silly, oracle program called pyWings (see Figure 8-10). pyWings will give you cryptic guidance in response to whatever questions you may ask it.

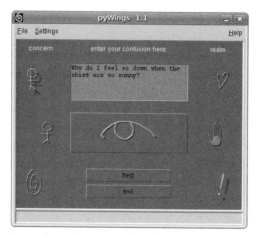

Figure 8-10: Seeking wisdom from pyWings

To use pyWings, type whatever your confusion is in the input box, click one of the concern icons on the left (self, another, world), one of the realm icons on the right (love, work, truth), and hit the big button that looks like half an eye. The oracle will then tell you what it has to say. As an example, I asked the oracle why I feel so down when the skies are so sunny, and I picked *self* as my concern and *truth* as the realm. Figure 8-11 shows the wisdom that was bestowed upon me.

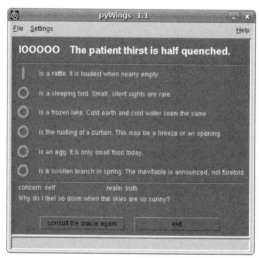

Figure 8-11: pyWings bestows its wisdom.

As you can see, the oracle told me, "The patient thirst is half quenched," which I will interpret as . . . well, I'm not sure what to interpret it as.

Hmmm.

pyWings was written in a programming language called Python, which actually creates scripts rather than true conventional programs. You will learn a little more about this distinction in Chapter 9, but one of the differences I can mention right off the bat is that you don't actually have to install pyWings; you are simply going to put it on your hard drive in your home folder and run it from there, more or less as is.

8B-1: Getting Ready for pyWings (Installing Tkinter)

As I mentioned, one difference between pyWings and most of the other applications you know is that pyWings is a Python script. In order to create a graphical interface for itself, pyWings uses a toolbox known as Tkinter, which is the de facto standard (though not the only) GUI toolbox for Python. Tkinter, however, no longer comes bundled with Ubuntu, so you will need to download and install it yourself. Fortunately, this is quite easily done.

While it is possible to whip open Synaptic and install Tkinter by the simple means learned in Chapter 5, it seems more appropriate in this command-line oriented chapter to . . . yeah, you got it, use the command line. That said, open a Terminal window, type **sudo apt-get install python.tk**, and then press ENTER. When asked for your password, type it, and then press ENTER. APT will search the online repositories and find your file, along with anything else it requires to function properly. Once it is ready, it will ask you if you want to continue. You do, so press **y**, and then press ENTER. When your username prompt reappears, you'll know the job is done and you can go on to the next step.

8B-2: Getting pyWings

You are just about ready to begin "installing" pyWings, but before you do, you've got to get it from http://sourceforge.net/projects/pywings/. Once there, click the **Download** button or tab. On the downloads page, download the file pywings-1.1.tar.gz (*.tar.gz* tells you that this is a *tarball*—the Linux world's answer to Zip files). Then place the file in your home folder so that you can follow along easily with the rest of this project.

8B-3: Creating a LocalApps Folder for pyWings

As I mentioned before, you will be installing the pyWings program locally in your home folder. Installing a program *locally* means that you are installing the program and all its support and data files in your home folder. This makes things a bit easier, but it also means that the program will not be available to other users. It also means that, if you're not careful, you might inadvertently delete it.

To make things a bit easier and safer for you, you are going to create a folder in your home folder in which to place pyWings and all other applications that you install locally on your machine in the future. You will, logically enough, call the folder LocalApps.

Let's make the folder by command, in order to get some more practice. Go to the Terminal, make sure you are in your home folder, type the following command, and then press ENTER:

```
mkdir LocalApps
```

8B-4: Extracting the pyWings Tarball

Now it is time to extract the tarball. You can do this by the double-click method you learned in Chapter 6, but since we're working with the command line, let's use that instead.

To start out, we're going to place the tarball in the same folder into which we extract its files. Usually this isn't necessary because the contents of most tarballs are already packaged in a folder of their own. By double-clicking the tarball to open it up in File Roller, you can see whether things are packed in a folder or simply as a group of files. In the case of pyWings, it is the latter, so follow these steps:

1. Create a pywings folder by typing **mkdir pywings** and pressing ENTER.
2. Move the pyWings tarball into that folder by typing **mv pywings*.gz pywings** and pressing ENTER.

   You can see that in this step we used an asterisk (*) to save some wear and tear on our fingers. The asterisk is a wildcard character that in this case told your system to move any file beginning in *pywings* and ending in *.gz*. Fortunately we had only one item matching those criteria.
3. Move over to the new pywings folder by typing **cd pywings** and pressing ENTER.
4. Now we get down to the process of extracting the tarball itself using the tar command. To do this, type **tar -xzvf pywings*.gz**, and press ENTER.

   Again, notice that we used the asterisk to save ourselves some keystrokes, though we could just as well have typed **-1.1.tar** in its stead.
5. Finally, type **cd**, and press ENTER to bring the Terminal back to your home folder.

8B-5: Moving the pyWings Folder to Your LocalApps Folder

The extraction process is now complete. Before going on to running pyWings, however, let's move it to the new LocalApps folder you created in Project 8B-3 on page 149. To do this, type the following command, and then press ENTER:

```
mv pywings LocalApps
```

8B-6: Running pyWings

Now that you have pyWings in place and ready for action, let's start up the great oracle right now so that you can get a better perspective on how to deal with the aspects of life that trouble you.

In the Terminal, make sure you are in your home directory, type the following command string, and then press ENTER:

```
python ~/LocalApps/pywings/pywings.py
```

Since pywings.py is a Python script, rather than an application, you are calling Python's attention to it so that it will know it needs to deal with it. If all went according to plan, pyWings should be up and running and will soon be making you a wiser person.

8B-7: Creating a Launchable Link for pyWings

The method of running pyWings that you've just used works well enough, but it is a pain in the posterior to open your Terminal and type that somewhat lengthy string every time you want to find out what fate has in store for you. Let's find a way to make things easier in the future.

To run an application from the Terminal, you generally type the name of that application or, to put it more precisely, the name of that program's executable file; the application's name thus acts as a sort of command. In order for your system to recognize that command, however, the command (the executable file, or a link to it) must be in a location where the system can find it. Whenever you run a command of any sort, your system checks a series of locations (most of which are *bin folders*, where executable files are located) to find that command.

You can easily find out where these locations are by typing `echo $PATH` in a new Terminal window and then pressing ENTER. As you will see, on your Ubuntu system, these locations are:

- /usr/local/bin
- /usr/local/sbin
- /sbin
- /usr/sbin
- /bin
- /usr/bin
- /usr/games

If the command you typed is in one of those locations, the program, or script, will run. As you no doubt know, however, pyWings is not in any of those locations. It is in /home/*username*/LocalApps/pyWings and is thus, in a sense, out of your system's sight.

To remedy this situation, you could add the path of your pyWings script to the list of paths that the system checks for run commands, so as to make the system aware of your new application's existence. However, let's try another method that I think is easier. What you will do is create a link to pyWings, a sort of launchable alias, in one of the locations your system does check for commands.

To create this link, you will be using three commands: cd (to change directories), sudo (to give yourself write access to the destination folder), and ln -s (to create the link).

1. In the Terminal, type **cd /usr/games**, and press ENTER. This puts you in one of the folders your system searches when you enter commands.

2. Type **sudo ln -s /home/***username***/LocalApps/pywings/pywings.py pywings**, and press ENTER. (Note that there is a space between the words pywings.py and pywings at the end of that command string.)

   The pywings at the end of that command string is the name that you are giving the link; the name of the link thus becomes the command you will use to run the application. If you type nothing, the link will be called pywings.py, which would mean three more keystrokes for you every time you wanted to start the program.

3. Type your password when prompted to do so, and then press ENTER.

4. Type **cd**, and press ENTER to return the Terminal to your home folder.

8B-8: Running pyWings Again

Now that you have created the link, you should be able to run the pyWings program much more easily. To try it out, quit pyWings (if it is still running), type **pywings** in the Terminal window, and press ENTER. Your personal pyWings oracle should appear again.

You've managed to cut down on the number of keystrokes required to run pyWings from the Terminal. However, if you are really into this pyWings thing and want to use it often, it will probably be handiest to add a launcher to your panel, a drawer, or the Applications menu.

To add a pyWings panel launcher, for example, right-click any open space in the panel, and select **Add to Panel**. When the Add to Panel window appears, click the **Custom Application Launcher** item and click **Add**. In the Create Launcher window that appears, type **pyWings** in the Name section, anything you want in the Comment section (**Your Obtuse Guru**, for example), and, assuming you created a launchable link in Project 8B-7 on page 151, type **pywings** in the Comment section. For an icon, click the **No Icon** button, and then look around until you find an icon that suits your fancy. I like gnome-eog.png myself. Once you've made your selection, click **OK** in the Browse icons window, and then click **OK** in the Create Launcher window.

8B-9: Adding Emblems to Your LocalApps Folder

Now that pyWings is successfully installed and working, it is probably a good idea to add an emblem to your new LocalApps folder so that you don't inadvertently dump it in the Trash someday. You have already learned how to do this in Chapter 7, so I won't give you the step-by-step instructions.

Project 8C: Command Practice Review with Briscola

If you would like to reinforce the skills you've put to use in the previous project, why not go a bit Continental, and try out Briscola—a simple, yet very traditional, Italian card game (see Figure 8-12). Unlike pyWings, which is a Python script, Briscola is a script of a different flavor, written in a scripting language called Tcl, which uses something called Tk to create its graphical interface.

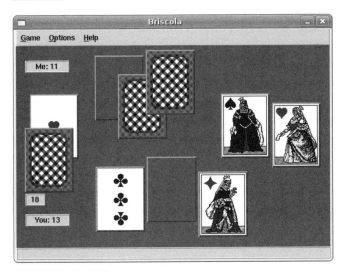

Figure 8-12: Briscola

8C-1: Getting Briscola

You are just about ready to begin "installing" Briscola, but before you do, you must get it. You can get Briscola by going to the project's home page at www.rigacci.org/comp/software and downloading in the traditional manner, but since we're working with commands, let's instead get Briscola by using a new command: wget.

To do this, just open a Terminal window, type the following command string, and then press ENTER:

```
wget http://www.rigacci.org/comp/software/briscola/briscola-4.1.tar.gz
```

In your Terminal window you will see wget in action as it connects to the site where Briscola is stored and then downloads the file. When it's done, you will find the Briscola tarball in your home folder.

8C-2: Extracting the Briscola Tarball and Renaming the Briscola Folder

Extracting the Briscola tarball is essentially the same process as that for pyWings; however, Briscola is already packaged within its own folder, so you won't have to create a special folder for it.

Although I am sure you now know the drill, I'll tell you again. Just open a Terminal window, type the following command, and press ENTER:

```
tar -xzvf briscola*.gz
```

A new folder, Briscola-4.1, will now appear in your home folder with all of the Briscola files in it. To make things easier to deal with in the future, let's shorten the name of the folder to simply *briscola*. We already know how to do this via the right-click method, but this time around let's to do it via the command line. To do this, you use, perhaps surprisingly, the mv command followed by the name of the file whose name you are going to change, followed by the new name of the file.

Give it a go by typing the following command and pressing ENTER:

```
mv briscola-4.1 briscola
```

8C-3: Preparing the Briscola Script

Most applications that come in tarball form include a README file, which includes information on what you need to do in order to install and use the application. If you double-click the **README** file in the briscola folder in Nautilus, you will see that the "HOW TO START" section tells you to adjust the first line of the briscola.tk script to point it to your Tk shell, and to adjust the second line of the script to point to the directory where the various Briscola files are located.

To perform the adjustments as instructed in the README file, just follow these steps:

1. Find the Tk shell, called Wish, by typing **locate wish** in the Terminal window and pressing ENTER, and then note the location given on a piece of paper. You may get a number of locations in your search results, but the one you want is /usr/bin/wish.
2. Direct the Terminal to the briscola folder by typing **cd briscola** and pressing ENTER.
3. Use the Pico editor, which we used in Project 8A on page 146, to edit the briscola.tk file by typing **pico briscola.tk** and pressing ENTER. The briscola.tk file will appear in the Pico editor in your Terminal window.
4. Change the very first line of the briscola.tk file from #!/usr/local/bin/wish to **#!/usr/bin/wish**.
5. In the second line, change /usr/local/games/briscola to **/usr/share/games/ briscola**, which is where you will place Briscola in just a bit.
6. Press CTRL-X on your keyboard.

7. Type **Y**, and press ENTER to save your changes.

8. Type **cd**, and press ENTER to return the Terminal to your home folder.

8C-4: Moving the Briscola Folder to a Global Location

We could move the briscola folder to the LocalApps folder and play it from there, as we did with pyWings, but this time around, let's do things a bit differently by moving the whole thing to global territory. This not only keeps it safe from our obsessive housekeeping tendencies, but also allows all users on the same computer to play the game. We will need to use the sudo command to do this so that we can have write access in those protected folders.

To do this, just type the following command in the Terminal window, and press ENTER:

```
sudo mv briscola /usr/share/games
```

When you are prompted for your password, type it, and press ENTER.

8C-5: Creating a Launchable Link for Briscola

Even though we've moved Briscola to a global location, we still can't run it with a simple one-word command because the briscola.tk file itself is not in the system's command search path. Just as we did for pyWings, we will now create a launchable link for Briscola to solve that problem. Here are the steps:

1. In the Terminal, type **cd /usr/games**, and press ENTER.

2. Now create the link by typing **sudo ln -s /usr/share/games/briscola/ briscola.tk briscola**, and press ENTER.

3. Type **cd**, and press ENTER to return the Terminal to your home folder.

You can now easily run Briscola by typing **briscola** in the Terminal and pressing ENTER.

Can I Do the Same Thing with pyWings?

Sure. If you want to move pyWings to a global location, just follow the same procedure for moving the pywings folder and creating the link as you did for Briscola, making the necessary substitutions, of course. You will have to remove the previously created pyWings link, though, by typing the following command and pressing ENTER:

```
sudo rm /usr/games/pywings
```

After that, move the pywings folder to global territory by typing **sudo mv ~/LocalApps/pywings /usr/share/games/pywings**, and pressing ENTER. When prompted for your password, type it, and press ENTER. You can then create the launchable link by typing **cd /usr/games**, pressing ENTER, typing **sudo ln -s /usr/share/games/pywings/pywings.py pywings**, and pressing ENTER once more.

Playing Briscola

As I already mentioned, Briscola is easy—about as easy a card game as there is. It is a trick-taking game, which means that you put out a card, then your opponent puts out a card, and the one who puts out the higher point-value card wins the hand, or *trick*. Points are awarded on the basis of the cards involved in that trick. The winner of the trick then goes on to *lead* the next trick, meaning that the winner puts out his or her card first the next time around. When all the cards are played, the points for each player are then tallied, and the player with the higher points wins. All much simpler to do than it is to describe.

The Cards and Their Rankings

Like many other Italian and Spanish games, Briscola is played with a 40-card deck, consisting of the following cards: K, Q, J, 7, 6, 5, 4, 3, 2, and the Ace. Traditionally, it is played with either French-suited cards (hearts, diamonds, clubs, and spades) or Italian-suited cards (swords, coins, batons, and chalices), usually dependent upon the region in which it is played. In the software version you have just installed, you will be playing with French-suited cards in the regional pattern of Tuscany.

Unlike most card games you are probably familiar with, the ranking and point values of the cards in Briscola is somewhat different, as you can see in the following chart.

Ranking of Cards	Point Value
Ace	11
3	10
King	4
Queen	3
Jack	2
7, 6, 5, 4, 2	0

While this ranking arrangement might seem odd, it is actually fairly common in card games from the southern and Catholic regions of Central Europe. With that bit of information in mind, it should all be pretty easy enough to fathom, taking a religious view, that God (Ace) and the Holy Trinity (3) rank higher than the quasi-mortal royals (K, Q, J) and their decidedly mortal subjects (7, 6, 5, 4, 2). The rankings are thus quite sensible, albeit slightly ironic, given that some religions frown upon playing cards, calling them "the devil's tool."

Game Play in Briscola

Once Briscola starts up, it will deal three cards to each player. It will then take the seventh card and place it face up under the downward-facing pile of undealt cards, known as the *stock* or *talon*. That seventh card is called the *Briscola* (from which the game gets its name), and it determines the *trump suit* for that particular game. This means that any card of the same suit as the Briscola will beat any card of any other suit, even one of a higher ranking. Of course, when you play a trump card against another trump card, the normal rankings of the cards come back into play.

It is important to note at this point that unlike many other trick-taking games, you are neither required to follow the suit of the card led in a trick in Briscola, nor are you required to beat it if you can. This means that if your opponent plays a club card, you can play a card of any suit you like, even if you have a card that can beat it, all depending on your own strategy for ultimately winning the game.

Before getting started, it is a good idea to first go to the **Options** menu and select **Show Score**. This will allow you to know how you're doing as you play. Once you've done that, you are ready for action, and as your computer opponent is always kind enough as to allow you to lead, you can begin by clicking the card you want to put into play. Your compu-opponent will then play its card.

Once you've assessed the situation, click one of the blank spaces in your hand, and the points for that trick will be displayed in the box labeled *You* (if you won the trick) or the box labeled *Me* (if the computer won the trick). Of course, if the trick only involved the 7, 6, 5, 4, or 2 cards, no points will appear, as those cards have no point value.

Want to Know More?

If you would like a more detailed set of rules for playing Briscola (and just about any other card game in the world), check out www.pagat.com.

Customizing the Terminal

As you now well know, the Terminal is a very simple application in terms of looks. It doesn't have to be, however, because you can spice things up a bit if you're so inclined. Not only can you change the background and text colors in the Terminal, but you can even display one of your favorite photos as a background (as shown in Figure 8-13) or make the background transparent . . . well, kind of transparent anyway.

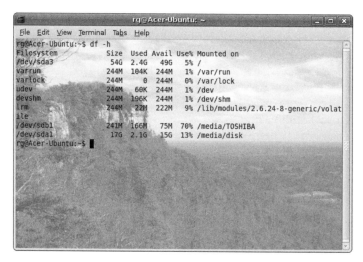

Figure 8-13: A Terminal window with customized background and font colors

To change the Terminal background, go to the Terminal **Edit** menu, and select **Current Profile**. When the Editing Profile window appears, click the **Effects** tab, select **Background image**, and then click the **Browse** button to navigate your way to the image you want to use (Figure 8-14). Depending on the image you use for your background, you may find it rather difficult to see the text once your image appears in the Terminal. If so, try moving the slider under the words *Shade transparent or image background* in the Editing Profile window. If that still doesn't do the trick, click the **Colors** tab, deselect **Use colors from system theme**, and then try some of the preset Foreground and Background combinations from the menu button next to the words *Built-in schemes.*

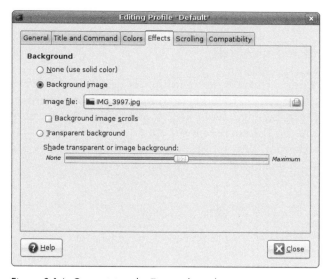

Figure 8-14: Customizing the Terminal window

If you just want to make the background transparent, go back to the Effects tab, select Transparent background, and drag the slider near the bottom of the Editing Profile window. You can also use the slider to adjust the shading of your background image if you choose to go that route.

NOTE   *The transparency effect used in the Terminal is a pseudo-transparency, as it is really just a mirroring of the desktop image. You will thus find, if you have any icons on your desktop, that when you pass the transparent terminal across such icon-laden areas, those icons will not appear in the seemingly transparent Terminal window—all you will see is the desktop wallpaper or background color.*

Depending on the colors present in your background image or in your desktop wallpaper (if you've gone the transparent route), you may also want to change the font color for your Terminal to make things easier to see. To do this, click the **Colors** tab, deselect **Use colors from system theme**, and then make the appropriate font color selection.

Tabbed Shell Sessions in the Terminal

To wrap things up in this chapter, I thought I might mention one particularly convenient feature of the GNOME Terminal: tabs. Just as you can view multiple web pages in one Firefox web browser window through the use of tabs, tabs in the Terminal application allow you to have more than one shell session running at the same time without having more Terminal windows open (see Figure 8-15). This reduces the amount of desktop clutter and generally makes things easier to deal with. You can open a new tab within the Terminal by going to the Terminal **File** menu and selecting **Open Tab**.

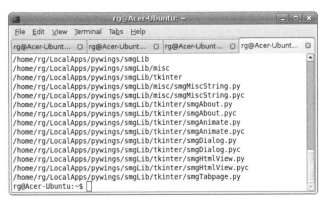

Figure 8-15: Running multiple shell sessions in tabs within the GNOME Terminal

9

ALIENS, TARBALLS, A GLASS OF WINE, AND A CUP OF JOE

More Ways to Install Programs

In the past few chapters, you learned how to install applications via Synaptic and run script-type applications from the command line, which gives you quite a variety of applications to choose from. It is now time, however, to expand your application-gathering repertoire even further.

In this chapter you will learn how you can add applications to your system in even more ways, including one of the most manual and traditional ways to install an application, that is, compiling it from source. You will also learn how to convert Red Hat Package Manager (RPM) packages for use in your Debian-based system environment, run Java-based applications, and—say it ain't so—even run some Windows applications. When you are done, you will have more options at your disposal than you'll know what to do with . . . and that's not a bad position to be in.

Project 9A: Installing the Java Runtime Environment and Running Java Apps: Risk

To start, let's go back to the topic of scripts. In Chapter 8 you learned to run a few applications based on scripts, such as the Python-based pyWings and the Tcl/Tk–based Briscola, but it just wouldn't be right to leave out what might be considered the granddaddy of all scripting languages—Java. In this project, you'll learn how to install the Java Runtime Environment and how to install and run the Java-based version of the classic board game Risk.

9A-1: Installing the Java Runtime Environment

In order to run Java-based applications, or *scripts*, you need to first install the Java Runtime Environment. You can do this via Synaptic by searching for and installing *sun-java6-jre*. The whole set of Java packages is pretty hefty in terms of download weight, so don't get freaked out if it seems to take longer than you're used to.

After the download is complete and the installation has begun, a graphical configuration window, like the one shown in Figure 9-1, will appear. In that window, read and then agree to the licensing terms by checking the box, and click the **Forward** button. Synaptic will then go back and finish up the installation.

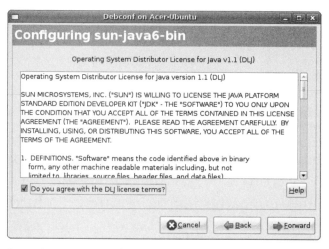

Figure 9-1: Accepting what you must in order to add Java support to your system

9A-2: Getting the Risk File

Once you've installed the Java Runtime Environment, you need to run a Java application in order to see it at work. One such application is the game Risk, which, like many other Java-based applications, is available from www.sourceforge.net. To make things easier, you can just point your browser directly to the Risk project home page at http://jrisk.sourceforge.net (don't forget the *j* at the beginning of that URL). On the main page, click the **Download** link. Then, on the Downloads page, click the **Risk jar and source** link.

A short while after the Download page opens in your browser, a window will appear asking you what to with the Risk Zip file. Your choices are to save it to disk or open it with Archive Manager. Since you're going to have to unzip the package once you download it anyway, you might as well choose the top option, *Open with Archive Manager*, and then click **OK**. The Archive Manager window will appear, and since Risk is already packed in its own folder, all you have to do is click **Extract**. When the Extract window appears, select your home folder as the destination, if it isn't already, by double-clicking its icon, and then click **Extract** again. Once the file is extracted, you can close the Archive Manager window.

You will now have a new Risk folder within your home folder. If you take a look in that folder, you will notice the file Risk.jar. This is the game that you will be running via the command line. (Should you choose to download other Java-based applications in the future, the file with the .jar extension will be the one you will be trying to run.)

9A-3: Running Risk

Now that you've installed the Java Runtime Environment and downloaded and extracted the Risk Zip file, you are ready to run Risk. To get going, open a new Terminal window, and do the following:

1. Move into the Risk folder by typing **cd Risk** and pressing ENTER.
2. Type **java -jar Risk.jar** (be sure to put a space between java and -jar), and press ENTER. Risk (shown in Figure 9-2) will soon appear, and you can start playing.

In case you're wondering, here's what you did in that last line: The first part of the command string, java, calls the Java Runtime Environment into action; the -jar flag after that tells Java that you are going to be running a JAR file; and the last part is the actual file you are going to run, Risk.jar. (In the future, if you choose to run other Java-based applications, just follow the same pattern: java -jar *application_name*.jar.)

Figure 9-2: Risk

Project 9B: A Little More Hands-On Java Experience: Schnapsen

Ever since I moved over to the world of Linux, I have been continually bellyaching about the fact that there was no Linux version of my favorite game, the Austrian card game Schnapsen. Eventually, I got Schnapsen to work under Wine (which you'll learn about in the next project), but now I've found something easier to deal with—a Java version of Schnapsen (Figure 9-3). If you would like a little bit more hands-on experience with Java and wouldn't mind learning about a pretty cool card came, just follow along with the instructions here.

9B-1: Getting and Extracting Schnapsen

To get started, you will need to download and extract Schnapsen. Here's what you need to do:

1. Open your web browser and go to http://home.pages.at/tjger/en.
2. On that page, click the **Schnapsen** link in the left frame.
3. In the right frame, click **Schnapsen.zip**.
4. On the following page, click the **Schnapsen_1.00.zip** link (not Schnapsen_1.00_exe.zip) to download the file.

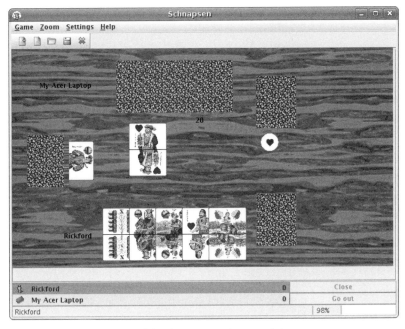

Figure 9-3: A Java version of the Austrian card game, Schnapsen

5. Once the download of the Zip file is complete, double-click it to bring up the File Roller application.

6. In File Roller, click the **Extract** button, which will bring up the Extract window.

7. In that window, click the **Create Folder** button, and create a folder within your home folder called *Schnapsen.*

8. Click the **Extract** button in that window, and when the extraction process is complete, close File Roller.

9B-2: Running and Anglicizing Schnapsen

Now that Schnapsen is in your home folder, it's time to run it, which you do pretty much the same way you did for Risk. Open a new Terminal window, and then do the following:

1. Move into the new Schnapsen folder by typing **cd schnapsen** and pressing ENTER.

2. Type **java -jar Schnapsen.jar** (be sure to place a space between java and -jar and use a capital *S* at the beginning of *Schnapsen*), and press ENTER. Schnapsen will soon appear, after which you can start playing . . . if you speak German.

3. To switch the interface into English, go to the **Einstellungen** menu, and select **Sprache ▸ Englisch**.

4. If you are not familiar with the German card faces and suits, you can switch them over to the ones you probably know (diamonds, hearts, spades, and clubs) by going to the **Settings** menu (assuming you are now in English mode) and selecting **French** in both the **Cards' set** and **Trump sign** menus.

You are now set to play. There are some basic rules in the Help menu, but you can also learn the rules of Schnapsen (and any other card game in the world) in greater depth at www.pagat.com. Have fun!

Project 9C: Say It Ain't So, Joe—Running Windows Applications with Wine

You've now learned many different ways to add applications to your system, so I might as well throw in yet another—running Windows applications. Despite the fact that there is a Linux equivalent for most of the Windows programs that you use or need, there may be one or two programs that you will miss. Fortunately, it is possible to run some Windows applications from within Linux with the help of a program called *Wine*.

The folks at Wine seem keen on pointing out that Wine is not a Windows emulator, preferring to call it a *Windows compatibility layer*. In fact, even the name itself drives home the point, as *Wine* is a recursive acronym for *Wine Is Not an Emulator*. Whatever way you choose to look at it, its function is to allow you to run Windows apps without having Windows installed on your machine.

It is only fair to point out that Wine continues to be a work in progress. It works well with some programs and not at all with others. Things are improving, however, and Wine now seems to work better with more applications. If you are curious as to which apps are known to run under Wine and to what degree of success, check out the Wine home page at www.winehq.org, and click the **AppDB** link.

9C-1: Installing and Checking Out Wine

You can get Wine via Synaptic by doing a search for and installing *wine*. Once the installation is complete, you can check it out by selecting **Applications ▸ Wine ▸ Programs ▸ Accessories ▸ Notepad**. After a few seconds (longer the very first time you use Wine), the Windows Notepad will appear (Figure 9-4).

9C-2: Installing a Windows Application in Wine

Now that you've seen a Windows application in action under Wine, you might as well learn how you can install more yourself. I will point you to one application that will definitely work—a pretty cool tabbed text editor called *NoteTab Light* (Figure 9-5).

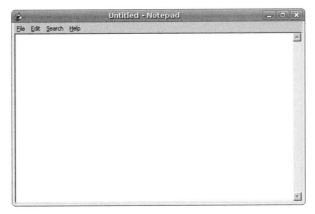

Figure 9-4: Windows Notepad running under Wine

To get NoteTab Light, go to www.notetab.com, right-click the **EXE Package** button in the NoteTab Light 5.61 section, and then select **Save Link As** in the popup menu.

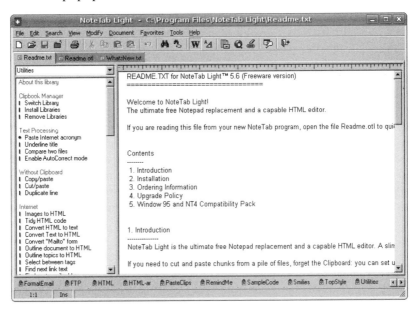

Figure 9-5: NoteTab Light

When the download is complete, find and then double-click the **NoteTab_Setup.exe** file. A few moments after that, the same sort of setup wizard that you would see if you were installing NoteTab Light in Windows will appear (Figure 9-6). Go through the wizard, accept the license agreement, and then accept all the defaults along the way until the installation is complete.

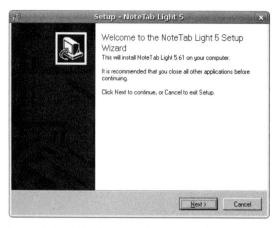

Figure 9-6: A Windows installation wizard running under Wine

Running NoteTab Light is quite easy because it provides you with a desktop launcher. Just double-click that launcher, and NoteTab Light will soon appear, just like a regular Linux app would. You can also run NoteTab Light and other Windows applications under Wine by going to the **Applications** menu, selecting **Wine ▸ Programs**, and then selecting the program you want to run. You might find, however, that Wine-dependent applications will not appear in this menu until you restart your system after installing them.

9C-3: Installing Microsoft Internet Explorer

Although more and more people are trying to get away from Microsoft Internet Explorer, there are times when you just have to have it. There are, after all, sites that won't let you use anything else. For Linux users, this used to be a problem, because getting IE to work via Wine could be quite a geeky chore. Not so anymore, thanks to IEs 4 Linux, which is a simple utility that helps you easily download, install, and set up Internet Explorer for use with Wine on your Linux system.

Before using IEs 4 Linux, you need to have two things installed: Wine, which you should have installed at the beginning of this project, and cabextract, which you can download via Synaptic. Once both packages are installed, you are ready to proceed, and you don't even need to go to the project home page to do so (it's www.tatanka.com.br/ies4linux, in case you're wondering). Here are the steps:

1. Download the IEs 4 Linux package by opening a Terminal window and typing the following:

   ```
   wget http://www.tatanka.com.br/ies4linux/downloads/ies4linux-latest.tar.gz
   ```

If you're not all that enamored with the command line, you can point your browser to www.tatanka.com.br/ies4linux/page/installation, and click the rather tiny **download IEs 4 Linux** link near the bottom of the page to download what you need.

2. Once you've downloaded the tarball, double-click it and extract its contents to your home folder.

3. Next, go to your home folder and double-click the newly created ies4linux folder.

4. Inside that folder, double-click the **ies4linux** launcher, and in the window that then appears (Figure 9-7), click **Run**.

Figure 9-7: Letting Ubuntu know what you want to do with the file you've just double-clicked

5. A window like the one shown in Figure 9-8 will appear. Accept the defaults, or make whatever choices you favor, and then click **OK**.

Figure 9-8: Setting up the IEs 4 Linux installation

After that, IEs 4 Linux will begin downloading, installing, and setting up Internet Explorer, showing its progress in a window like the one in Figure 9-9. When it is done, it will tell you, at which point you can click the **Close** button that appears at the bottom of that window.

Figure 9-9: Checking the progress of the IEs 4 Linux installation

You should now find an Internet Explorer–like launcher on your desktop. Double-click that, and you will soon be looking at your own Wine-run version of Internet Explorer 6 (shown in Figure 9-10).

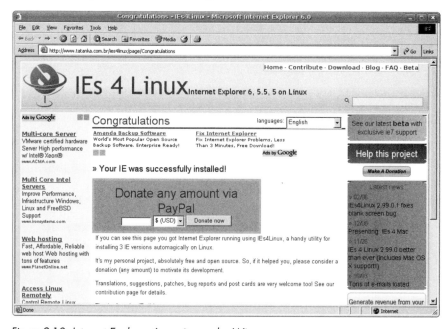

Figure 9-10: Internet Explorer 6 running under Wine

As you may recall, the applications you install from the various Ubuntu repositories via Synaptic or Add/Remove Applications are in the form of DEB packages—and the repositories are filled with such packages. Unfortunately, although these repositories seem to contain just about every piece of software out there, for different reasons not every package finds its way into these repositories, even if it is available in DEB form. At the present time, the application Skype is one of these.

In case you don't already know, *Skype*, shown in Figure 9-11, is voice over IP (VoIP) software that allows you to speak to other Skype users over the Internet with the clarity of a regular telephone line. And it doesn't cost anything— even if you call users overseas. There are also for-fee services, such as SkypeOut, which allows you to call regular mobile and landline telephone numbers from your computer at a fraction of what it would normally cost from a regular telephone.

While it is true that Ubuntu comes bundled with a VoIP package of its own called Ekiga Softphone, it is not compatible with the much better known and more widespread Skype. Since it is very likely that the majority of people you know who are using a VoIP software package are using Skype, it only makes sense to use Skype so that you can easily communicate with them. It's nice software anyway.

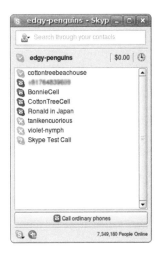

Figure 9-11: Internet telephony made easy with Skype

9D-1: Getting and Installing Skype

Because Skype is not available from the Ubuntu repositories, you will need to get it yourself from the Skype website (www.skype.com). Once there, click the **Download** button, which will automatically take you to the download page for Linux versions of Skype. On that page, click the link for Ubuntu, and then click the **Save File** button in the window that appears.

Once the download is complete, you will find the Skype DEB package on your hard disk, either on your desktop or in your home folder, depending on how you have things set up. Double-click that package, after which Package Installer, yet another APT front end, will appear with information about the package you are about to install (Figure 9-12) and any other packages that it is going to download in order to make the first one work. In that window, click the **Install Package** button, after which you will be prompted for your password. Once the password formalities are complete, things should start looking rather Synaptic-esque, with the same orange bars zipping back and forth in progress windows until the process is complete. Then, just click the **Close** button in the progress window, and close the Package Installer window. Mission accomplished.

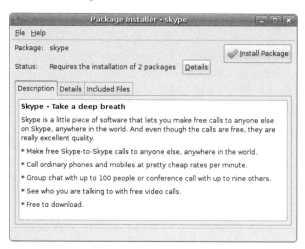

Figure 9-12: Installing individual DEB packages via Package Installer

NOTE   *As is the case with all APT front ends, you cannot use Package Installer while another APT front end is open. Be sure to close Synaptic or Add/Remove Packages before using Package Installer.*

Once all the pieces have been installed, you can run Skype by going to the **Applications** menu and selecting **Internet ▶ Skype**. After setting up a Skype user account, I would advise you to restart your computer—Skype seems to have better sound quality after an initial restart. Also, while we're on the topic of sound quality, remember that it is best to use Skype with a headset. Trying to talk with a stick microphone could cause feedback or echoes because the microphone will pick up and transmit sounds from the speakers.

Project 9E: Converting RPMs to DEB Packages Using Alien

While it is true that not all DEB packages make their way into the Ubuntu repositories, it is also true that some, albeit few, applications are not available as DEB packages at all. Some, however, are available as RPMs, which are the packages used in Red Hat, Fedora, Mandriva, and a few other Linux distributions. While this may not sound particularly promising to you as an Ubuntu user, there are a few rays of hope emanating from a handy utility by the name of Alien.

If you haven't guessed already, what Alien does is convert RPM packages to DEB packages that you can install and run in your DEB-based system. It doesn't work perfectly 100 percent of the time, and it isn't as desirable an alternative as a properly compiled DEB-from-source package, but if there's an application you really need, it might just get the job done. To give Alien a try, we'll convert and install an application called TuxCards (shown in Figure 9-13) that calls itself a *hierarchical notebook*.

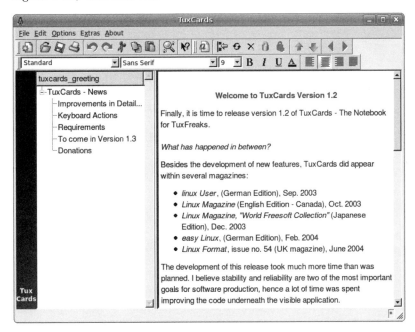

Figure 9-13: TuxCards—a hierachical notebook

9E-1: Installing Alien

Before downloading, converting, and installing the TuxCards RPM, you have to first install Alien. Fortunately, Alien is available via Synaptic, so all you have to do is perform a search for *alien*, and then follow the standard installation procedures. If you prefer, you can download and install it by using the apt-get command you learned about in the previous chapter. If you go this route, first type sudo apt-get update, and press ENTER. After the repository database update is complete, go ahead and install Alien by typing sudo apt-get install alien and pressing ENTER.

9E-2: Installing Qt GUI Library

If you used Synaptic in 9E-1 and it is still open, check to see if you have already installed one of the files that TuxCards needs to run by searching for *libqt3-mt*. If your search shows that it is already installed, you are ready to move on. If not, install it.

9E-3: Getting the TuxCards RPM

Once Alien is installed, you need to download the TuxCards RPM. You can get this from www.tuxcards.de/requirements.html. On that page, right-click **tuxcards-1.2.1mdk.i586.rpm**, and then select **Save Link As** in the popup menu. There are other versions on the page that might work, but for the sake of this project, stick with the one I just mentioned.

NOTE   *Be aware when attempting to download any RPM file that the .rpm extension is interpreted by your system as a RealMedia file. Thus, if you simply single-click a .rpm link, your system might try to play it in a media player, rather than trying to download it. Right-clicking such links avoids this problem.*

Once the download is complete, make sure to place the RPM in your home folder so you can follow along easily.

9E-4: Converting the TuxCards RPM

Now that the TuxCards RPM is in your home folder, you can use Alien to convert it to an Ubuntu-friendly DEB package by typing the following command and pressing ENTER:

```
sudo alien --scripts tuxcards*.rpm
```

After you type your password, nothing much will seem to happen. Once Alien is done doing its thing, however, you will get the message tuxcards_1.2.2_i386.deb generated (or something like that) in the Terminal window. If you look in your home folder, you will find the newly generated DEB package along with the original RPM.

9E-5: Installing the Newly Generated TuxCards DEB Package

You can now install the TuxCards DEB package by using the dpkg (Debian package) command with the -i (install) flag and then pressing ENTER. The command should be:

```
sudo dpkg -i tuxcards*.deb
```

If I haven't won you over to the world of commands (not that I'm trying to), and you still prefer going about things graphically whenever possible, you can install the TuxCards DEB package the same way you installed Skype in Project 9D—by double-clicking the DEB package and using Package Installer. It all works out the same in the end, so it's strictly up to you.

9E-6: Running TuxCards

Once TuxCards has been installed, you can run it via the Run Application applet. Just type tuxcards in the command box, and then click the **Run** button.

Project 9F: Compiling and Installing Programs from Source: Xmahjongg

Though it was far more common in the earlier days, *compiling programs from source* seems to be a phrase you still hear more in the Linux world than in any other. For the beginner, just the mention of compiling a program from source seems off-putting enough. The words *compile* and *source* seem to instill a sense of foreboding in the heart of the new user. That certainly was the case for me, anyway.

However, this method of installing programs is a lot easier than it sounds. In fact, now that you have some experience using the Terminal and command line, it is just plain easy—a sort of one, two, three, and you're done process.

Of course, you can live long and prosper without ever bothering to compile anything on your system. You can move along quite happily with your system as is, or you can just install programs by means of the numerous and very convenient APT front ends that you've learned about thus far, such as Syanptic, Add/Remove Programs, and even Package Installer.

So why would you want to bother compiling programs from source? Well, although there are a lot of DEB packages that Synaptic can ease into your system, not every bit of software in Linuxdom is available in that file format. Or perhaps you want the newest version of the software you have your eyes on, but the version available via Synaptic is a slightly older version. Of course, there is that good old human nature factor at play as well—there may well come a time when curiosity gets the better of you, and you will want to move just one step beyond the way you've grown accustomed to doing things. After working through this short project, you will be able to do just that, and I am sure you will find that your initial worries will have been for naught. Before getting into the hands-on thing, however, read through the following little primer first, so that you know just what is going on.

What Is Source?

In order to understand what *source* is, you should understand a bit about how a program actually gets from its primitive state on the programmer's computer to an up-and-running application on your machine. First the programmer writes a program in a programming language. You have probably heard of programming languages such as BASIC or C, and there are many others. What the programmer actually writes with such a language is a set of instructions called the *source code*, or *source.* Your computer, however, cannot actually understand any of that source on its own. It is as if the computer speaks ancient Greek, and the source code is all written in French. The computer therefore needs some sort of interpreter to help it out.

The various languages that programmers use are called *high-level languages*—they are relatively easy for programmers to read. The computer, on the other hand, only understands *low-level languages*, which are quite difficult for most mere mortal programmers to deal with. To convert the high-level language instructions to a low-level language, the computer needs some other program to translate.

This can be done while a program is running, in which case the translator program is called an *interpreter*. Applications that run using an interpreter are usually *scripts*. The pyWings and Briscola applications in Chapter 8 are examples of such script applications.

The problem with such scripts is that they can be slower than most of the applications you're familiar with because the computer must run an interpreter, interpret the source code, and run the actual application all at the same time. This is like having a French book translated into Greek by a live interpreter—very slow indeed.

As an alternative, most programs use a compiler instead of an interpreter. A *compiler* translates the high-level source code into low-level *machine code*, or *object code*, that the computer can understand before the application is actually run. Once this translation is done, the computer never has to bother with the high-level instructions again; it can merely read the translated version each and every time it runs the program. This is like having a translated version of a foreign book that you can read any time you want to. Because computers can run compiled programs without simultaneously using an interpreter, compiled programs run faster than scripts. Most applications for all operating systems are, therefore, compiled.

Tarballs: The Containers of Source

Almost all source packages come in the form of tarballs (tarballs, DEBs, and even the RPMs, such as those used in Red Hat–based systems, are all referred to as *packages*, which is why the icon for such files looks like a little parcel-post box). As you learned in Chapters 6 and 8, tarballs consist of a group of files that have been archived into a single file, which is most often compressed to save disk space, much like Zip files on Windows systems or SIT (StuffIt) files on Macs. In Linux, the most common method for creating such archives is through the *tar program*, from which the tarball gets its name, while the compression of that archive is usually accomplished by means of the gzip program. Compressed tar files, or *tarballs*, can thus be recognized by their file endings, which are .tar.gz, or when compressed with the bzip program, tar.bz2.

As you learned in Chapter 8, the files archived in tarballs can be extracted by using the command line, but to keep things easy in this chapter, you can just use the simple double-click method that you used in Chapter 6, if you prefer.

The Basics

As I mentioned before, the process of compiling an application from source and then installing it is actually simple. Basically, after untarring the source tarball, you would use the following commands to accomplish the task:

`./configure`   To configure a *makefile*, which provides instructions for the make command

`make`   To translate the source code into object code that the computer can understand

`sudo make install`   To give yourself write privileges in protected folders and then install the application

`make clean`   To clean up the leftovers once the process is complete (to clean up the mess)

I know that sounds like a lot of commands, but as I always say, it is easier to actually do than it looks like on the page, so fear not.

9F-1: Installing the Tools You Need

Before doing anything else, you have to get your system ready to do what you're about to ask of it. Because Ubuntu is designed with the average computer user in mind, it does not come with the various applications and libraries you need to compile applications from source. Fortunately, however, everything you need to get the job done is available via Synaptic. To get ready for the work at hand in this chapter (and many other jobs you are likely to do on your own in the future), perform searches for and install the following packages:

- build-essential
- libgtk2.0-dev

9F-2: Downloading and Extracting the Xmahjongg File

To get down to some hands-on experience with compiling a program from source, you will be working with a game called *Xmahjongg*, which you can see in Figure 9-14. If you've tried out the version of Mahjongg that comes with your Ubuntu distribution, you will notice that this one is much easier on your eyes and is a bit more colorful (check out the project site at www.lcdf.org/ xmahjongg to catch a glimpse of it in its full-color glory).

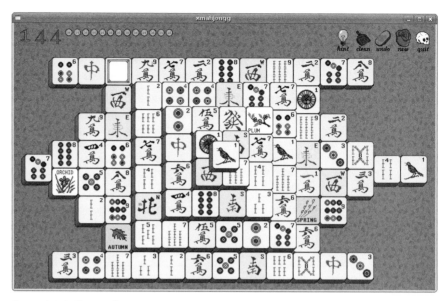

Figure 9-14: The Xmahjongg game

Xmahjongg is available via Synaptic, so it is not absolutely necessary to install it in the way you are about to, but doing so provides a perfect opportunity to learn how to compile a program from source. The amount of source code isn't all that great, so it won't take too much time to do, and it requires no tinkering.

In case you are not already familiar with this genre of Mahjongg game, the idea is simple enough. Each tile has an image and there are four of each tile in the pile. You must match pairs of like tiles that are open on at least one side. When you click two matching open tiles, they will disappear. The object of the game is to remove all the tiles from the board.

To get started, you will first have to download the Xmahjongg source code. You can get this from the Xmahjongg project page at www.lcdf.org/xmahjongg. Download the tarball xmahjongg-3.7.tar.gz or a newer version if there is one. Do not download any of the other file types available on that page.

If you prefer, you can instead download the Xmahjongg tarball by using the wget command that you learned in Chapter 8. Just open a Terminal window, type the following command, and then press ENTER.

```
wget http://www.lcdf.org/xmahjongg/xmahjongg-3.7.tar.gz
```

Once you have the file on your hard disk, untar the xmahjongg-3.7.tar.gz file either via the command line, as you learned to do in Chapter 8, or via the simple double-click method. To make it easier for you to follow along with the directions I'll be giving you, be sure to place the untarred Xmahjongg folder in your home folder. Then you will be ready to roll.

Normally at this point, you would look through the folder to find some instructions for dealing with the package, just as you did in Chapter 8 for Briscola. In most source code packages, this information is included in an INSTALL file like that in the xmahjongg-3.7 folder (Figure 9-15). To read the INSTALL file, just double-click it, and it will open in Gedit.

In this case, you can simply close the INSTALL file, as it prescribes the same steps I've listed below. However, in the future, when you install other programs from source, you will need to follow the instructions in the INSTALL files that come with the source files. With most INSTALL files, the instructions will match those that follow, though I would suggest using the alternative method I'll be presenting as a substitute for the make install step.

Of course, it may well happen that you take a look at the contents of the INSTALL file and start wondering what alien tongue it is written in. In cases when you have no idea what the INSTALL file is going on about, just look for a configure file in the package folder. If you find one, you should be able to just do things the way you will learn in this project.

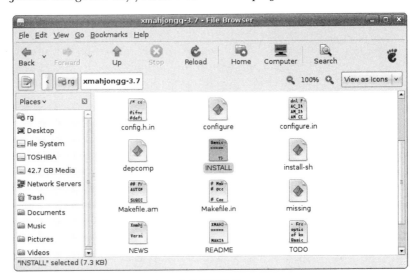

Figure 9-15: Identifying a package's INSTALL file

9F-3: Running configure and make for Xmahjongg

Now that you have downloaded and untarred the Xmahjongg tarball, installation is pretty standard. Here's what you need to do:

1. Open a Terminal window, and then move into the new folder by typing **cd xmahjongg*** and pressing ENTER.

    The next step is sort of a setup phase that runs the configure script in the xmahjongg-3.7 folder. The configure script checks what files, compilers, and other things it needs, and then it searches your computer to see if those things are there, and if so, where. Based on this information, it writes a file called a *makefile*, which is a set of instructions that will tell the make command in the subsequent step how to set things up specifically for your system configuration.

2. Configure the program by typing **./configure** and pressing ENTER.

    While you are running configure, you will see lots of odd and mysterious things flowing through your Terminal window; this is essentially a running account of what is going on, each step of the way. Depending on the program you are dealing with, this could take a bit of time—a few seconds or a few minutes. Either way, you needn't worry. As long as the mysterious text keeps flowing and you don't get an error message at the very end of the whole process, all will be well.

    When configure has done its thing, you will see your prompt again, and you can go on to the next step, which is the translation, or *compilation*, step. The make command reads the makefile created by configure to see how things need to be set up on your machine. Then it proceeds to call on the compiler to translate the high-level source code into low-level, machine-readable files that can be installed in the subsequent step.

3. To perform this translation, type **make**, and press ENTER.

    Again, you will be treated to more mysterious text flowing through the window and a short wait, usually a tad longer than for the configure process. Once make has done its job and you see your prompt again, you are ready to install the program.

Up to this point, you have not changed your system in any way. All the changes thus far have taken place in the xmahjongg-3.7 folder only—your system is still as pure as the day you started. Of course, all that is going to end right now when you perform the final installation step.

9F-4: Installing and Running Xmahjongg

Now you've come to the last step in this part of the process, make install. Here you are telling your system to install what you have created, or compiled, in the make step. Oh, and please note that because installation takes place in permissions-protected parts of your system, you will need to add sudo to the command string in order to give yourself administrative privileges.

To perform the installation, type **sudo make install**, and press ENTER. You will then be prompted for your password. After typing it and pressing ENTER, the installation process will take place (and very quickly, at that). Once your Terminal brings you back to your user prompt, Xmahjongg will be installed and ready to run. As a general rule, programs compiled from source do not automatically install a launcher in your Applications menu;

you must instead run them by command. Although you can run a program for the first time by typing a command in the Run Application panel applet, it is better to run the program for the first time by typing the command in your Terminal window. If anything has gone amiss during installation, the Terminal will tell you what the problem is, whereas the Run Application method would just leave you wondering what's going on.

To run Xmahjongg, just type **xmahjongg** in a Terminal window, and then press ENTER. If everything goes as it should, you can create a program launcher for Xmahjongg in your Applications menu, on the GNOME Panel, or in a panel drawer.

9F-5: Cleaning Up and/or Uninstalling Xmahjongg

Once you are done and everything seems to be working as it should, you would normally tidy things up in the Xmahjongg folder by getting rid of any unnecessary files. You can do this via the Terminal by using the cd command to go back into the Xmahjongg folder, typing **make clean**, and then pressing ENTER.

If you want to uninstall Xmahjongg, open a Terminal window, go back to the Xmahjongg folder by using the cd command, type **sudo make uninstall**, and finally press ENTER. The routine is essentially the same for any applications installed in this way; however, as you might imagine, uninstallation isn't always as smooth and simple a process as what I've just described (and it's definitely not as easy as it is via Synaptic or other APT front ends).

The make uninstall routine also requires that you keep the original project folder, which means you have to keep a bit of clutter you normally wouldn't need to bother with. Oh, and to make matters . . . a little more disconcerting, some projects do not provide a make uninstall routine at all. This means that you have to keep track of where everything has been installed in your system and then remove each item piece by piece using a series of sudo rm commands. A geek's dream, as one friend likes to put it.

All that negativity aside, go ahead, have some fun, and put your command-line skills to one more workout. You'll have something to tell your grandkids about in the future.

10

GUTENBIRD

Setting Up and Using Your Printer and Scanner

Two of the most common computer peripherals are printers and scanners. This only makes sense, as it is those two tools that turn a web-surfing, game-playing, music-churning, number-crunching box of chips into a meaningful production tool—a virtual publishing house, if you will. These two tools help your computer convert digital information into hard copy (in the case of printers) and hard copy into digital information (in the case of scanners). It is not surprising, therefore, that these tools often come together these days in the form of multifunction printers.

In this chapter, you will learn how to connect these useful devices to your computer, how to set them up, and how to use them. If you're more into working with your digital camera than with a scanner, you might want to sneak a peek at Chapter 14; otherwise, put on your printer's smock, and follow on. . . .

Printers

Unless the only thing you use your computer for is playing games, listening to MP3s, or stopping doors on hot, breezy days, you will no doubt want to hook up your machine to a printer. Despite the paperless office era that the personal computer was supposedly going to usher in, it seems that the computer's strength as a desktop-publishing and general work tool has made producing high-quality printed documents an even more attractive proposition than ever before.

Confirming That Your Printer Is Supported

Setting up a printer to work with your new system is a pretty easy task, and it seems that printer support in the Linux world gets better with each release. In general, support for Epson, Brother, Samsung, and Hewlett-Packard printers is good, while support for other makers and other printer types is a bit spottier, though improving.

If you really want to make sure your printer is supported, just try it out by following the instructions in the next section. If you are thinking about buying a printer or are trying to decide whether or not to switch to Linux, go to www.linuxprinting.org. On that site, you can check out the online database to see if your printer is currently supported and, if so, to what degree. Listings for supported printers also include information on what drivers are best for your purposes. There is also a page of suggested makes and models, in case you're considering buying a printer with the intent of using it with your Linux system. Read this before making your purchase decision. You might also want to consult Ubuntu's list at https://wiki .ubuntu.com/hardwaresupportcomponentsprinters.

Getting Ubuntu to Automatically Recognize and Set Up Your Printer

Printer handling in Ubuntu is now pretty much a no-brainer, because most printers are automatically detected. If you have a USB printer, get started by connecting it to your computer and then powering up the printer (vice-versa should work just fine, too). Assuming Ubuntu recognizes your printer, and chances are it will, a small printer icon will appear in the upper-right panel while the system goes through its automatic setup routine. When it is done, a small warning window like the one in Figure 10-1 will appear, telling you that your printer has been recognized. There is nothing more for you to do in this case other than close that window—your printer is set up and ready to roll.

Figure 10-1: Ubuntu lets you know that it has automatically recognized and configured your printer.

It is also possible, however, that Ubuntu will recognize your printer, but it will not find a driver that is an exact match for it. In this case, it will offer up a substitute driver instead, and the auto-recognition window (Figure 10-2) will look slightly different from the one in Figure 10-1.

Figure 10-2: Ubuntu lets you know that it has automatically recognized your printer but couldn't find an exact driver match for it.

If you find yourself in this situation, it wouldn't be a bad idea to print a test page to see if the substituted driver works as it should. You can do this by clicking the **Find Driver** button in that window, which will bring up the Printer configuration and Change Driver windows. Click **Cancel** in the Change Driver window (you won't be needing that window at this point), and then click the **Print Test Page** button in the Printer configuration window. If the test print page looks normal (something like Figure 10-3), things should be fine and you can close the Printer configuration window.

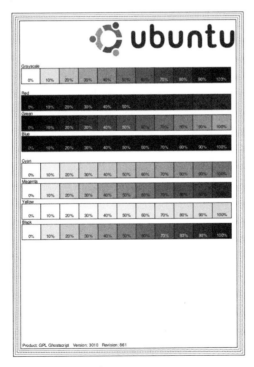

Figure 10-3: An Ubuntu test print page

If you have a printer that connects to your computer's parallel port, auto-detection and setup should also work if your printer was connected to your computer at startup. If it was not, shut down your system and turn your computer off, connect your printer to the computer, turn on the printer, and then start your computer again. With luck, your printer should be recognized and set up automatically this time around. You can also try this same approach with a USB printer that was not recognized at initial plug in.

Manually Configuring Printers

If your printer isn't automatically recognized, you can still set things up manually. Here's what you need to do:

1. Go to the **System** menu, and select **Administration ▸ Printing**. A Printer configuration window will appear, showing the printers that have already been recognized and/or configured.

2. Click the **New Printer** button, after which the system will show any new finds in a New Printer window.

3. To select a printer from the list in the left pane, click the entry for that printer once, and then click the **Forward** button.

4. Your system will begin scanning to see if there are any new printers connected, after which it will display its findings in a new window (Figure 10-4). Click the entry for your printer in the left pane of that window, and then click **Forward**.

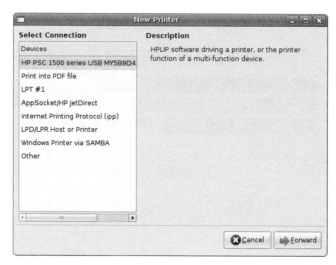

Figure 10-4: Setting up a printer manually

5. The system will then begin searching for drivers for your printer and will identify the make of your printer in the next screen of the wizard. Check that the correct make is selected, and then click **Forward**.

6. In the next screen, your printer model should appear in the left pane, while the recommended driver will appear in the right pane (Figure 10-5). Click **Forward**.

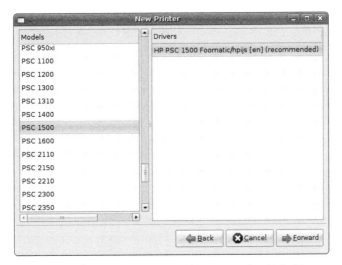

Figure 10-5: The printer setup wizard recommends which driver to use.

7. In the final screen of the Wizard, fill in the blanks to suit your needs, and then click **Apply**, after which the wizard will close and your new printer will appear in the left pane of the Printer configuration window.

Your printer should now be set up and ready for use. However, just to make sure that everything is hunky-dory, it is always a good idea to print a test page. You can do this by clicking the entry for your printer in the left pane of the Printer configuration window. After that, click the **Print Test Page** button in the Settings tab that opens (Figure 10-6).

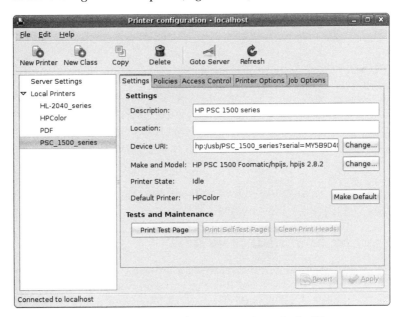

Figure 10-6: Printing a test page with your new printer via the Printer configuration window

Your system will send a test document to your printer and let you know it's done so in a small window, which you can close. The printer should print out the test document shortly.

NOTE   *If your test page didn't come out the way it should, or if your printer wasn't configured automatically or correctly by the system, check out www.linuxprinting.org, and see if there are any special requirements or caveats for your model.*

Setting Up Printers Connected Over a Network

If you would like to use a printer connected via a home or office network, just follow these steps:

1. Go to the **System** menu, and select **Administration ▸ Printing**. A Printer configuration window will appear, showing the printers that have already been recognized and/or configured.

2. Click the **New Printer** button, after which the New Printer window will appear.

3. Select **Windows Printer via SAMBA** in the left pane of that window by clicking that entry once, and then click the **Browse** button in the top-right corner of the page.

4. In the SMB Browser window that appears (Figure 10-7), navigate your way to the printer you wish to use, and then click **OK**.

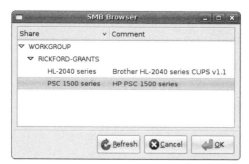

Figure 10-7: Browsing for printers connected over a Windows Network

5. Once you're back in the New Printer window, click the **Forward** button.

6. Now continue from step 5 in the previous section, "Manually Configuring Printers" on page 186.

For the Driverless Among You

As I mentioned, there are some printers for which Linux does not yet have built-in support. For those of you who find yourselves with such printers, there are a few routes you can take in order to get things to work.

Checking the Connections

You'd be surprised how many times I have triumphantly solved someone's printer problems by simply turning on the printer or wiggling or replugging the USB or parallel connectors. Printers that are powered down and/or that have loose connections are often to blame when the printer's model name fails to appear in the first page of the printer setup wizard.

If that approach fails, browse to www.linuxprinting.org, as it is sometimes the case that Linux can only support certain printers if they are connected via the parallel port, even if they work via USB in other systems.

Trying Your Windows Drivers

If your printer came with an installation disk, you might want to see if you can find a driver for it there. The driver on such a disk should end in *.ppd* (for *PostScript Printer Description*). To use one of these drivers, try to add your printer as described earlier, but when you get to the New Printer window where you select your printer's make, click the radio button next to the words *Provide PPD file*, and then try to locate the file in the drop-down menu button at the bottom of the page. When and if you find a driver, click the **Forward** button, and then continue the printer setup.

Third-Party Drivers

Recently, more and more Linux printing drivers are becoming available. If you don't find your printer on that second page of the printer setup wizard, just trying googling the make and model of your printer plus the word *linux*. In the past, for example, I had a laser printer that did not appear at www .linuxprinting.org, so I googled the printer, *samsung+SCX4100+linux*, which led me to www.driverstock.com, a site that provides free printer drivers for most operating systems, including Linux. On that site, I found not only the driver for my printer, but also the driver for its built-in scanner.

You might also want to check the website for the manufacturer of your printer, as many now provide Linux drivers for a number of their printers. Brother, Lexmark, Hewlett-Packard, and Samsung do, to name a few. Canon seems to be the main holdout as far as the big boys go. There is also a German company (www.turboprint.info) that provides Linux drivers, albeit for a fee, for machines that are really hard to deal with and for high-quality graphic solutions.

If you happen to find and download a driver for your printer that does not come with its own installer, just follow the directions given for trying Windows drivers. Finally, don't forget to give the Ubuntu forums (www .ubuntuforums.org) a try to see if anyone there has any experience getting the printer in question to work on their system.

Trial and Error

Finally, there is always the old trial-and-error approach, which works on occasion. When setting up your printer via the wizard window, try choosing from one of the other models and/or drivers available for printers from your printer's manufacturer.

After you are done with the wizard, click the printer you added in the left pane of the Printer configuration window, click the **Settings** tab, and then click the **Print Test Page** button to see what happens. If nothing happens, click the **Change** button at the far right end of the *Make and Model* row in the Settings tab, select a different printer model and/or driver, and then, back in the Settings tab, click the **Print Test Page** button again. Repeat that process until something works. With any luck, something will . . . might . . . well, just give it a try if you're desperate.

Printing Details

Now that your printer is set up, you will no doubt want to start printing. This is an easy task, and it isn't very different from how it works in the Windows and Mac worlds, so you shouldn't need much explanation. In fact, printing in Ubuntu has become easier than ever, because all the settings you would normally want to toy with are all in their own tabs within the Print window that appears when you select Print in an application's File menu. I would even dare to say that figuring out printing options in Ubuntu is now easier than it is in Windows or OS X.

You should be aware that the function of the tabs can vary depending on the application you happen to be printing from. Thus, the tabs you'll see when printing from the GIMP will be slightly different from those you will see when printing from Firefox. Generally, however, the Settings and Page Setup tabs will always be there, no matter from whence you came. All that said, I'll give you an idea of some of the settings that are available within some of the Print window's tabs.

General   Printer selection, pages to print, number of copies, order of printing, collating

Page Setup   Pages per sheet, scaling, paper type, paper source, output tray

Options   Print frames, shrink to fit page, print background, headers and footers

Image Settings   Size, resolution, page positioning

Job   Print timing (now, later, at time), cover page

Image Quality   Output resolution (DPI)

Printing in OpenOffice.org

Occasionally, you will come across an application that has a slightly different way of handling printing—like OpenOffice.org. Fortunately, the differences may actually make printing in OpenOffice.org more Windows-like, and thus easier for newbies from the Windows world to follow along with. As you can see in Figure 10-8, the main Print window for OpenOffice.org applications allows you to select the printer you want to use, the range of pages, and how many copies you want to print. You can access other options by clicking the Properties and/or Options buttons.

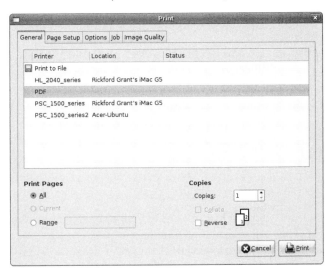

Figure 10-8: Print settings in OpenOffice.org modules

Printing to PDF

One of the nice features of Linux is that you can save most documents or web pages as PDF files. In some cases, such as in OpenOffice.org, you do this by exporting the document to PDF. In most other applications, however, you do it via the Print dialog box, in which case you are said to be "printing to PDF." Whether you are *saving as* PDF, *exporting to* PDF, or *printing to* PDF, you are essentially doing the same thing: creating a PDF file of your document.

This is very handy, as it allows you to create documents that cannot be altered by others and yet can easily be read regardless of the word processor program or computer platform the reader is using. Best of all, this feature, which you would have to pay a pretty penny for in the Windows world, costs you nothing, as it is built in to your system.

In most GNOME applications (and now in Firefox, too), you can print to PDF by going to the **File** menu of the application in question and selecting **Print**. When the Print window (Figure 10-9) appears, select **PDF** in the list of printers, and then click the **Print** button. The PDF file will be saved to the PDF folder within your Home folder by default.

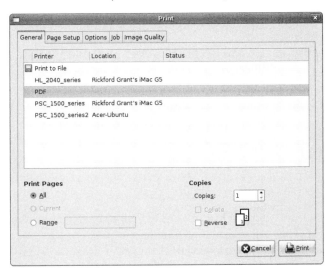

Figure 10-9: Printing a file to PDF in most GNOME applications

Canceling a Print Job

It happens to all of us. You wanted to print just 1 page of a 57-page document, but you accidentally started printing the whole thing. What can you do to save your ink and 56 sheets of paper? Fortunately, the solution is simple.

Once you've clicked the Print button and the print job is sent to your printer, a small printer icon will appear somewhere at the right end of the top GNOME Panel (usually to the left of the other items there), as you can see in Figure 10-10.

Figure 10-10: A printer icon appears in the GNOME Panel while printing.

Just click that icon once, and a window showing your current and queued print jobs will appear (as shown in Figure 10-11). Your errant print job will be listed in that window, so right-click the name of the job to select it, and then, in the popup menu, select **Cancel**.

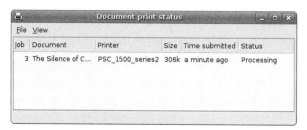

Figure 10-11: Canceling a print job via the print queue window

After you do this, the print job listed in the queue window will disappear, and your printer will stop printing. You can then close the print queue window. This is a very easy process that you may well find is more effective than what you've experienced in other operating systems.

In some cases, things will be even easier, particularly if you installed your printer driver yourself by means of the installer that came packaged with the driver. In many such cases, the driver will provide its own progress window that will appear whenever you print a document. If so, you can simply click the **Cancel** button (or equivalent) in that window to cancel the printing job.

NOTE   *In some cases you may have to clear your printer after canceling a print job. You can do this by turning your printer off, waiting a few seconds, and then turning it on again.*

Scanners

Scanners are extremely useful and about as cheap a peripheral device as you can get. They allow you to take images or pages of text and input them, in digital form, into your computer—in much the same way as you would duplicate a document on a copy machine. However, even as digital cameras are rapidly overtaking traditional film cameras as the photographic device of choice for the masses, the number of people using scanners to transfer their non-digital images into digital form is slowly decreasing.

Despite this trend, scanners are not in immediate danger of extinction because there are more images around than those you photograph yourself. In some ways, you could even argue that scanners are becoming a bit more common due to the fact that they now often come as part of the increasingly popular multifunction printers.

Even though scanners have been around for a relatively long time, support for them in Linux is still a bit spotty. Fortunately, this is changing for the better with every new Linux release. The back end, the essentially hidden part of your system that handles scanner recognition and support in Linux, is called Sane, while the graphical interface for Sane is called XSane (shown in Figure 10-12). If you are wondering whether Linux will be able to recognize your scanner, or if you are trying to figure out what type of scanner to buy, you will probably want to go to the Sane website, www.sane-project .org/sane-mfgs.html.

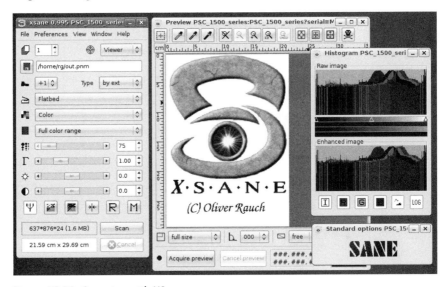

Figure 10-12: Scanning with XSane

There you will be able to see whether your scanner is supported or get tips about what scanner to buy. As I have mentioned before, you can also try out the Ubuntu forums (www.ubuntuforums.org) and ask for Ubuntu-specific recommendations there.

Scanning with XSane

To run XSane, go to the **Applications** menu, and select **Graphics ▶ XSane Image Scanner**. XSane will then perform a search for an attached scanner. If it finds one, it will start up. If it doesn't, it will pop up a tiny window that says, "No devices available." You can do little else at that point other than click the **Close** button.

If you do run up against this problem, you can try running XSane as root by running the Terminal (Applications ▸ Accessories ▸ Terminal), typing sudo xsane, pressing ENTER, typing your password when prompted, and pressing ENTER. If your stars are in alignment, XSane should detect your scanner, pop up a message that it is dangerous to run XSane as root, and then open up in its full multi-windowed glory. If your scanner still isn't detected, a trip to www.sane-project.org or www.ubuntuforums.org might be in order to see if there are any known workarounds for your particular scanner model.

To actually scan something, place the photo, document, or whatever it is you are planning to scan on the scanner bed, and then click the **Acquire preview** button at the bottom-left corner of the XSane Preview window (which usually opens up at the right end of your screen). Once the preview appears, use the selection tools in the same window to define the exact area you want to scan, and then choose your resolution and color depth settings in the main XSane window (which usually opens up at the top left of your screen). When everything is ready, click the **Scan** button, after which your scanned image will appear in a new Viewer window (as shown in Figure 10-13).

Figure 10-13: The results of your scan are displayed
in a separate Viewer window.

In that window, you can perform some minor tweaks of the scanned image using the buttons and menu items provided, and then save the image by going to the **File** menu and selecting **Save image**. If you scanned a document that you want to convert to text, click the second button from the left (the one that says **ABCDEF**), and you will also be able to save the file as a text document, though you will have to have a package called *gocr* installed in order to do so.

If you happened to download and install a driver for your scanner or multifunction printer from the device manufacturer's site (or elsewhere), you may find yourself with another scanning application provided within the driver package. If you prefer, you can use that application instead of XSane to perform your scanning chores.

Why Are My Scanned Images So Big?

To wrap up this section on scanning (and, for that matter, this chapter), let me address a question that seems to confuse a lot of people. One of the first areas of confusion is that there is a general blurring of how the terms *ppi (pixels per inch)* and *dpi (dots per inch)* are used. Most applications use these terms interchangeably, and yet they aren't really the same thing. To make things simple, when you are talking about images on your screen, you are talking about *pixels* (the little squares that make up your screen image) per inch, and when you are talking about printer resolution, you are talking about *dots* (of printer ink) per inch.

Your computer screen generally has a resolution of 96ppi, while most modern inkjet and laser printers have a resolution range of 300 to 1200dpi, or sometimes even more. This means that a photo scanned at 96ppi, which looks just fine on your screen, ends up looking pretty lame when you print it out. On the other hand, when you scan a picture at 300ppi, the image will look much better in your printout but will seem gigantic on your screen. This makes sense, as the resolution of your image is more than three times that of your computer screen's resolution. The result is that your computer can accommodate the higher resolution of the image only by displaying that image at three times its original size.

As an example, have a look at Figure 10-14, where you can see an identical image scanned at three different resolutions: 96ppi, 150ppi, and 300ppi. As you can see, the 96ppi image at the far left (measuring 5 × 6 inches—about the size of the hard copy itself) is the smallest, while the other two images are proportionally bigger (about 10 × 12 inches for the 150ppi image and about 22 × 25 inches for the 300ppi image).

Figure 10-14: The same image scanned at three different resolutions

What Resolution Should I Use When Scanning?

What resolution you use when scanning really depends on a variety of factors, the most important of which is what you plan to do with the image when you're finished. When I look at Figure 10-11 on my computer screen, the smallest image looks best, the middle image looks okay, and the largest looks a bit odd, not as sharp as the other two. Basically, when scanning images for display on a computer—on web pages, for instance—it is probably best to stick with a ppi similar to typical screen resolutions or slightly larger: 96 to 150ppi.

When it comes to printing, a whole new set of considerations comes into play. First of all, there are the limitations of your scanner, since different models have different maximum resolutions. The resolution limits of your printer itself are also, naturally enough, a major consideration. For example, laser printers and inkjet printers have different characteristics; laser printers will produce better-quality images than inkjet printers, while inkjet output will be more greatly affected by the type of paper used than a laser printer will be. Of course, your printed output is not going to suffer if you scan your images at higher resolutions than those at which you plan to print them out, but you will end up with a lot of files taking up too much disk space. Remember: *The higher the resolution of a scanned image, the greater the file size in terms of disk space.* If this is of concern to you, you can simply resize the images after you're done printing using an application such as the GIMP (more on that in Chapter 14), but if you would prefer not being so cavalier with your use of disk space from the get-go, you can follow these very general guidelines:

- If you are using a laser printer, scan at the same resolution at which you are going to print.

- If you are going to use an inkjet printer with photo-quality paper, scan at about 80 percent of your target printout resolution—about 240ppi for a 300dpi printout.

- If you are using an inkjet printer with regular paper, scan at about 65 percent of your target printout resolution—about 195ppi for a 300dpi printout.

Needless to say, these are just suggestions to get you started. What works best for you and your particular scanner/printer setup may be slightly different. Nothing works better than a bit of experimentation and trial and error. In this case, you can't really go wrong. Just give yourself some time, don't get frustrated, and, most importantly, don't wait until you desperately need to scan something before trying things out—stay ahead of the game.

11

FONT FEATHERED FRENZY

Adding New Fonts to Your System

Your Ubuntu system comes with a wide variety of very usable and, at least to my eyes, rather handsome TrueType fonts. However, these tend to be a bit on the conservative side of the aesthetic spectrum, and many users will want to add a few more distinctive fonts to the system repertoire. In my own case, I had this really cool idea of writing messages to my friend in old Scandinavian runes. (Of course, my friend wet-blanketed the idea, so it all came to naught. . . .)

You probably won't be interested in sending cryptic, runic messages to your friends, but you may want to print out an award for an event using some sort of Gothic font, or you might be preparing a newsletter for the local chapter of your snail-breeders society and want to use a font that is round, bubbly, and slimy. Whatever your penchant, purpose, or desire, you will probably come to the point when you want to install some other TrueType fonts on your system, and in this chapter I'll tell you how to do just that.

Before you install anything, of course, you have to find some fonts. The Internet is always a good source, and there are many sites that have a variety of freeware, shareware, and for-sale TrueType fonts available for download. When choosing and downloading fonts, it is best to select those designed for Windows rather than those designed for Mac. Fonts designed for the Windows world will most likely be in the form of Zip files, which will pose no problem for you, because you can extract them with File Roller. Simply double-click them, just as you have with the other archived files you have used thus far, and click the **Extract** button in the File Roller window when it appears. The font file will appear on your desktop (or wherever your Zip file happened to be) as an icon showing an upper- and lowercase sample of the first letter in that font (Figure 11-1).

Figure 11-1: Font icons display the first letter in the font.

In addition to getting a glimpse of what the fonts look like through these icons, you can also see all, or at least almost all, of the characters in a given font by double-clicking the font icon. A window, as shown in Figure 11-2, will open, showing you most of the characters in A-to-Z format and then in the traditional "The quick brown fox jumps over the lazy dog" format that you may well remember from your junior or senior high school typing classes.

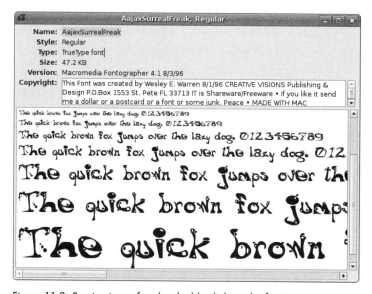

Figure 11-2: Previewing a font by double-clicking the font icon

How you install fonts depends on who is going to use them. If you have only one user account on your machine, the easiest way is to install the fonts locally. Locally installed fonts are ones that only you or someone logged in to your user account will be able to use. On the other hand, if you have more than one user account and want the fonts to be available to all of the users on your machine, use the method described in Project 11B on page 200.

11A-1: Getting the Font Files

The Internet is awash in free fonts. For this project, I will point you to the www.fontfreak.com site, which has a very nice collection of fonts. Once you get to the FontFreak splash page, click **ENTER SITE HERE**. The next page will ask you if you want to download all the free fonts on the site in one single file; click **No thanks, I will download them one by one**. This will lead you to the main page, where you can click any of the links beneath the words *FREE FONTS* in the box on the upper-left side of the page. You can browse through the various pages until you find some fonts to your liking. Which fonts you download is completely up to you, but be sure to choose the PC version of them, not the Mac version. You can do this by clicking the Windows icon to the right of any font sample.

Since you will also need fonts for Project 11B, you might as well download them now too. All in all, for the two projects, you will need at least four fonts. When you've finished downloading, drag the font files to your home folder so it's easy to follow along with my instructions. Also be sure to unzip your font files before going on to the installation steps.

11A-2: Installing the Fonts

To get started, you need to set up your system by providing it with a location to place your fonts. You will only need to do this the very first time out. Here's what you need to do:

1. Open a Nautilus window by going to the **Places** menu in the GNOME Panel and selecting **Home Folder**.
2. In that window, create an invisible fonts folder by going to the **File** menu and selecting **Create Folder**.
3. When the folder appears, name it **.fonts** (the period before the name means that it will be invisible).
4. Hide the new folder by clicking the **Reload** button. Your .fonts folder should no longer be visible. If this is the case, you can close the window— your setup was successful.

Now that everything is set up, let's continue with this project using one of the fonts you downloaded. After you've decided which font to use, follow these steps:

1. Open a Nautilus window by going to the **Places** menu in the GNOME Panel and selecting **Home Folder**. Once you've done that, open another Nautilus window by doing the same thing.

2. In one of the Nautilus windows, go to the **Go** menu, and select **Location**. A Location input box will then appear below the button bar in that window. You can also achieve the same result by pressing CTRL-L.

3. In that Location box, open your invisible .fonts folder by typing `/.fonts` after the location already listed for your home folder—for example, /home/username/.fonts. (If in doubt, replace the location with `~/.fonts`.) When you're done, press ENTER.

    Once you've set this up, all of the fonts installed locally on your system will appear. The first time around, however, there won't be any, because you just created the folder. (Oh, and to make your life easier, it wouldn't be a bad idea to bookmark this window for future use.)

4. From the other open Nautilus window (your home folder window), select the unzipped font you want to install, and drag it to the .fonts folder window (or use the copy-and-paste method if you prefer).

Now that you have installed your font, you can go ahead and give it a try in one of your applications, such as OpenOffice.org Writer. (Any running applications need to be restarted before the new font will appear in that application's font menu.)

11A-3: Uninstalling Locally Installed Fonts

You can uninstall any fonts installed locally by opening the .fonts folder and then dragging the fonts you want to remove to another folder or to the Trash.

Project 11B: Installing TrueType Fonts Globally

As I mentioned already, the fonts you have installed thus far can only be used by you when you log in under your usual username. If, however, you want to install fonts that can be used by you and anyone else who has an account on your computer, the process is slightly different. We'll use another one of the fonts you downloaded for this part of the project.

11B-1: Installing Individual Fonts Globally

The font folder for globally installed fonts is in root territory, so you will need to put the sudo command to use in order to install fonts in this way. Here are the steps:

1. Open a Terminal window, and then create a new folder for your fonts within the global location (let's call it *MyFonts*) by typing the following and pressing ENTER:

```
sudo mkdir /usr/share/fonts/truetype/MyFonts
```

2. Type your password when prompted to do so, and press ENTER.

3. Copy the font you want to install globally to your newly created global font folder by typing the following and pressing ENTER:

```
sudo cp fontname.ttf /usr/share/fonts/truetype/MyFonts
```

Be sure to include spaces on both sides of *fontname*.ttf. Also, be sure to use the name of your font in place of the word *fontname*. For example, if your font is called arachnid, you would type sudo cp arachnid.ttf /usr/share/fonts/truetype/MyFonts.

You shouldn't have to enter your password after step 3 since you already provided it in step 2, so the process is now complete. That being the case, go ahead and test things out by opening OpenOffice.org and looking for the font in the font menu. Remember that you will need to restart OpenOffice.org if it was already open when you installed the font.

11B-2: Installing Multiple Fonts Globally

If you want to install several fonts globally at the same time, you can do so quite easily. The process is essentially the same as in Project 11B-1, with a slight variation. Here's what you've got to do:

1. Create a new subfolder in your home folder window. You can call it anything you like, but I'll be using the name *fonts2go* in this project.

2. Unzip the fonts and then place the ones you want to install via this method into the new fonts2go folder.

3. Open a Terminal window, and then copy all of the fonts in your fonts2go folder to your new global font folder by typing the following and pressing ENTER:

```
sudo cp fonts2go/*.ttf /usr/share/fonts/truetype/MyFonts
```

4.   Type your password if prompted to do so, and press ENTER.

Now that you are done, check your results in OpenOffice.org. You should also back up the font files in the fonts2go folder to CD or floppy (just in case you need to install them on another system) and then trash the files. Keep the folder, however, so that you can use it again in the future.

11B-3: Uninstalling Globally Installed Fonts

If you want to remove any fonts that you installed using either of the global installation methods introduced in this project, you can do so in the following manner:

1.   Open a Terminal window, type `sudo rm /usr/share/fonts/truetype/MyFonts/`*fontname*`.ttf`, and press ENTER. Be sure to replace *fontname* with the name of the font you are uninstalling.

2.   Type your password, and press ENTER when prompted to do so.

Project 11C: Installing Microsoft Windows Core Fonts via Synaptic

Like it or not, the computing world is still pretty much a Microsoft world, and that means that the vast majority of users, even Mac users, are using Microsoft core fonts. That being the case, it is inevitable that you will have to deal with documents using fonts such as Georgia, Verdana, Times New Roman, and Courier, to name a few. Of course, your system can substitute the fonts it has for those used in the document, but in order for you to see things as they were intended and to allow others to see your documents the way you intended (web pages are good examples), it will probably behoove you to install those Microsoft core fonts on your own system.

Fortunately for you, there are two ways to get these fonts. One is to download and install them via Synaptic, while the other, for those of you with a dual-boot setup, is to simply copy them from your Windows partition. In this project, I will explain how to perform the first of these procedures, so if you're a Windows-less Ubuntu user (or a dual-booter who thinks the Synaptic approach is easier), here's what you need to do:

1.   Run the Synaptic Package Manager (**System ▸ Administration ▸ Synaptic Package Manager**), and provide your password when prompted.

2. Click the **Search** button. In the Search window that appears, type `msttcorefonts`, and then click the **Search** button in that window.

3. The msttcorefonts package should now appear in the list pane of the main Synaptic window, so right-click the package name, select **Mark for Installation** in the popup menu, and then follow the standard procedures you learned in Chapter 5 for installing a package via Synaptic.

When the process is complete, your new Microsoft fonts will have been successfully installed and ready for immediate use by every user account on your machine.

Project 11D: Installing Microsoft Core Fonts from Your Windows Partition (for Dual-Booters)

If you're a dual-booter with Windows installed on another partition of your hard disk, you can take advantage of the fonts you already have on your Windows partition. This can be as easy as what you did in Projects 11A and 11B; however, before you can do anything involving your Windows partition, you need to mount it.

11D-1: Mounting Your Windows Partition

Mounting your Windows partition in Linux used to be a bit of a chore, but that isn't the case anymore, at least not in Ubuntu. In fact, all you have to do is open a Nautilus window and double-click the Windows partition in the side pane.

You will most likely find two hard disk icons in the side pane, so it is possible that you won't be sure which one your Windows partition actually is. That said, just remember that your Linux partition is represented by the hard disk icon named *File System*. If your Windows partition is NTFS formatted, its name will be the size of your Windows partition followed by the word *Media*. This means that if your Windows partition is 80GB in size, it will appear as *80GB Media* in the left pane. If your Windows partition happens to be FAT32 rather than NTFS formatted, it will appear with the partition label instead. Now that you know which disk icon is which, it's time to get mounting. Just double-click the icon for the Windows partition in the Nautilus side pane and an Authenticate window will appear (Figure 11-3). In that window, type your Ubuntu password, and click the **Authenticate** button. A new window showing the contents of your Windows partition will appear.

NOTE *If you hibernated rather than quit Windows, you will most likely receive a* Cannot mount volume. You are not privileged to mount this volume. *error message when trying to mount your Windows partition. This is a form of protection because hibernated volumes cannot be safely read-write mounted in Linux.*

Figure 11-3: Mounting your Windows partition is easier than ever.

11D-2: Installing Fonts from Your Windows Partition

Now that your Windows partition is mounted, you can copy the fonts you have there and install them for use within Ubuntu. Depending on whether you want to install your Windows fonts locally or globally, the next steps will be different.

Installing Windows Fonts Locally

There are two ways you can go about installing your Windows fonts locally. The easiest is to just do a variation on what you did in Project 11A-2—that is, double-click your way to the Windows Fonts folder in one Nautilus window, copy the TrueType fonts you want, and then paste them into the .fonts folder within your Ubuntu home folder in another Nautilus window.

The other option is to use the command line. Start by using the `cd` command to move into your Windows Fonts folder via the Terminal (`cd /media/disk/Windows/Fonts` and then ENTER, for example), then type **cp** **fontname.ttf ~/.fonts** and press ENTER. Be sure to replace *fontname* with the name of the font you want to install.

NOTE *The location of the Windows Fonts folder can vary slightly, depending on the version of Windows you are using. Most likely, the path to your Fonts folder will be /media/disk/ WINDOWS/Fonts or /media/disk/windows/Fonts. When in doubt, try double-clicking your way to the Fonts folder in your Windows partition, then press CTRL-L to reveal the file path in the Location box of the Nautilus window.*

If you want to go wild and copy all of the fonts in your Windows fonts directory (that's a lot of fonts, mind you!) via the command line, you can use the asterisk as a wildcard by typing ***.ttf** instead of *fontname*.ttf. Be sure that you have a space between cp and *fontname*.ttf and between *fontname*.ttf and ~/.fonts/. Once you're done, you're done.

Installing Windows Fonts Globally

To install your Windows fonts so that all users on your machine can use them, just return to the still open Terminal window. Then copy the font you want to the personal system font folder you created in step 1 of Project 11B-1 on page 201 (and if you didn't perform that step then, do so now) by typing **sudo cp** *fontname***.ttf /usr/share/fonts/truetype/MyFonts**. If you want to copy and install all of the fonts in your Windows font directory, you can do so by typing **sudo cp *.ttf /usr/share/fonts/truetype/MyFonts** instead. After typing either of those strings, press ENTER, after which you will probably be prompted for your password, so type it, and press ENTER again. The job will then be done.

Unmounting Your Windows Partition

If you mounted your Windows partition manually, you can unmount it immediately after finishing your work with it, or you can just wait until you shut down your system, whereupon it will be automatically unmounted. Before you can unmount it yourself, you must first be certain you aren't accessing the directory, either from the Terminal window or from Nautilus. So, before unmounting, close any Nautilus windows open to that partition or, if you are using the Terminal, type **cd** to change back to your home directory. Once you've done that, right-click the Windows partition icon in the side pane of a Nautilus window, and select **Unmount**.

Customizing Your System Fonts

Now that you know how to get and install fonts, you might be itching to use some of them to further customize your system. To get started doing this, just select **Preferences ▸ Appearance** in the **System** menu, which will bring up the Appearance Preferences window. Click the **Fonts** tab in that window to see the options available to you (Figure 11-4).

As you can see, you can specify font preferences in five categories: applications, documents, desktop, window titles, and the Terminal (fixed width font).

The choices you make take effect immediately, so you will soon know whether or not you can live with them. Unlike the other aspects of customization, those choices could drive you stark raving mad. Sure, it is easy and fun to live with the gaudiest desktop imaginable, the wildest and most mismatched color scheme on the planet, and the goofiest icons ever to be seen by post-Neanderthal man, but if your font selections get too out of hand, watch out! You do have to be able to read the results, after all.

Figure 11-4: Setting system font preferences

Making Things Look Better

The fonts you see on your screen generally look quite smooth and clean. If you are using an LCD monitor, however, you may find that fonts will look even better if you select **Subpixel smoothing (LCDs)** in the Fonts tab of the Appearance Preferences window. If you're not sure whether you need to do this, just give it a try, and see if you notice any difference. GNOME applies changes immediately upon selection, so if you keep a window with text in it open behind the preferences window, you can easily see the effect of each of your selections as you make them.

Creating Your Own Fonts with FontForge

After all this font talk, it seems only appropriate that I end this chapter by giving you the means to create your own fonts (or at least modify someone else's). FontForge (previously known as PfaEdit) allows you to create or modify TrueType, PostScript, and bitmap fonts (see Figure 11-5). The interface itself seems a bit dated, but don't let that fool you; FontForge is quite capable and easy to use.

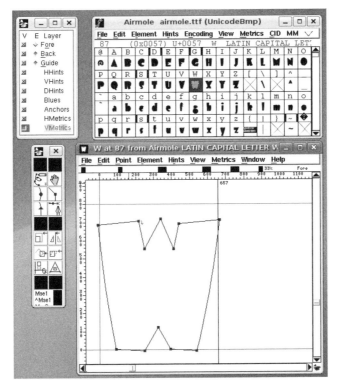

Figure 11-5: Using FontForge to create and modify fonts

Downloading, Installing, and Running FontForge

You can easily download and install FontForge via Synaptic. Just do a search for *fontforge*, mark the **fontforge** and **fontforge-doc** packages for installation when they appear in the list of search results, and then follow the usual procedure for installing packages via Synaptic. You can run FontForge by going to the **Applications** menu and selecting **Graphics ▶ FontForge**. An Open Font window will appear, in which you can select the font you want to work with. Make sure that it is not an installed font, but rather a font located within the home folder itself, or within another visible folder.

After that, I think I had better leave you to your own resources (and those of others). Font creation and modification is, after all, too complex a topic for this book, but those of you already into this stuff probably just needed a pointer to the right tool and not my meager instructions. If you do need more than a pointer, the FontForge help files are a good place to start, as is the FontForge project page at http://fontforge.sourceforge.net.

12

POLYGLOT PENGUINS

Linux Speaks Your Language

These days, almost all operating systems are multilingual, or at least capable of becoming so. This is true of Linux as well. Just open your web browser, and, without performing any special installations, you can read pages in any European language, including those with Cyrillic alphabets, such as Russian. You can even view pages in Chinese, Japanese, Thai, Arabic, and Hebrew, to name but a few.

But the multilingual capabilities of Linux are much greater than this, and the way that GNOME-based distros, such as Ubuntu, handle multilingual matters makes it quite easy to take advantage of these capabilities. As you will soon see, you can even set up your system to give you a totally foreign language environment, allowing you to function completely in the language of your choice. Add to this the ever-expanding number of free programs available for language study, and you have a truly meaningful language-learning tool.

Read-Only Language Support

If all you want is to be able to read web pages or documents written in a foreign language, you don't need to install any additional language support except in some rare cases. From the get-go, you will be able to view documents in just about any language you happen to throw at your system—doesn't matter if it's Swedish, Italian, Chinese, Japanese, Arabic, Hebrew, Russian, Vietnamese, Armenian, or Thai. You will be able to read whatever you are linguistically capable of reading (see Figure 12-1 for an example).

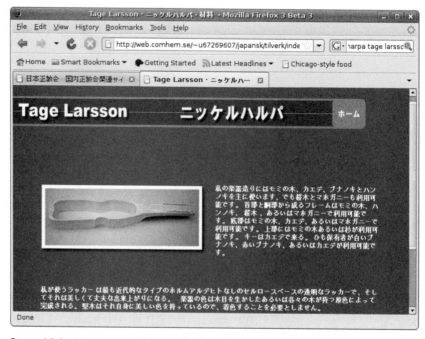

Figure 12-1: A Japanese web page displayed in Firefox

Changing the Character Encoding in Firefox

Firefox usually automatically recognizes the language in which a web page is written and thus displays the page correctly. Sometimes, however, the author of the page may neglect to include the character coding for that page in the HTML, in which case Firefox, not knowing that the page is prepared in another language, will open it in the default language of your system. The result is a page in which you see nothing but odd combinations of symbols and letters that have no meaning. In this case, try changing the character coding in Firefox to the language encoding you believe the page to be in. Some languages employ more than one encoding scheme, so if you're not sure, give each one a try. You can make your choices by going to the Firefox **View** menu and selecting **Character Encoding**. From the submenu there, you can select the appropriate coding for the language of that page.

Typing Nonstandard Characters

Typing characters that are not standard in English, such as é, ç, ß, ø, æ, and å, can be done quite easily in Linux without any modifications. In most situations, you can do this by using the Character Map utility included in your system, which can be found at **Applications ▸ Accessories ▸ Character Map**. Upon running Character Map, a window like the one shown in Figure 12-2 will appear.

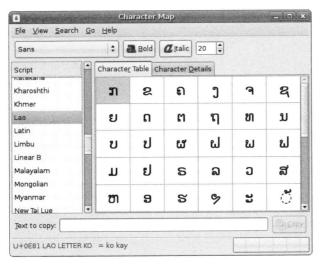

Figure 12-2: Inputting characters with the Character Map utility

To input the character you want, just select the language or character set in the left pane of the window, and then, in the right pane, double-click the character you want to input. The character will appear in the little input box next to the words *Text to copy* at the bottom of the window. Just click the **Copy** button, and then paste the character wherever you want to place it.

OpenOffice.org modules offer a method of their own that can also be used. Click **Insert** in the menu bar and then select **Special Character**. A selection window will open, and you can select the character you want there. Once you've done that, click the **OK** button, and the character will appear in your document, after which the selection window will close by itself.

Using the Compose Key Option

If you only need to type an accent or umlaut once in a while, and don't feel particularly keen on opening an application or going to a special menu to do so, using the *compose key option* for your keyboard is a good way to go. Basically what this means is that you use one of the lesser-used keys on your keyboard in conjunction with six symbols (` , ' ~ " ^) to help in the creation, so to speak, of accented characters. By default, the compose key is the right ALT key.

Let's say, for example, that you wanted to type an umlauted u (ü). While pressing the right ALT key, you would press ". Then you would release the right ALT key, press u, and . . . voilà, you'd have yourself an ü. Here are some more examples:

á   right ALT + ' then a
ç   right ALT + , then c
è   right ALT + ` then e
ñ   right ALT + ~ then n
ô   right ALT + ^ then o

NOTE   *These sequences are based on US keyboard layouts. Combinations for other layouts may differ.*

Using the Keyboard Indicator

If you often type in a particular foreign language, it might be more convenient for you to use the Keyboard Indicator GNOME Panel utility. This utility lets you switch quickly among various keyboard layouts. For example, if you often type in Swedish, and thus use the characters å, ä, and ö regularly, using the appropriate keyboard layout would be easier than repeatedly using the Character Map. Of course, you will have to familiarize yourself with the keyboard layout, or *keymap*, for each language you choose, but this is a relatively easy task.

The Keyboard Indicator is already included in your system, so there is no need to install it. To access it, simply right-click somewhere on the GNOME Panel where you would like to place a launcher for it. Then, from the popup menu select **Add to Panel**. When the Add to Panel window appears, scroll down and click **Keyboard Indicator**, and then click the **Add** button. The letters *USA* or *GBr* will then appear on the panel.

Now, this alone will give you nothing except your default keymap, so you must configure Keyboard Indicator if you want to be able to use other keymaps. To do so, just right-click the icon, and from the popup menu select **Keyboard Preferences**, which will open the Keyboard Preferences window.

To add a keymap, click the **Layouts** tab in that window, and then once in the new tab, click **Add**. After you do this, the Choose a Layout window will appear with a list of the keymaps available to you (Figure 12-3). In the drop-down menu next to the word *Layouts*, select the country or language you wish to add. If you wish to choose an alternative keymap for that language, make your choice, if available, in the drop-down menu next to the words *Variants*. Once you've made your selection, you might want to consider clicking the Print button to get a handy hard copy of your new keyboard layout (for reference purposes) before clicking the **Add** button, which will bring you back to the Keyboard Preferences window. In that window, you will find your new keymap listed along with the original.

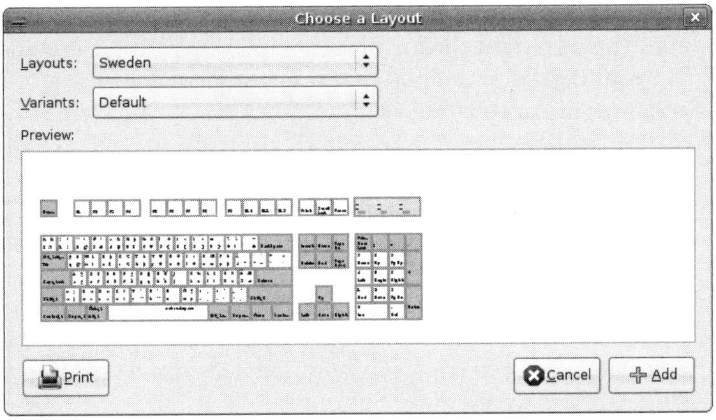

Figure 12-3: Adding keyboard layouts to the Keyboard Indicator

At this point, you can choose which of these layouts you want to make your default by clicking the radio button next to that keymap (as shown in Figure 12-4). It is also possible to print a hard copy of any of the keymaps you have listed here by selecting the keymap and then clicking **Print**. Once you're done, click the **Close** button to complete the setup.

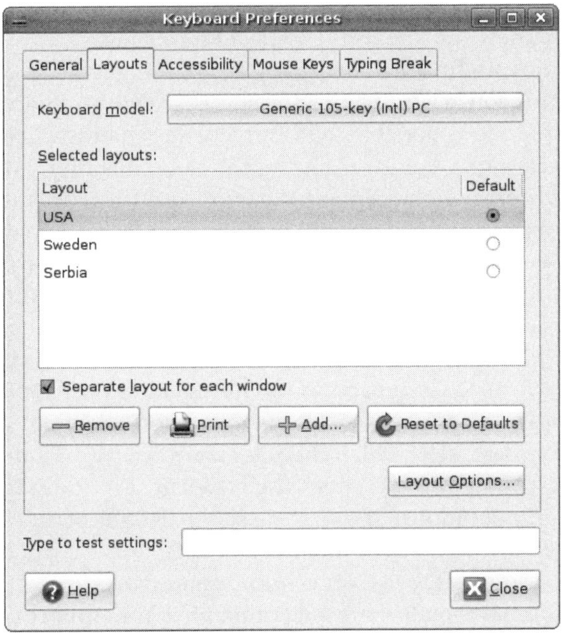

Figure 12-4: Selecting the default keyboard layout in the
Keyboard Preferences window

After closing the Keyboard Preferences window, you can change the keyboard layouts by clicking the Keyboard Indicator icon in the panel. If you are not sure where the keys are located in your current keymap (and you didn't print out a hard copy of that map, as suggested earlier), you can get some help by right-clicking the panel Keyboard Indicator and selecting **Show Current Layout** in the popup window, after which a map of the new layout will appear in a separate window. The keymap shown in that window can be rather hard to make out, so you will probably need to expand the window by dragging the window by one of its bottom corners. You can also print a copy of the layout from this window by clicking the **Print** button.

If you just want to choose a single keyboard layout to replace your present one (such as British English instead of American English or German instead of Spanish), you can do so from the Keyboard Preferences window by adding the keyboard layout you want to use, clicking the *Default* radio button for your language, removing any additional layouts by clicking each once, and then clicking the **Remove** button.

Viewing Your System in Another Language

One of the many things that originally attracted me to the Linux world was being able to install language support for languages other than English. On one of my machines, I have installed support for Chinese, Japanese, Swedish, and my default, English. With just a simple logout and a few more clicks, I can log back in with an interface in a totally different language. I can have a Chinese, Japanese, or Swedish system whenever I want.

This is very useful if you are going to be doing a lot of work in a foreign language, or if you are studying a foreign language and want to give yourself as much exposure as possible to it. It is also very handy when you have users with different native languages using the same machine. At my former university, for example, where my Japanese and Chinese students sometimes used my computer, the additional language support allowed them to log in using their own language. All in all, it is a very useful feature.

Taking advantage of this feature in the GNOME environment is very easy and, depending on the language you wish to use, requires little in terms of special installation measures. Basically all you have to do is install a group of support files for each language you want to add to your system. You can do this quite easily by going to the **System** menu and selecting **Administration ▸ Language Support**, after which the Language Support window (Figure 12-5) will appear. In that window, check the boxes next to the languages for which you want to install support. If you are installing language support for languages with complex writing systems, such as Japanese, be sure to also check the box next to the words *Enable support to enter complex characters*.

Once you have made your selections, click the **Apply** button. You will be prompted for your password at this point, so provide what is required, and the Language Support tool will begin downloading and then installing the support packages you specified. Once it is done, it will tell you to reboot your computer in order to activate the language support modules you've just installed.

Figure 12-5: Installing additional language support

NOTE   *Language Support is another graphical front end for APT, and that being the case, be sure to close all other APT-related tools before using it.*

Multilingual Login

Once you have installed support for any additional languages you want, you will be ready to start typing in the newly installed languages (following a restart of your machine). If you like, you can also log out of your current session and log in to a new one in a different language environment. The actual switch is made from your login screen.

Just below the text box where you would normally type your username, select **Options ▸ Select Language**, after which a small window will appear with a menu button labeled *Last language.* Select the language you want to use in the next session in that menu, and then click the **Change Language** button. The small language-selection window will then close automatically, after which you will be asked if you wish to restart with the language you've just selected. What you do at this point is up to you, but I would just click **No** in order to get on with things.

After that, proceed as usual by typing your login name and password (pressing the ENTER key after each, of course). A little window will then pop up asking you if you want to use the language you've chosen as your default language forever and ever. You can either click **Just For This Session** or **Make Default** depending on your personal preferences. Whatever you do end up choosing, fear not; it's no big deal to change back at a later point in time by logging out of your system, logging back in to your system under your previous default language, and clicking **Make Default**.

Your startup process will then continue, and everything will progress as it usually does. Depending on what language you've chosen, once your desktop appears you will be in another linguistic world. Your menus, applications, and even the little Tips windows that pop up when you run your mouse over a panel icon will all be in the newly selected language (Figure 12-6).

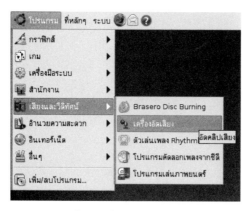

Figure 12-6: The Applications and Sound & Video menus shown in Thai

Your folder names, however, will not appear in the newly selected language without your say-so. As you will surely notice when you first log in, a window like the one shown in Figure 12-7 will appear asking you whether or not you want to change your standard folder names (Pictures, Public, Music, etc.) to the language you've just logged into. The choice is yours, but if you're only in the new language environment for a look around, it's probably best to click **Keep Old Names**. If, on the other hand, you are setting up a new user account in the new language for another user, then go ahead and click **Update Names**.

Figure 12-7: To change or not to change folder names after logging in to a new language environment

Chinese, Japanese, and Korean Input

For most European languages (and many other alphabet-based non-European languages), pressing a letter on the keyboard simply prints that letter to the screen. However, Chinese, Japanese, and Korean require a kind of conversion process that is handled by a special application (actually a set of applications) called an Input Method Editor (IME). Of course, this is a Windows-world term, but I will use it here for convenience's sake. In any case, each of these languages has its own IME, and each is quite different due to the basic differences in the three writing systems.

Chinese

While most people (at least those in the linguistic know) would think that Chinese would be the most complicated system, because the writing system consists of thousands of characters, it is in fact the simplest. The Chinese IME simply takes the romanized keyboard input, known as *pinyin*, and converts it into Chinese characters, or *Hanzi*. For the IME, it is essentially a simple dictionary lookup task—big dictionary, simple IME. In the event that there is more than one character for the pinyin input, a list of possible candidates will appear, and the user can then simply select the appropriate character from that list. More recent Chinese IMEs also have predictive capabilities, by which they judge what you are trying to type on the basis of what you've typed so far (Figure 12-8). Although these more "intelligent" IMEs can be a bit squirrelly to use at first, they prove to be rather handy once you get the hang of things.

Figure 12-8: Newer Chinese IMEs can predict what you're going to write . . . kinda.

Japanese

The Japanese IME has a considerably more complicated task to perform, as it has three writing systems to deal with: *Kanji* (ideographic characters borrowed long ago from China), *hiragana* (the phono-alphabetic system used mainly for tense and case endings), and *katakana* (used mainly for words borrowed from other languages). Still, the standard input method for Japanese is primarily via the standard Roman keyboard layout, plus a few extra special-function keys. Thus, typing in Japanese is a two-step process whereby the IME first converts the romanized text into hiragana as it is typed and then converts it to appropriate Kanji, katakana, or hiragana elements after the spacebar is pressed.

You can see an example of these steps in Figure 12-9. In the first line, the IME has already converted the romanized input on the fly. It has converted rinakkusdenihongonyuuryokumodekimasu (which means *You can also input Japanese in Linux*) to hiragana. The fact that line is underlined means that it has not yet been converted beyond that. In the second line, however, the user has subsequently pressed the spacebar, which caused the IME to convert the hiragana string into the appropriate Kanji, hiragana, and katakana elements. The first word, *Linux*, has been converted to katakana text, as it is a borrowed word, while *Japanese input* has been converted to Kanji; the rest stays in hiragana.

りなっくすでにほんごにゅうりょくもできます。

リナックスで日本語入力もできます。

Figure 12-9: IME conversions while typing in Japanese

Korean

The job of the Korean IME is again quite different from that of the Chinese and Japanese IMEs, as the language itself is written in a very different way. Korean is written either entirely in alphabetic letters, called *Hangul*, or in a combination of Hangul and ideographic characters borrowed from Chinese called *Hanja*. While the Hanja characters are essentially the same as their Chinese and Japanese counterparts, Hanzi and Kanji, the Korean phonetic alphabet, Hangul, has it own unique appearance, as you can see in the Korean word for Korea, *Hangug(k)*, in Figure 12-10.

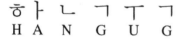

H A N G U G

*Figure 12-10: Korea (Hangug) written
horizontally in Hangul*

This seems simple; however, the representation is not quite correct, as Korean is very unique in the way that its alphabetic characters are put to the page. Unlike the usual side-by-side positioning of hiragana, katakana, and most other languages written with an alphabet, Hangul letters are grouped in pairs, triplets, or even quadruplets, which are written, as a general rule, clockwise. The IME, therefore, must take the input (usually based on a Korean alphabetical keyboard layout) while it is being typed, and it must adjust the size, spacing, and positioning of each of the letters as it puts them into appropriate clusters (see Figure 12-11).

*Figure 12-11: An example of the
clustering process in the Korean IME*

Project 12: Installing Asian Language Input Support for SCIM

So what do you do if, for example, you want to be able to type Chinese, Japanese, Korean, Hindi, Thai, or Nepali while still in your usual English environment? What if you want to be able to type all of those languages in the same document? Can you do it?

You bet.

There are actually several ways of going about this, but the easiest and arguably most straightforward to use is Smart Common Input Method (SCIM), the base for which comes preinstalled in Ubuntu. SCIM supports most Asian languages, including Chinese, Japanese, and Korean, and it provides a number of input methods for many of these, though you must install the appropriate modules first.

12-1: Downloading and Installing SCIM Input Method Modules

Despite coming preinstalled on Ubuntu, SCIM will not be able to do anything for you right out of the box in terms of Chinese/Japanese/Korean (CJK) input. In the previous section, I said that SCIM's "base" comes preinstalled in Ubuntu; this does not mean, however, that CJK support also comes preinstalled. As is, SCIM only allows you to type in a few less complex languages, such as Russian and Thai. For Chinese, Japanese, Korean, and certain other languages, you have to install support yourself. In order to enable SCIM so you can input CJK and other similar types of characters, you will need to install the appropriate input modules for the language you wish to use.

The easiest way of getting these packages is via the Language Support utility. Just go to the **System** menu, select **Administration ▶ Language Support**, and then install support for the languages you want. This approach downloads and installs not only the input support modules, but also a number of other packages required if you want your system and major applications to appear in the languages in question. If you only want to input CJK characters from within your own language environment, it is probably simpler to download and install the specific modules for those languages yourself via Synaptic. Depending on the language you want to use, you need to do a Synaptic search for *scim*, and then install one or any combination of the following modules:

- For Japanese input support, install scim-anthy.
- For simplified Chinese (pinyin) input support, install scim-pinyin.
- For traditional Chinese (zhuyin/Bopomofo) input support, install scim-chewing.
- For Korean input support, install scim-hangul.

There are also sets of additional input methods available for each of these languages. If, for example, you type Korean based on the standard English keyboard layout or if you need Hangul-to-Hanja conversion capabilities, you should also install scim-tables-ko. Additional Japanese methods are available in the scim-tables-ja package, while those for Chinese are available in scim-tables-zh.

You can also use SCIM as a convenient means by which to type in other Asian languages that do not require special conversion routines, such as Thai, Hindi, Telugu, Bengali, and Punjabi. To use SCIM for input support for these languages, install scim-tables-additional.

After the installation of the language support modules is complete, it is a good idea to restart your machine to ensure full functionality of the language modules you've installed. The SCIM panel utility will appear in the right side of the top panel, and the languages you added will then appear in the menu that comes up when you click that applet, thus letting you know that SCIM is ready for CJK input action.

12-2: Typing in Asian Languages with SCIM

To get a feel for how SCIM works, try using it with Gedit (**Applications ▸ Accessories ▸ Text Editor**).

Once Gedit appears, click the SCIM panel applet. A list of the available languages that can be handled via SCIM will then appear in a drop-down menu (Figure 12-12). Remember, however, that the number of languages appearing in that menu is dependent on the number of language packages you installed.

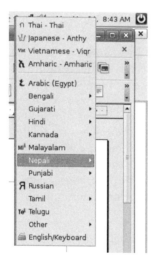

Figure 12-12: A list of the languages that can be handled by SCIM

From that list, select the language you want to use, and then, for those languages where you are given a choice, select the input method you prefer. The icon for the SCIM panel applet will reflect the change by showing the icon for the language you have chosen. You can then start typing.

At this point, a small input palette like the one in Figure 12-13 will appear at the bottom-right corner of the screen. This palette, in addition to displaying the language and input method currently in use, also allows you to easily switch between English and the current language of input, or to switch from the language in which you are currently typing to another. By clicking the red button at the far-right end of the palette, you can also find out what the hotkeys are for the input method you are currently using.

Figure 12-13: The SCIM input palette

Regardless of the input method you are dealing with, probably the most important hotkey combination you will want to use is SHIFT-spacebar, which toggles you back and forth between English and the language you currently have selected in SCIM.

13

PENGUINS BACK AT WORK

Getting Down to Business in Linux

I have to admit it: When I think about the joys of computing, I tend to think of the more hedonistic, self-indulgent areas like gaming, music, and graphics. Still, as is the case for most computer users, what I usually end up doing on my computer is work, and writing this book falls into that category.

Fortunately, Linux can get down to business and do it as well as the next OS. I think it's safe to say that you are missing nothing and are probably gaining quite a bit in terms of home and office productivity programs in the world of Linux. In this chapter, I'll walk you through the Linux offerings in this department.

OpenOffice.org

Whether they should be or not, people are quite obsessed with office suites, even though most people seldom need more than a word processor. The de facto standard among office suites is Microsoft Office, which is available in both the Windows and Macintosh worlds. Of course, as it is a Microsoft product, you can be quite sure that there is no Linux version available.

Fortunately, Linux does have an exceedingly capable office suite in the form of OpenOffice.org, which is, incidentally, also freely available (as in *free*) in Windows and Mac OS X versions. OpenOffice.org is not some lightweight sour-grapes substitute for the Microsoft Office–less Linux world; it is a full-featured contender, and in some cases, OpenOffice.org is a clear winner.

OpenOffice.org Applications

The entire OpenOffice.org office suite consists of a number of application modules, and the most commonly used ones come bundled with Ubuntu. These include a word processor (Writer), a spreadsheet (Calc), and a presentation creator and player (Impress), all of which you can find in **Applications ▸ Office**. In addition, there is a very handy vector drawing program (Draw), which you'll find in **Applications ▸ Graphics**. The database module (Base) and the mathematical formula editor (Math), though no longer packaged with Ubuntu, are still available as separate downloads via Synaptic (by searching for and marking *openoffice.org-base* and *openoffice.org-math*, respectively).

Since giving full and detailed instructions on how to use each of these applications would take up an entire book (and there are entire books on the subject), I will simply introduce each module to you.

Writer

As I mentioned earlier, the word processor is the office application that the majority of users turn to most often. Fortunately, OpenOffice.org Writer is a good one (see Figure 13-1). It is chock-full of features and can read and save Microsoft Word files. Like Word, it will even let you save your documents as HTML files so that you can easily change your documents into web pages.

As I said, Writer is a very straightforward word processor, so I won't go on about it, but if you would like an introduction to using Writer, check out the First Steps tutorial at the OpenOffice.org website (www.openoffice.org/writerfirststeps/writerfirststeps.html).

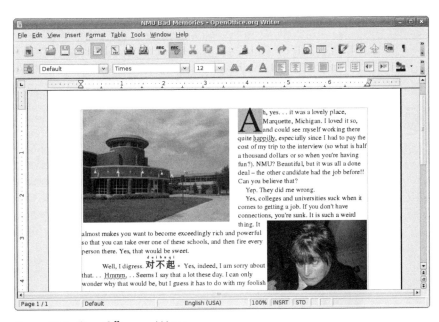

Figure 13-1: OpenOffice.org Writer

Calc

Calc is the OpenOffice.org spreadsheet application, and it is similar to Excel in terms of capabilities and general layout (see Figure 13-2). It can also, quite importantly, read and save Microsoft Excel files.

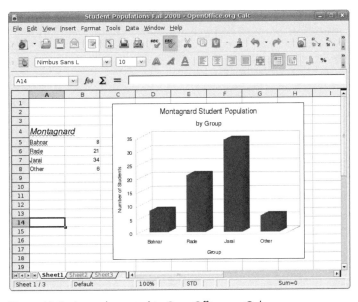

Figure 13-2: A graph created in OpenOffice.org Calc

Since most people who use spreadsheets generally understand what they are all about and, after a bit of poking around, can figure out how to use them, I won't go into any sort of primer about using Calc. However, as there are many others who don't see any need to even try using spreadsheets, I will mention a few of the simpler things that can be done with Calc, in the hope of enticing some of you into trying it.

Most people who don't use spreadsheets think of them as a sort of giant calculators used for computing uncomfortably large sets of numbers, like payrolls (which was the original purpose of such applications). That's right, of course, but spreadsheets can be used for everyday tasks too, such as projecting household budgets, calculating grade point averages (by teachers or students), figuring out how long it will take you to save up for your trip to Hungary, or even for something as weird as comparing the seat heights for the four or five motorcycles you are trying to choose among. And when doing any of these minor mathematical tasks, you can easily create graphs in order to make all the abstract numbers speak to you visually.

If numbers are just not your thing, you can still use Calc for creating lists of information, such as birthday lists, class rosters, shopping lists, address lists . . . whatever. You can even have Calc put the lists into alphabetical order, or sort them by date of birth, and so on. Everyone eventually seems to find some use for Calc, so don't ignore it entirely.

Impress

Impress is OpenOffice.org's answer to Microsoft's PowerPoint, with which it is compatible. It allows you to create graphically attractive slides for use in presentations and also allows you to create notes or handouts to accompany them. While these features make Impress quite handy in business and education settings, you may not find as much value in it as a home user.

Draw

More useful to the home user is OpenOffice.org Draw. Although Draw isn't all that great a program for creating true graphics in the artistic sense, it is very useful for creating flowcharts, organizational diagrams (like seating arrangements for wedding receptions or conferences), or any other document in which you want a bit more control over the placement of text and graphics (especially when the two are combined), such as for fliers, awards, diagrams, and newsletters. In this sense, Draw can be used quite effectively as a simple page layout program, as you can see in Figure 13-3.

Microsoft Office and OpenOffice.org File Compatibility

Although I mention the point throughout this section, it is worthwhile to re-emphasize that OpenOffice.org can read and write Microsoft Office files. This compatibility is quite good, though tables sometimes prove slightly problematic.

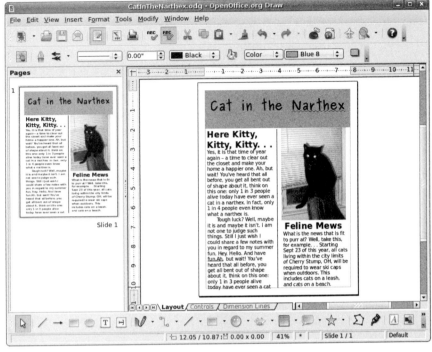

Figure 13-3: A newsletter created (and displayed) in OpenOffice.org Draw

In order to read Microsoft Office files, all you need to do is double-click the file in question, and it will open in the appropriate OpenOffice.org module. When saving files within OpenOffice.org to use within Microsoft Office, however, you must save them into the appropriate format, as OpenOffice.org will otherwise save files into its native format (.odt for Writer documents, .ods for Calc documents, and .odp for Impress documents) by default.

To do this when saving a file, click the small arrow next to the words *File type* in the Save window, and select the appropriate Microsoft Office format from the list of available file formats listed in the pane that then appears—**Microsoft Word 97/2000/XP** for a Writer document, for example.

OpenOffice.org Features

The three main applications in OpenOffice.org (Writer, Calc, and Impress) are, respectively, quite similar to their equivalents in Microsoft Office (Word, Excel, and PowerPoint), so switching over to the OpenOffice.org applications should be relatively easy.

If you don't have any experience with Microsoft Office, you should still find it all pretty straightforward, as the basic layout is pretty intuitive. And if you are lacking in the intuition department, the built-in Help files are pretty good, too. To further help you along, the Tips system works just like tooltips in the Windows and Mac worlds. In case you aren't sure what I'm talking about, tooltips are those little yellow boxes that pop up to tell you what a button or menu item does when you place your mouse over that button or menu item.

Despite all the straightforwardness I am speaking of, there are a few interface items that will most likely be unfamiliar to you. That being the case, I will briefly discuss those items. I'll be using the word processor, Writer, as I describe these things, so if you want to run OpenOffice.org while following along, Writer might be a convenient starting point for you too.

Getting to Know the Buttons

Although you should pretty much be able to figure out what all of the buttons on the OpenOffice.org toolbars do, there are a few buttons common to all OpenOffice.org modules that most likely require, or at least deserve, a bit more explanation.

Export to PDF

This first button is situated to the left of the two printer buttons (Print and Page Preview). You can use this button to *export*, or save, your document as a PDF file, in a manner that is similar to (albeit easier than) the one in Chapter 10.

Hyperlink

Clicking the Hyperlink button, the button to the left of the Table button, brings up the Hyperlink window, from which you can assign links to specified documents—not only to web pages, but also to documents on an individual computer, and even targets within that document. While a hyperlink on a web page is something we have all come to take for granted, the idea of hyperlinking between text documents sounds like a pretty radical concept. It is, in fact, a rather old one that has been around since before you or I even heard of the Internet.

Navigator

The fourth to the last button in the top row (the one that looks like a starburst) is the Navigator button. Clicking this button brings up the Navigator window (see Figure 13-4), which is a pretty cool navigational feature that comes in handy when working with lengthy or otherwise complex documents.

The Navigator allows you to easily bounce back and forth between pages in a document or even between elements therein, such as sections, links, and so on. Let's say that you have a document with lots of illustrations in it (like this chapter), and you want to jump directly from graphic to graphic. In this case, you would double-click the word Graphics in the main pane of the Navigator window and then click the jump buttons (the odd little buttons to the left of the page number selector) to begin jumping.

Figure 13-4: The Navigator window

If you are dealing with a document containing various heading levels, like all of the chapters in this book, you can also use Navigator to switch among those levels. Say you've decided to add a new main heading at the last minute to a document you've been writing. All of the headings you had before thus need to be dropped down a notch; the former main heading becoming a subheading, and so on. By double-clicking the word Headings, the text of all the headings you have listed in the document would then appear. You could then select a heading in that list, and then click the Demote Level button (that's the one at the far right of the second row of buttons) to move it down a notch.

Gallery

 To the right of the Navigator button is the Gallery button. By clicking this button, the Gallery, a library of graphical elements for use in your documents or web pages, will appear in a separate pane at the top of your document window (see Figure 13-5). The elements within the Gallery range from various types of lines to buttons to colored three-dimensional doughnuts, and you can even add items of your own.

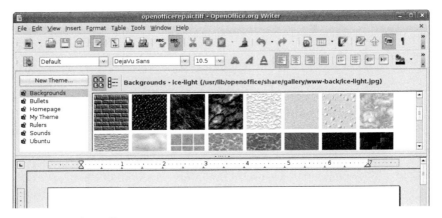

Figure 13-5: The Gallery

Inserting a graphic into your document is a simple enough task even when not using the Gallery. All you need to do is go to the **Insert** menu, select **Picture ▸ From File**, and then locate the image file you want to insert. It can be handier to use the Gallery, however, when you intend to use certain graphics frequently. Once in the Gallery, your graphics are always only a click or two away and can be conveniently viewed in the Gallery browser window.

The collection of artwork that comes with OpenOffice.org is mostly geared toward building web pages, but there is other clipart available, all of which can be easily downloaded via Synaptic. Just search for and install *openclipart-openoffice.org*. Once the rather lengthy download and installation process is complete (there's a lot of clipart in the collection), you will find it all nicely organized and waiting for you in the Gallery (Figure 13-6).

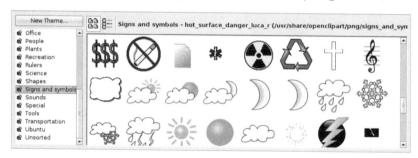

Figure 13-6: Viewing clipart collections in the Gallery

If you prefer to see what you're getting before you get it (and to only get exactly what you want), you can also visit the Open Clip Art Library by pointing your browser to www.openclipart.org. The site has all of the clipart available via the downloads mentioned in the previous paragraph, and more. Best of all, everything there is in the public domain, so it is all free to use. Be sure to check out the "Game baddie" collection—it's yet another one of my faves.

Adding your own graphics to the Gallery is also relatively easy to do. First you have to create a new category (called a *theme*) for each group of images you wish to add. To create a Gallery theme of your own, just click the **New Theme** button in the Gallery window. This will open the Properties of New Theme window, where you should first click the **General** tab and give your theme a name. Once you've done that, click the **Files** tab, and then the **Find Files** button, which will bring up a Select Path window. From there you can navigate to the folder in which you are storing your clip art, photos, or other graphics. Once you have found the folder, click the **OK** button, after which a list of all the files in that folder will appear in the Properties of New Theme window.

You can easily add images to your new Gallery theme by clicking the name of each image you wish to add (you might want to make sure that the box next to the word *Preview* is checked to make things a bit easier), and then clicking the **Add** button. Once you have done that, a copy of the image will immediately appear in the Gallery browser, where it will remain for future use. To use one of the images in the Gallery, just right-click the image you wish to insert into your document, choose **Insert**, and then select **Copy** or **Link** in the popup menu.

Styles and Formatting

 The final stop on our tour through OpenOffice.org's unfamiliar buttons is the Styles and Formatting button, which is located at the far left side of the second row of buttons. This button acts as a toggle for the Styles and Formatting window (Figure 13-7), from which you can select and then apply styles to any of the various elements within your document. Oh, and if you just can't take your hands off the keyboard for a moment to fiddle with the mouse, you can also open the window by pressing the F11 key.

Figure 13-7: The Styles and Formatting window

To give you an example of how convenient using styles can be, imagine that you are typing a bibliography page for some document you've prepared. You typed each entry as you might any paragraph, as in:

Smythe, W. (2004). Reconsidering the need for speech between non-human interlocutors beyond the age of seven. The Journal of the Society of Elves, Faeries, and Garden Gnomes, 20 (2), 125-147.

Like most paragraphs you type, the entry is formatted as a first-line indent, which is fine and dandy except for the fact that you want a hanging indent, which is the norm for bibliography entries. Rather than messing around with tabs or margins to get things the way you want, all you have to do is click your mouse anywhere within the paragraph, and then double-click the **Hanging Indent** entry in the Styles and Formatting window. After that, as if by magic (though you know better), the transformation is made:

Smythe, W. (2004). Reconsidering the need for speech between non-human interlocutors beyond the age of seven. The Journal of the Society of Elves, Faeries, and Garden Gnomes, 20 (2), 125-147.

You could follow the same procedure for each of your other entries, or, with Hanging Indent selected, click the **paint can** button in the Styles and Formatting window, after which your mouse cursor, when placed over the document, will appear as a paint can. Click that paint-can cursor in any other paragraph in your bibliography, and that entry, too, will be formatted in the new style. The process is essentially the same when applying different styles to any other document elements.

Word Processing Done Lightly with AbiWord

If OpenOffice.org's Writer is a bit more powerful than what you need for your everyday word processing chores, and you would prefer something that pops up as soon as you click the launcher, then you might want to consider giving another word processor, AbiWord, a try (Figure 13-8).

AbiWord has a very straightforward and easy-to-use interface, which you should be able to figure out without much, if any, help. It also has a couple of rather interesting features, such as its auto-resize function, which magnifies the onscreen document size (fonts, images, and everything) or shrinks it as you increase or decrease the size of the program window. And in case you're wondering, AbiWord can save and read Microsoft Word DOC files and save documents as PDF files.

You can easily install AbiWord via Synaptic by performing a search for *abiword*, and then installing **abiword-gnome**. Once you have AbiWord installed, you can run it by going to the **Applications** menu and selecting **Office ▸ AbiWord Word Processor**.

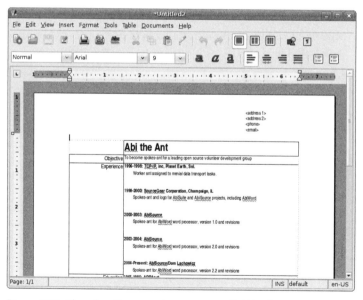

Figure 13-8: The other Linux word processor—AbiWord

Some Other Cool Productivity Apps

In addition to the more traditional office applications, there are a number of other applications either included with or available for your system that can be grouped together under the "productivity" label. I will introduce a few of those to you here.

Sticky Notes

Mac users will be well familiar with the digital version of the now ubiquitous little yellow Post-It–like notes called Sticky Notes (Figure 13-9) that come as part of the GNOME desktop. GNOME's Sticky Notes is a panel applet that you can add to your own panel by right-clicking on any open panel space and then selecting **Add to Panel** in the popup menu that then appears. When the Add to Panel window appears, click **Sticky Notes**, and then click the **Add** button. You will then be ready for note-taking action.

Figure 13-9: GNOME's Sticky Notes

Tomboy

If Sticky Notes just doesn't cut it for you and your more dramatic note-taking needs, then perhaps you will find yourself better served by another application that comes with your system by the name of *Tomboy* (Figure 13-10). Like Sticky Notes, Tomboy also works as a panel applet, but it is a bit more full featured, albeit without making any claims to stickiness. Instead, the various notes you create can be viewed by selecting them from the menu that appears when you click the Tomboy panel applet itself. All in all, a very handy approach.

What really gives Tomboy its bragging rights, however, is its search and hyperlink functions. These allow you to search for entries within your entire Tomboy note library, and create hyperlinks that connect text in one note to another linked note. In fact, Tomboy will automatically create a hyperlink whenever you type a word that matches one of your existing note headings. To make matters even more exciting (or at least more useful), Tomboy, by means of its plugins feature, allows you to export notes to HTML or print them out, either as hard copy or as PDF docs.

If you'd like to give Tomboy a try, start it up by going to **Applications ▶ Accessories ▶ Tomboy Notes**, after which Tomboy will appear in the top GNOME Panel.

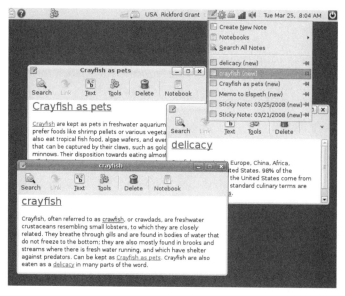

Figure 13-10: Notes taken seriously—Tomboy

GnuCash

If you are familiar with the personal financial management software Quicken, then you might be interested in GnuCash (Figure 13-11), which is the Linux world's best-known offering in the personal finance arena. It reads Quicken and Intuit QIF files, which makes things even nicer should you be making the transition from another operating system. Unfortunately, unless you live in Germany, you cannot use GnuCash for online banking; but as the GnuCash folks themselves say, don't blame them, blame your bank.

To install GnuCash, just do a Synaptic search for *gnucash*, and then mark both **gnucash** and **gnucash-docs** for installation. Once these are installed, you can run the application by going to **Applications ▸ Office ▸ GnuCash Finance Management**.

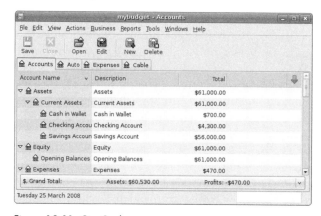

Figure 13-11: GnuCash

Scribus

To round things out, we come to the open source desktop publishing application, Scribus (Figure 13-12), for those times when OpenOffice.org Writer and Draw just don't cut it. Scribus is designed to produce commercial-grade output, with support for professional publishing features, such as CMYK colors, PostScript handling, and creation of color separations, to name but a few.

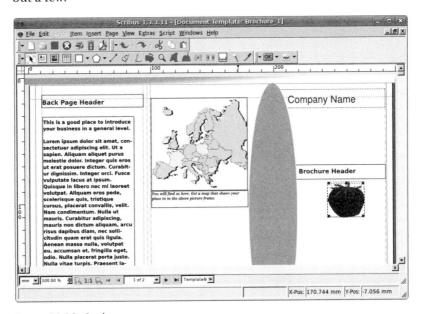

Figure 13-12: Scribus

You can download and install Scribus by doing a Synaptic search for *scribus*. Once the installation is complete, you can run the application from **Applications ▸ Office ▸ Scribus**.

14

BRUSH-WIELDING PENGUINS

Linux Does Art

Now that you know that you can get down to business in Linux, it is time to don that beret of yours and address the artistic side of things. Yes, Linux does art, and as you will soon find out, there are a good number of programs on your system that allow you to create and manipulate graphic files. These days, however, there is perhaps nothing as important to most users' graphical repertoires as their digital cameras, so that is where we'll begin.

Project 14A: Importing Images from Digital Cameras

While scanner support for Linux is still a bit spotty, support for digital cameras is practically a worry-free affair. In fact, if Ubuntu can't figure out what kind of camera you have, it just treats it as if it were an external hard drive or flash drive plugged into your computer's USB port. And even if your camera doesn't seem to communicate with your computer when connected directly, you can still transfer your images to your hard disk by removing the memory card from your camera, inserting it into a USB flash memory card reader, and plugging that reader into one of your computer's USB ports. In that case your system will mount the card reader as if it were an external drive (which is pretty much what it is), thus allowing you to copy the images to your hard disk. Of course, you can use this method even if your camera works just fine with Ubuntu—some people find it the easiest way to deal with things, anyway.

14A-1: Importing Images from Camera to Computer Somewhat Automatically via F-Spot

When you connect your camera to your computer via a USB cable, put your camera in play mode, and power it on, Ubuntu will usually automatically recognize it and pop up a window asking if you want to import the photos on the camera. To import the photos in this way, here's what you need to do:

1. Click the **Import Photos** button in that first window, after which thumbnails of the photos present on your camera will appear in another window (Figure 14-1). By default, all of the images are selected, but if you prefer to only copy the images you want, you can do so by pressing the CTRL key and clicking the desired images.

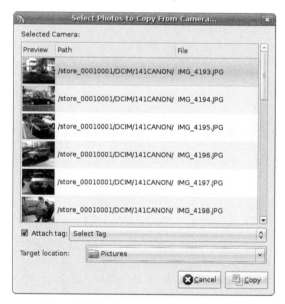

Figure 14-1: Using F-Spot Photo Manager to import photos from your digital camera

2. Once your selections are made, use the menu button next to the words *Target location* to designate the folder to which you wish to copy your photos. Since you already have a Pictures folder, that folder, or a specially created subfolder within it, might be a logical spot.

3. Finally, click the **Copy** button.

4. F-Spot will then begin the copying process, showing its progress in a separate window. When the download is complete, the words *Download*

Complete will appear within the progress bar of that window. Click the **OK** button. You can now view your images within the main F-Spot window (Figure 14-2).

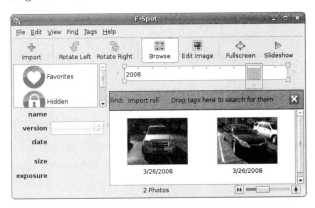

Figure 14-2: Viewing your digital camera images in F-Spot

14A-2: Transferring Images from Camera to Computer via Nautilus

As I mentioned, if Ubuntu doesn't recognize your camera, it will treat it as if it were an external drive, making the process of transferring photos from camera to computer an intuitive one. Just plug your camera into one of your computer's USB ports, and within a matter of seconds it will appear in the side pane of any Nautilus window (Figure 14-3) and on your desktop as a double-clickable launcher.

After that, simply double-click the entry for your camera in the Nautilus side pane, and then just drag-and-drop or copy-and-paste the images from your camera to any logical spot in your home folder. Pretty sweet, you've got to admit. Oh, and when you're done with your transfer chores, right-click the icon for your camera in the side pane of a Nautilus window (or on the Desktop), select **Unmount**, and then turn off your camera, after which it will disappear from the side pane and desktop.

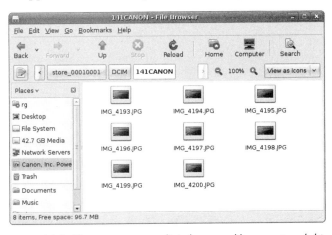

Figure 14-3: Ubuntu treats your digital camera like an external drive.

F-Spot not only works to import images from you camera to computer, it also acts as a handy photo-organizing, browsing, viewing, and editing tool. And working in conjunction with Evolution, the default email software in Ubuntu, F-Spot allows you to easily send images via email (**File ▶ Send by Mail**) without fiddling around with attachments.

14B-1: Exporting Images to Online Albums and Galleries

Another cool feature of F-Spot is that it also allows you to export images to numerous online gallery or album sites, such as Flickr and Picasa. Exporting an image to an online gallery or album is pretty simple, and we'll use a Picasa Web album for our example. Here's what you need to do:

1. Select the photos you want to place into your online album by holding down the CTRL key and clicking each photo once.

2. In the main F-Spot window, select **File ▶ Export to ▶ PicasaWeb**, after which an Export window like the one in Figure 14-4 will appear.

Figure 14-4: Exporting images to online galleries via F-Spot

3. The first time out, you will need to click the **Add** button at the top of the window (to the right of the word *Gallery*) in order to set things up so that F-Spot can access your online gallery.

4. In the small window that appears, type the username and password for your online album/gallery service (not your username and password for Ubuntu). Click **Add** in that window when you're done.

5. Now back in the Export window, click the **Export** button.

F-Spot will then start uploading your images to your online gallery site, letting you know what it's doing in a progress window. Once done, your web browser will open to your online gallery page, revealing your newly uploaded images.

14B-2: Organizing Your Photo Collections with Tags

As your photo collection grows and grows, it can get rather tough to sort things out and find exactly what you're looking for. Fortunately, F-Spot has a few ways of making this easier to deal with, one of which is the timeline slider, located immediately above the thumbnail viewing pane, which allows you to locate images by year and month.

An additional and interesting way of organizing things is by using *tags*, which allow you to identify images thematically. Applying tags and using such tags to narrow down your photo searches is pretty easy to do.

First, to apply tags to your images, just drag the appropriate tag icon in the left pane of the F-Spot window directly onto the image you want to tag. You can place more than one tag on a picture. Once you have added the tag, a small version of the tag icon will appear below the image, as you can see in Figure 14-5.

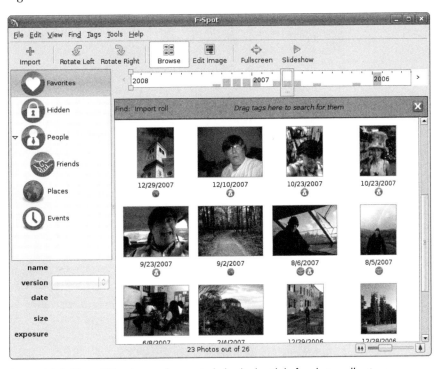

Figure 14-5: Using F-Spot's tags feature to help deal with hefty photo collections

Searching for images by tag is perhaps even easier than adding the tags to the images in the first place. Let's say you wanted to find all of your images that were tagged as *Events*. Just drag the icon for the Events tag to the orange find bar above the thumbnail viewing area. Almost immediately, images tagged as *Events* will appear in the thumbnail area below. Sweet.

Getting Arty with the GIMP

The Windows and Mac worlds may have Photoshop, but the Linux world has the GIMP. While arguably not as powerful as Photoshop, the GIMP is a capable contender, which may explain why it has been ported over to both Mac and Windows. The GIMP allows you to create bitmap graphics and, quite importantly, retouch or completely doctor image files. With the GIMP you can get rid of red-eye in your digital photos, airbrush out unwanted shadows (or even facial blemishes), give your image a canvas texture, change a photo into an oil painting, and even add a bell pepper here and there—and with drop shadows no less (see Figure 14-6). To run the GIMP, go to the **Applications** menu, and select **Graphics ▸ GIMP Image Editor**.

Figure 14-6: Manipulating a digital image in the GIMP

Using the GIMP to Resize Images and Convert File Formats

The GIMP is also a very handy tool for resizing images. This can be done by simply right-clicking an image opened in the GIMP and then selecting **Image ▸ Scale Image** in the popup menu. This will bring up the Scale Image window, where you can set the new size of the image.

The GIMP is also an excellent tool for converting images from one file format to another. You can, for example, open a bitmap (.bmp) file and save it as a PNG (.png) file, or save a JPEG (.jpg) file as a GIF (.gif) file, and so on. While this can also be done with other graphics apps, the GIMP supports an extremely wide variety of file formats, and it even lets you save an image file as a compressed tarball, which makes it a true file-conversion king.

To perform a file conversion, just right-click an image opened within the GIMP and then select **File ▸ Save As** in the popup menu. You can make the same selection from the **File** menu if you prefer. Either way, the Save Image window will then appear. In that window you can specify the new file format by replacing the original file extension in the Name box at the top of that window with the extension for the format you want to convert the image to. If you're not sure what formats are available to you, click the small arrow to the left of the words *Select File Type (By Extension)*, and then choose from the options in the pane that appears below. To save a work in progress, use the GIMP-native XCF format, so that you can continue working on the image later.

Dialogs

The GIMP interface, as you might have noticed, is based on a series of dialogs, two of which appear when you first run the application. You can, however, open still others, and, more importantly, you can dock those together to form larger single dialogs. While this is quite easy to do, figuring out how to do it is something that leaves many GIMP newbies at a loss.

The various dialogs available to you in the GIMP can be found by going to the **File** menu in the main GIMP window (that's the one that usually appears at the left of your screen, as in Figure 14-6), and selecting **Dialogs**. From the submenu that appears, make your choice from the list of dialogs shown.

After you've opened a couple of dialogs, you can dock them together by clicking and then holding the name of the dialog, located just below the title bar, and dragging that name to the bottom of the dialog you wish to dock it to. The name of the dialog will appear as a floating icon/name tab as you do your dragging (Figure 14-7).

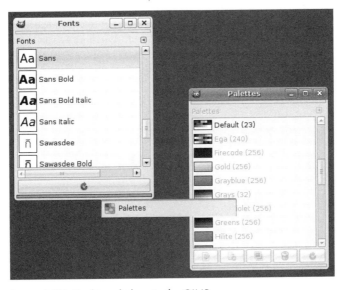

Figure 14-7: Docking dialogs in the GIMP

When the thin, gray band near the bottom of the target dialog turns brown (compare the bottom of the two dialogs in Figure 14-7 to see the difference), release the mouse button, and the dialogs will be joined as one, as you can see in Figure 14-8.

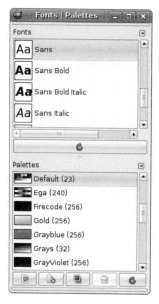

Figure 14-8: Docked dialogs in the GIMP

Taking Screenshots with the GIMP

As I mentioned in Chapter 7, you can also use the GIMP to take screenshots. Using the GIMP for this purpose has certain advantages, one of which is not having to turn off the Compiz-generated screen decorations in order to take single-window shots with borders intact. Another advantage is the ability to capture regions (as shown in Figure 14-9) rather than just a particular window or the full screen. If you have ever used the Mac OS X application Grab, you may be familiar with this feature.

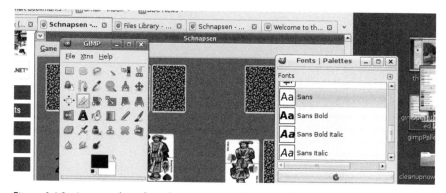

Figure 14-9: A screenshot of a selected region taken with the GIMP

Taking screenshots with the GIMP is very straightforward. Just go to the File menu, and select **Acquire ▶ Screenshot**. A window like the one in Figure 14-10 will appear. In that window, make your choices, and then click **Snap**. If you're taking a full-screen shot, all you have to do is wait until the shot is taken and the image appears in a new GIMP window. If you're taking a single-window shot, your cursor will turn into a white crosshair. Click the crosshair on the window you want to capture, and . . . well, that's all there is to it.

Figure 14-10: Taking screenshots with the GIMP

Learning More

It is lots of fun to learn to use the GIMP by just playing around with it for a while. Most of the fun stuff, to get you started, is located in the Filters menu of any image window. Of course, you should make a backup copy of any file you are planning to experiment with before altering it.

If you prefer working through manuals and tutorials to just finding things out by goofing around, you can download and install the GIMP User Manual via Synaptic by searching for *gimp* and then marking **gimp-help-en** for installation. Once it is installed, you can access the manual from within the GIMP from the Help menu. If you prefer, you can just view the manual online at http://docs.gimp.org/en. You can also find a series of skill-level-based tutorials at www.gimp.org/tutorials.

gpaint

If the GIMP comes across as a bit overwhelming for you, or if it seems to be overkill for your simpler tasks, you might want to try out an application known as gpaint (or GNU Paint), which you can download and install via Synaptic (search for *gpaint*). As you can see in Figure 14-11, gpaint is very similar to Windows Paint and MacPaint, and just as simple.

Once you have installed gpaint, you can run it by going to **Applications ▶ Graphics ▶ GNU Paint**.

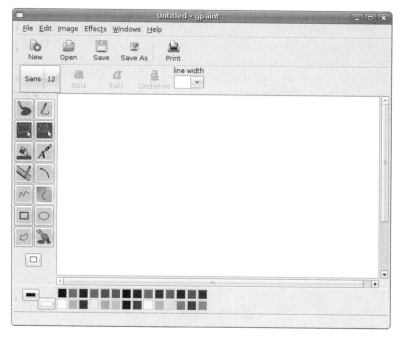

Figure 14-11: Art done simple—gpaint

Inkscape

The GIMP, like other so-called *paint programs*, creates bitmap images in various file formats. These are images in which the location and color of every single pixel is recorded. The image is essentially a collection of dots, or *bits*. The file you create is a rather hefty map of these bits (hence its name), and this map tells your system where everything in your image is supposed to go when it is displayed or printed.

Drawing programs, on the other hand, create vector images, or drawings. The vector image file is a collection of mathematical formulae representing the various shapes in your image. This may sound rather unimportant to you, but such drawings have advantages in certain cases. One of these advantages is that vector image files take up less space on your hard disk than bitmaps. Another, and perhaps the most important, advantage is that shapes in vector images retain their smooth edges when the images are enlarged. A smooth circle created as a bitmap, for example, would begin to show jagged edges ("the jaggies") when enlarged to any extent, while the same circle in a vector image would remain smooth and round no matter how much you increased its size.

If you're interested in giving a drawing program a go, then try Inkscape (see Figure 14-12). To download and install it, do a Synaptic search for *inkscape*, and then mark the file for installation. Once it is installed, you can run it from the **Applications** menu by selecting **Graphics ▸ Inkscape**.

If you would like to learn how to use Inkscape, go to the Inkscape home page at www.inkscape.org. Be sure to click the **Galleries** link on that page to see examples of what you can create with the program, such as the image shown in Figure 14-12, which is from http://plurib.us/svg_gallery.

Figure 14-12: Inkscape

Project 14C: Installing Picasa

It wouldn't be right to dedicate a whole chapter to Linux's graphical capabilities without mentioning one of the newest entries in the Linux application arena—Picasa. Those of you coming from the Windows world are no doubt familiar with this very popular image viewing, organizing, and editing application from Google, and you will no doubt be pleased to discover that it is now available for Linux. Picasa is not an open source application, which may cause some Linux diehards to turn away, but it is free, feature rich, nice to look at, and decidedly cool (Figure 14-13). It also gives you easy access to various online photo blogs, photo finishers, and product providers, such as PhotoStamps, Shutterfly, Kodak, and even Walgreens.

14C-1: Downloading and Installing the Picasa Package

Picasa is free and getting it is relatively easy—just point your browser to http://picasa.google.com/linux/download.html, click the **Free Download (.deb)** link, and then save the file to your hard disk.

After the download is complete, locate the Picasa DEB package on your hard disk, and double-click it. Click the **Install Package** button in the Package Installer window that appears. You will then be prompted for your password, so provide it, and then click **OK** to begin the installation. When the installation process is complete, you will be notified in the installation progress window. After that, you can close both that and the Package Installer windows.

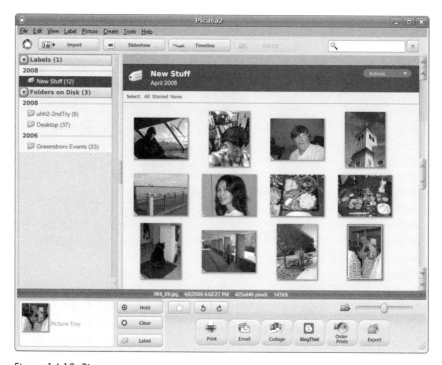

Figure 14-13: Picasa

14C-2: Running and Setting Up Picasa

Once Picasa is installed, you can run it by going to the **Applications** menu and selecting **Graphics ▸ Picasa**. The first time you do this, you will be greeted by a Picasa License Agreement window. Agree to what you're asked by clicking **I Agree**.

You will then be asked in another window, and again only the first time out, whether you want it to scan your entire computer for images (the default selection) or just your desktop. Do not, I repeat, do not accept the default (*Completely scan my computer and all network directories for pictures*).

The reason for this warning is that even though you may have yet to add a single image to your computer, your system is already chock-full of them. If you were to accept the default, Picasa would be filled with all sorts of stuff that you really wouldn't want there. It is supposed to be an organizer for *your* photos, after all. With that in mind, select **Only scan the Desktop**, and then click the **Continue** button. Picasa will then scan your desktop for images and add any images it finds to its library.

Working with Picasa should be very straightforward, but if you want to find out more, check out http://picasa.google.com/linux. On that page, you will find a basic overview, links to more Linux-specific information (including FAQ and forum pages), and a Picasa tour.

A Few Other Graphics Apps to Consider

In addition to the graphics applications I have covered in this chapter, there are still more available. All of these can be grabbed via Synaptic (or for some easy browsing, via the Add Applications tool). While you can experiment with what's available, I will point out a few others worth noting. If nothing else, these applications will give you an idea of the breadth of stuff out there waiting for you.

gThumb Image Viewer

In earlier editions of Ubuntu, an application called gThumb (Figure 14-14), handy for use in photo-handling chores, used to come preinstalled. Some folks wish it still did. It has almost all of the same features as F-Spot and a few of its own (like creating original web album pages). That said, it all really boils down to whether you prefer F-Spot or gThumb (or even Picasa, for that matter). They're all free and easy to use, so have a go at them all, and see which you like. If you do install gThumb, you can run it from **Applications ▸ Graphics ▸ gThumb Image Viewer**.

Figure 14-14: gThumb

Blender

Perhaps one of the most impressive open source applications available today is Blender. Blender (Figure 14-15) is a professional-level 3D modeling, animation, and rendering program. It is rather complex, but that is the source of its power and popularity (it comes in versions for just about every operating system out there). If you would like to find out a bit more about Blender before taking the time (and disk space) to install it, go to www.blender3d.org. Find it via Synaptic by searching for *blender*; once the program is installed, you can run it from **Applications ▸ Graphics ▸ Blender 3D modeller**. There are selections for either windowed or full-screen versions, so suit yourself.

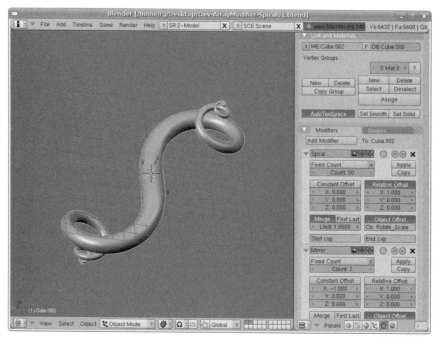

Figure 14-15: Blender

QCad

Another open source application that has found its way into almost all operating systems is QCad (Figure 14-16). QCad is a 2D computer-aided design (CAD) program with which you can create technical drawings such as room interiors, machine parts, or even musical instruments (I've seen a plan for a Nyckelharpa done on QCad!). To find out more, go to the project home page at www.ribbonsoft.com/qcad.html. Search Synaptic for *qcad*, and install the application. Once it is installed, you can run it from **Applications ▸ Graphics ▸ QCad**.

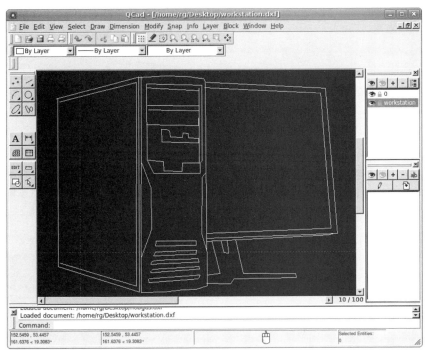

Figure 14-16: QCad

Tux Paint

To wrap things up, let's turn to an application for the kids (or the kids within us) and have a look at Tux Paint. With its big colorful buttons and fun and funky tools, Tux Paint, shown in Figure 14-17, is an app that your children can handle and enjoy. The best of Tux Paint's features (at least in my opinion) are its stamps, of which there is a good variety—everything from apples to seahorses, and euro coins to boot! Oh, yes, and it talks to you. Click a duck stamp, and you will not only hear a voice say *duck*, but you will also hear that *quack quack* that we've come to associate with our green-necked friends. Search Synaptic for *tuxpaint*, select it and *tuxpaint-stamps-default*, and, once installed, launch it from **Applications ▸ Education ▸ Tux Paint**.

Figure 14-17: Tux Paint

15

TUX ROCKS
Music à la Linux

It's now time to move on to the audio side of things. Yes, Linux does indeed rock, and in this chapter you will find out about those musical talents that your system possesses. You will learn how to rip CDs, create MP3 and Ogg Vorbis files (files which you can recognize by their .mp3 and .ogg filename extensions), add album cover art, change file tags, play music files, and burn files onto audio CDs that you can play in any CD player. You'll also learn how to play a variety of audio streams. If you're interested in learning how to work with your iPod in Linux, how to deal with podcasts, and how to convert audio files from one format to another . . . well, you'll have to wait until Chapter 16.

Audio File Formats

Before we go any further, it is probably best to discuss the various formats in which audio data can be stored on your computer. For the longest time, the de facto standards have been WAV (created by Microsoft/IBM and using the

.wav extension), AU (from Sun/Unix and using the .au extension), and AIFF (from Apple and using the .aiff extension), all of which are uncompressed formats. Files saved in these formats are, therefore, exceedingly large, with an average WAV file of CD-quality music weighing in at about 10MB per minute. To put that in perspective, back in 1988 my first Macintosh had a 40MB hard disk—more space than I thought I would ever need, but not enough space to store a WAV file of Nirvana's "Come as You Are."

As computers underwent their evolution into the multimedia machines they are today, it became clear that something was going to have to be done about those disk-space-devouring audio files. Audio compression formats were thus developed. These compression formats worked, to oversimplify things a bit, by cutting out the portions of a sound signal that the human ear cannot hear—sort of a dog-whistle approach. The most widely known and embraced of these audio compression formats is MP3. Audio files encoded in MP3 format can end up being as little as one-twelfth the size of the original WAV file without any noticeable loss in quality.

Another audio compression format that was developed was Ogg Vorbis. Ogg Vorbis was a product of the open source community, so, unlike MP3, which has always been used under the shadow of yet-to-be-exercised patent rights, it was free of patent and licensing worries from the get-go. Because of that, and the fact that it was the equal of MP3 in terms of quality and performance (if not, as many claim, better), Ogg Vorbis became the darling of the Linux community.

As you work with the audio rippers mentioned in this chapter, you are sure to notice yet another encoding option—FLAC. *Free Lossless Audio Codec (FLAC)* is an encoding format that, unlike MP3 or Ogg Vorbis formats, does not remove any audio information from the audio file during the encoding process. The downside of this is that FLAC only provides space savings of 30 to 50 percent, which is much less than the 80 percent neighborhood achieved by MP3 or Ogg Vorbis formats. The upside, of course, is that the FLAC files should be equivalent to CDs in terms of quality.

Given that retention of audio quality, FLAC becomes an ideal choice if you are not satisfied with the audio quality provided by Ogg Vorbis or MP3 files. It is also a good choice if you might want to create both Ogg Vorbis and MP3 files . . . or if you just don't know which one you want to work with yet. In such cases, you can just rip the file and encode it in FLAC format. You can convert the FLAC file later, when you know what you want or need. You'll learn how to easily convert audio files from one format to another in Chapter 16.

Project 15A: Installing MP3 Support for Audio Apps

All that talk about Ogg Vorbis and FLAC aside, there are still many people who like or need to deal with MP3 files. You may, for example, already have numerous MP3 files ripped from your music collection, or you may enjoy listening to one of the many Internet radio streams that are broadcast in MP3 format. Unfortunately, MP3 playback and encoding support is not included in Ubuntu due to licensing concerns. Even if you plan on using Ogg Vorbis format in your future ripping and encoding endeavors, installing MP3 support is a good idea so as to cover all your audio bases. It's also a very easy process.

The easiest way to install MP3 playback support is to double-click an MP3 file that you have on your hard disk. A window will appear, asking if you want to search for the codecs necessary to play the file. Click **Search**, after which another window will appear, showing you what you need to install (Figure 15-1). Check both boxes in that window, click the **Install** button, and then do what you're told until the packages are installed. You will then be able to play not only your MP3 audio files but also MPEG and WMV videos.

Figure 15-1: Ubuntu helps you find the codecs you need.

If you prefer, you can download and install these codec sets quite easily via Add/Remove Applications by doing a search for *gstreamer* and then installing the GStreamer ffmpeg video plugin and the GStreamer extra plugins.

As for MP3 encoding support, which enables you to rip CDs and create your own MP3 files . . . well, things aren't so automatic. But it's not much of a chore, either, because all you need to do is run Synaptic and search for and install *gstreamer0.10-plugins-ugly-multiverse*. If you also want to give yourself AAC encoding ability, you should install *gstreamer0.10-plugins-bad-multiverse* as well. You will then be ready for action, as described in the next section.

Audio Rippers and Encoders

The application you use to rip audio files from CD and encode them into space-saving MP3 or Ogg Vorbis formats is commonly referred to as a *ripper*. For some time now, the most commonly used non–command-line ripper was Grip, which still has its dedicated following. Other simpler-to-use rippers, however, have surfaced more recently, such as RipperX, Goobox, and the one that comes bundled with Ubuntu: Sound Juicer.

Sound Juicer

Sound Juicer (Figure 15-2) is pretty straightforward and quite capable in terms of what it does. It isn't perfect, though, and it still can be a bit quirky. In addition, unlike many of its ripping cousins, Sound Juicer does not automatically create a playlist for the songs you rip and encode, and it lacks a simple, newbie-friendly means by which to adjust the encoding bitrate.

Figure 15-2: Ubuntu's default ripping and encoding application—Sound Juicer

Despite these limitations, there are still many people who prefer Sound Juicer to the competition, so you might as well give it a try to see how you like it. To get started, just place the CD you want to rip in your drive, and then start up Sound Juicer by going to **Applications ▶ Sound & Video ▶ Audio CD Extractor**. Sound Juicer will then automatically display the title of your CD, the artist's name, and titles of all the tracks in the application window.

NOTE *It is important to mention at this point that if you are not connected to the Internet, these bits of album information will not appear because album and track data are not embedded in the CD itself. What happens instead is that the audio ripper or player on your machine sends the digital ID of the CD you're playing to an online database, such as MusicBrainz. In turn, the online database sends the album information for that CD back to the player or ripper.*

The Default Folder for Ripped Files in Sound Juicer

By default, Sound Juicer is set up to rip your CDs and encode audio tracks in Ogg Vorbis format, and the default location in which Sound Juicer saves these files is your Music folder. Each time Sound Juicer rips a CD by an artist it hasn't come across before, it will create a folder for that artist in your Music folder. Within that artist folder, it will also create an album folder. If you wish to change the default folder for your ripped files or the way Sound Juicer organizes things, you can do so in the Sound Juicer preferences (**Edit ▶ Preferences**).

Ripping and Encoding Sound Files in Sound Juicer

To start ripping the audio tracks from the CD you have in your drive, you first need to select the format in which you wish to encode the tracks. To do this, go to **Edit ▶ Preferences**, and then in the **Output Format** menu select the encoding format of your liking. The most of common of these is **CD Quality, MP3 (MP3 audio)** or, in the Linux world, **CD Quality, Lossy (Ogg multimedia)**. Once you've made your choice, click **Close**.

NOTE *If you have not installed the gstreamer0.10-plugins-ugly-multiverse package, the MP3 option will not appear in the Output Format menu.*

After that, all you need to do is click the **Extract** button at the bottom of the Sound Juicer window to rip and encode all of the tracks on the CD. If there are certain tracks you do not care to rip and encode, just uncheck the checkboxes next to the names of those songs before you click Extract. If you only want to rip and encode a few of the songs in the list, it might be better to first go to the Edit menu, select Deselect All, and then check the checkboxes next to the songs you do want to rip before clicking Extract.

While the songs are being ripped and encoded, Sound Juicer will show you its progress in the lower-left corner of the window. When that progress bar disappears and all of the songs you selected for ripping are no longer checked, you'll know Sound Juicer is finished with its work. You can eject the CD by going to the **Disc** menu and selecting **Eject**. If you want to rip and encode another CD, pop it into the drive; just as with the first CD, the album, artist, and song titles will all appear in the program window, and you can rip away yet again.

Once you're done with your ripping chores, you *could* check out the results of your efforts using one of the players discussed in the following sections, of course. But the quickest and perhaps the most interesting way to preview your newly ripped files is to open a Nautilus window, and then navigate to the new tracks within your Music folder. Once you're there, place your cursor over any one of tracks, and a little eighth note in one of those comic bubbles will appear (Figure 15-3), and the track, without so much as a single mouse click, will mysteriously start playing. Kind of cool, don't you think?

12 - No Hace Falta. mp3   13 - Te Voy A Mostrar.mp3

Figure 15-3: Previewing an audio file from within Nautilus

Audio Players

Now that you know how to rip your audio CDs and encode them to space-saving MP3 and Ogg Vorbis files, you need to use another application to play them. Fortunately, this is an area where Linux shines, as there is quite a selection of audio players available, one of which I will discuss here.

Rhythmbox

The default audio player in Ubuntu is called Rhythmbox (see Figure 15-4). Rhythmbox, using Sound Juicer as its ripper/encoder, seems to function pretty much like a simplified version of Apple's iTunes application, though, for better or worse, iTunes it is not. It is, however, a relatively easy-to-use audio player which, despite some quirkiness in its early stages, has developed quite a following in the Linux world. To run Rhythmbox, just go to the **Applications** menu and select **Sound & Video ▸ Rhythmbox Music Player**.

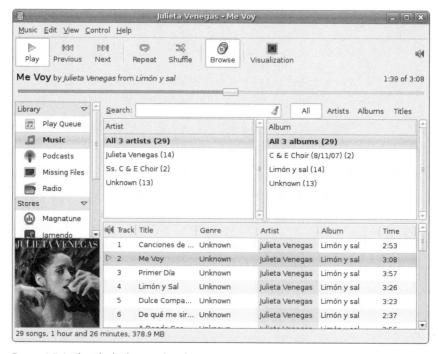

Figure 15-4: The Rhythmbox audio player

Adding Songs and Albums to the Rhythmbox Library

If you are familiar with Apple's iTunes, then you should understand the Library in Rhythmbox too, as it is essentially the same concept, though it does not physically move your files as iTunes does.

Rhythmbox should automatically import everything you have in your Music folder without any extra work on your part. If you prefer to add songs to the Rhythmbox library manually, you can open the preferences window

(**Edit ▸ Preferences**), click the **Music** tab, and then uncheck the box next to *Watch my library for new files.* After that, you can add new albums to your Rhythmbox Library by going to the **Music** menu, selecting **Import Folder**, and then navigating to the folder for the new album you want to add. If you want to add a number of albums by the same artist, just navigate to and select the folder for that artist instead. If you just want to add a single audio file, you can also do that—just select **Music ▸ Import File**, and then navigate to the song in question.

If you are not the navigating type, you can also add files and folders by other means. The simplest way is to drag the folder or song you want to add to the Library into the right pane of the Rhythmbox window. You can also add a song to the Library directly by right-clicking the file and selecting **Open with ▸ Open with Rhythmbox Music Player** in the popup menu that appears.

Rhythmbox also allows you to add songs to the Library directly from a CD. The steps are as follows:

1. Open the Preferences window, click the **Music** tab, and select the encoding format you wish to use (Ogg Vorbis is the default). Once you're done, click **Close**. Unless you change encoding formats often, you won't have to do this more than once.

2. Select your audio CD in the left pane of the Rhythmbox window.

3. Click the **Copy to library** button in the upper-right part of the Rhythmbox window. The ripping and encoding process will then begin, and the progress will show in the bottom-right corner of the Rhythmbox window. Once done, the ripped songs will automatically appear in the Rhythmbox Library.

Browsing the Rhythmbox Library

The Rhythmbox Library, which you can make visible by clicking **Music** in the left pane of the Rhythmbox window, is a collection of all of the music you add to it. This can prove to be a bit unwieldy as your collection grows. Fortunately Rhythmbox has a nice browser function, like the one in iTunes, which can be toggled on and off by clicking the **Browse** button. This function allows you to see lists of the artists and albums in two separate panes above the main Library list. If you click a specific artist in the Artist pane, a list of albums by that artist will appear in the right pane. You can then double-click one of the albums in that right pane to play it. If you want to play all of the albums you have by that artist, just double-click the artist's name in the left pane. All in all, a very handy feature.

If you would like to add an additional layer of categorization to the browser, you can do so by adding a Genre pane. To do this, just go to the **Edit** menu, select **Preferences**, select the **General** tab of the window that appears, and then select **Genres, artists, and albums**. After clicking the **Close** button in the Preferences window, you will have a three-pane browser in Rhythmbox (Figure 15-5).

Figure 15-5: The Rhythmbox browser

Creating Playlists in Rhythmbox

Of course, you can tailor things even further so as to match every situation and your every mood. There are days, after all, when you're feeling a bit too ethereal for Kelly Clarkson (and thank goodness for that). To prepare for such moments, you can create *playlists*, which are lists of songs to be played in a predetermined order. Just think of each playlist as an all-request radio station . . . where all the requests are your own.

To create a playlist in Rhythmbox, go to the **Music** menu and select **Playlist ▸ New Playlist**. When the Playlist icon appears in the left pane of the Rhythmbox window, type a name for the list, and then add the songs you want by simply dragging them from the Library pane to the Playlist icon. The songs themselves will remain in the Library, so you aren't really moving anything—just creating aliases.

You can also create *automatic playlists*, which are lists that automatically scan the Library for songs that match your creation criteria. You could choose to create a list for the all the songs in your Library by a particular artist or of a specific genre. To do this, just select **Music ▸ Playlist ▸ New Automatic Playlist**. A window will appear in which you can specify what the list is to contain. You can even specify how many songs you want in the list.

Once you've created your lists, you can play one by clicking the list once and then clicking the Play button near the top of the window, or by just double-clicking the list.

Other Cool Features in Rhythmbox

Rhythmbox includes a few cool features worth noting. In addition to being able to manage podcasts (discussed in Chapter 16), it also supports displaying album cover art. As you can see in both Figures 15-4 and 15-5, whenever you play a track in Rhythmbox, the album cover art for that track is automatically downloaded and displayed in the lower-left corner of the window (assuming that Rhythmbox can find it online).

Another cool and somewhat similar feature has to do with lyrics. To utilize this feature you must first activate it by going to the **Edit** menu and selecting **Plugins**. In the Configure Plugins window that appears (Figure 15-6), check the box next to *Song Lyrics* and then click the **Close** button. After that, go to the **View** menu and select **Song Lyrics**. Rhythmbox will then search the Net for the lyrics to the track you are currently playing and display them in a separate window (Figure 15-7).

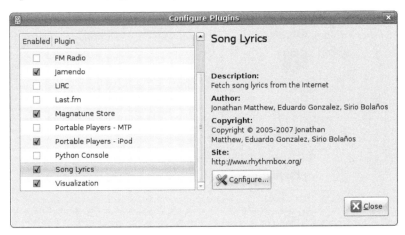

Figure 15-6: Activating Rhythmbox's lyrics function

Finally, if you are an iTunes user and attached to a bit of visual stimulation while playing your tunes, Rhythmbox can now satisfy you with a visualizer of its own. To activate it, go to the **View** menu and select **Visualization** (you can turn it off in the exact same way). The right half of the Rhythmbox window will then be filled with the wild, swirling shapes and colors of psychedelia that you've come to know and love.

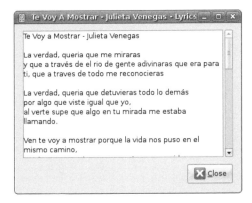

Figure 15-7: Rhythmbox displays the lyrics to the track currently playing.

In addition to allowing you to play audio CDs or the music you have stored on your hard disk, Rhythmbox also allows you to play Internet radio streams in either MP3 or Ogg Vorbis format. To add a stream, click the **Radio** icon in the left pane of the Rhythmbox window, and you will come face to face with . . . well nothing at all, the first time around. In this project, we will try to remedy this rather lonely situation by adding a few streams on our own.

15B-1: Adding Radio Streams to Rhythmbox

To get started, let's try adding FIP, a French music station specializing in the eclectic. The process for adding FIP is essentially the same for adding any other stream. Here are the steps:

1. Click **Radio** in the left pane of the Rhythmbox window.
2. In the upper-right corner of the window, click the **New Internet Radio Station** button.
3. In the window that then appears, type the following URL, and click **Add: http://www.tv-radio.com/station/fip_mp3/fip_mp3-128k.m3u**.
4. Double-click the new entry for your stream to play it.

The only problem with what you've just done is that the title of the stream appears in the Rhythmbox window as the URL you typed in, and the genre, for its part, appears as *unknown*. Needless to say, this isn't all that handy a way to have things, especially once you have more than a couple of streams listed and have to go wading through them to figure out what is what.

Remedying this state of affairs is a simple process. Just right-click the stream, and select **Properties**. In the window that appears, change the content of the Title and Genre boxes so that they represent something more meaningful to you. As you can see in Figure 15-8, I used *Radio France – FIP* for the title and *Eclectic* for the genre.

Figure 15-8: Changing a stream's title and genre properties in Rhythmbox

15B-2: Adding Additional Radio Streams to Rhythmbox

Now that you've had a taste of what Rhythmbox does with radio, you may well be hungry for more. Ah, but where do I find these radio streams, you ask? For the largest collection of MP3 streams, go to www.shoutcast.com, find a stream that seems interesting to you, right-click the **Tune In!** button for that stream, and then select **Copy Link Location** in the popup menu. After that, paste the URL in the URL box of Rhythmbox's New Internet Radio Station window, and click **Add**. You can then double-click the stream in the right pane of the Rhythmbox window to play it.

Creating Audio CDs

All this talk about encoding and listening to MP3 and Ogg Vorbis files on your computer is fine and dandy, but there are no doubt times when you would like to have your songs on a plain audio CD that you can play while you slog your way to work on the New Jersey Turnpike or the Ventura Freeway. Luckily, this is easy enough to do, and there are a couple of ways to go about it.

Burning Audio CDs with Rhythmbox

For Rhythmbox users, the easiest way of going about things is to do it all from within Rhythmbox. To do this, first create a playlist with the songs you want to burn to CD, and then click the **Create Audio CD** button. A confirmation window will appear, asking you if you want to create the CD you've just set out to create. You no doubt do, so click the **Create** button, and copies of your tracks will be created in WAV format. When that process is complete, you will be prompted for a blank CD, so pop one into your drive, click **OK**, and the burn process will begin. When it's done, the progress window will vanish, and your new audio CD should pop out of your drive. Simple.

Burning Audio CDs with Brasero

Another way to create play-anywhere audio CDs from your ripped MP3 and Ogg Vorbis files is with Brasero, which we first discussed in Chapter 6. To go this route, place a blank CD in your drive (and close the Nautilus window that pops up to handle it), and then go to the **Applications** menu and select **Sound & Video ▸ Brasero Disc Burning**. When Brasero appears, click **Audio project**. Now add any mix of songs (in any mix of audio formats) to the right pane of the window. You can do this by navigating to the songs you want in the left panes and then clicking the **Add** button (or just dragging the files over to the right pane). You can also drag files from any open Nautilus window to the right pane of the Brasero window.

As you add songs to the Brasero window, a bar to the right of the CD image at the bottom of the window will show you how much more space you have available on the disk (Figure 15-9). Keep an eye on that so as not to queue up more than your disk can hold. Once you are ready, though, just click the **Burn** button, and then click **Burn** in the setup window that appears after that. A progress window will appear, and once the burn is complete, Brasero will let you know and eject your disk. You can then take the disk, plop it in your car stereo or wherever else you want to play it, and enjoy the results.

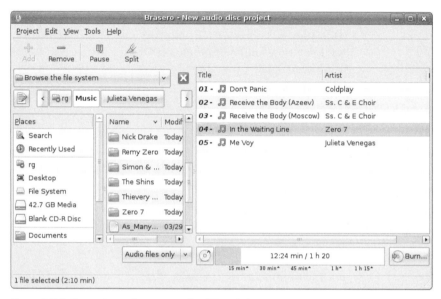

Figure 15-9: Preparing to burn an audio CD with Brasero

Project 15C: Listening to RealMedia Streams with RealPlayer

Now that you know how to play MP3 Internet broadcast streams, it is time to help your system go a bit more mainstream by installing RealPlayer 11 (Figure 15-10). RealMedia streams are widely available on the Internet and are provided by many mainstream broadcasters, both local and international. You can also use RealPlayer to play RealVideo streams, when they're available. Before we start, I should mention that there are actually three ways to install RealPlayer. In this project, I am going to focus on the easiest. It is also the standard and, without question, the most legal way of doing it.

Figure 15-10: RealPlayer 11

Downloading and Installing RealPlayer

Installing RealPlayer is fairly easy, though you will be resorting to the command line to do it. Here's what you need to do:

1. Open Firefox, go to www.real.com/linux, and click the **Download RealPlayer** button.
2. When the download is complete, place the RealPlayer file in your home folder in order to make it easy for you to follow along with these instructions.
3. Make the RealPlayer file executable by opening a Terminal window, typing the following, and then pressing ENTER:

```
chmod a+x RealPlayer11GOLD.bin
```

4. In the same Terminal window, run the installer by typing the following and pressing ENTER:

```
sudo ./RealPlayer11GOLD.bin
```

5. When asked to press ENTER to continue, press ENTER.
6. When asked to enter the complete path to the directory where you want to place RealPlayer, accept the default location by pressing ENTER.
7. When asked if you want to begin copying files, accept the default choice, [F]inish, by pressing ENTER.

In a few seconds, you will see the words *Succeeded* and then *Done* in your Terminal before being returned to the user prompt. You can then close the Terminal window.

Setting Up RealPlayer and Testing Your Installation

Once Real Player 11 is installed on your machine, you will need to go through the final setup steps and then test it all out. You can start by going to the **Applications** menu and selecting **Sound & Video ▸ RealPlayer 11**. A simple setup wizard will appear, which you will have no trouble with on your own, as all you really have to do is click the button in the bottom-right corner of the window a few times. Once you have completed the wizard, the RealPlayer window will appear—you can close it. Because most websites providing RealMedia streams these days utilize embedded players, this is what you will want to check in order to see if things were correctly installed. You should be aware that Firefox comes preconfigured in Ubuntu to use the Totem plugin to handle RealMedia streams. This, I am sure you will find, is a less-than-satisfying way of handling things. After installing RealPlayer and then restarting Firefox, however, the RealPlayer plugin should take over the job.

You can test it out by restarting Firefox and then making your way to the Radio Sweden P2 site at www.sr.se/p2. On that page, click the **SR Världen** button, which is the link to Radio Sweden's exceedingly cool, eclectic world music station, The World. A window will then appear asking you what sort of stream you want to use. Check the uppermost box next to the words *Real Audio* on that page, and then click **Spara** (*save*).

Soon after that, a small Firefox player window like those in Figure 15-11 will appear. If you can see the Real logo in the player control section at the upper-left of the window (like the one in the foreground of Figure 15-11), you are ready to roll. If, instead, you see a player component like the one shown in the background of Figure 15-11, you will know that the Totem plugin is still in control, and you will have to try again. Try restarting your system and then giving it one more go first, though.

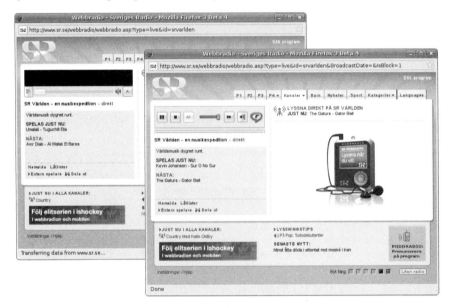

Figure 15-11: RealPlayer embedded in a web page

Going to Town with RealPlayer

Now that you are all set up, you probably want some more streams to try out. There are plenty of sites with RealMedia streams, but let me steer you to some of my favorites to get you started (you may already know some of these):

- Världen (world music from Radio Sweden)
  www.sr.se/srvarlden
- Car Talk (car talk)
  www.cartalk.com/menus/show.html

- Michael Feldman's Whad'Ya Know? (comedy/game)
  www.notmuch.com
- A Prairie Home Companion (Garrison Keillor, et al.)
  www.prairiehome.org
- Radio Netherlands (pop music)
  www.radionetherlands.nl
- Sounds Eclectic (alternative/world music)
  www.soundseclectic.com

Other Cool Audio Apps

The applications I have covered so far are only a taste of what Ubuntu has in store for you in its repositories. You can start out by browsing though the offerings listed in Add/Remove Applications. You can also perform searches in Synaptic for other applications you hear about on the Internet or that I mention in this section. Try them out, keep them if you like them, or remove them if you don't. After all, it doesn't cost you anything in Linux.

To give you a starting point, I will mention a few applications that I think might be worth investigating.

Other Audio Players

If the music players that I've covered in this chapter have whetted your appetite for more, you are in luck—there are plenty of others, as a browse through Add/Remove Applications's Sound & Video category will reveal. Check out Exaile, Audacious, and Listen to get started. Oh, and as you'll find out in Chapter 17, if you haven't discovered it already, the Totem video player that comes with your system also doubles as an audio player. Wow.

Other Audio Apps

If you are an Internet radio junkie, there is probably no application as useful to you as Streamtuner (Figure 15-12). Streamtuner is, as its name implies, an online radio stream tuner. It works by downloading lists of available streams from a variety of sources, which you can then easily browse. When you find something you like, just select the stream, click the **Tune in** button, and the stream will open in the player of your choice. The default player for most streams is XMMS, so to select a different player for playback, go to Streamtuner's **Edit** menu, select **Preferences**, and then in the right pane of the Preferences window, change the default applications for playback by typing the command for the application you wish to use. This is usually the name of the application, in all lowercase letters. For example, if you want your playback to be from Totem, you would click **Listen to a .m3u file**, scroll to the right, and change xmms %q to **totem %q**.

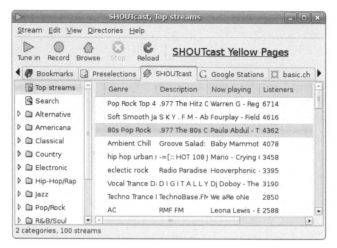

Figure 15-12: Browsing Internet radio streams with Streamtuner

If you're installing Streamtuner, you might as well install Streamripper, which is a sort of Internet audio stream recorder. It works in conjunction with Streamtuner, allowing you to rip the streams you are listening to (and even those you aren't listening to) and save them as MP3 files. Streamripper isn't listed in Add/Remove Applications, so you'll have to install it via Synaptic by doing a search for *streamripper*. Then, to record a stream from within Streamtuner, just right-click the target stream, and then select **Record** in the popup menu.

EasyTAG and Audio Tag Tool

For the true audio geek, these two applications allow you to alter the tags of your MP3 and Ogg Vorbis music files. EasyTAG (Figure 15-13) is the more full-featured of the two, but Audio Tag Tool has a friendlier user interface. Give 'em both a try and see what you think. Search Synaptic for *easytag* or *tagtool*, install one or both, and then locate either under **Applications ▸ Sound & Video**.

LMMS

Linux MultiMedia Studio (LMMS) is a combination tracker/sequencer/ synthesizer/sampler with a modern, user-friendly, graphical user interface— at least that's what the LMMS home page suggests. I can't swear to how easy it is to use, as I don't know much about apps in this genre, but there is a lot of hoopla about it out there in the Linux world, and it sure looks cool, as you can see in Figure 15-14. It sounds really cool too (try out the demos once you install it). Search Synaptic for *lmms*, install the program, and run the command `lmms`.

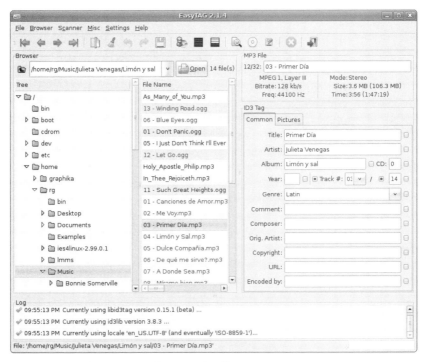

Figure 15-13: Editing MP3 and Ogg Vorbis file tags in EasyTAG

Figure 15-14: Creating music with LMMS

Audacity

If you're interested in podcasting, one application you will find repeatedly mentioned is Audacity. *Audacity* (Figure 15-15) is a multi-platform audio recording and editing application that is frequently used not only in the Linux world, but in the Mac and Windows worlds as well. It allows you to cut and paste bits of sound, raise pitch, increase speed, add echo and other effects, and . . . well, all sorts of other neat stuff. Get it via Synaptic by doing a search for and then installing *audacity*. Audacity will then be available from **Applications ▸ Sound & Video**.

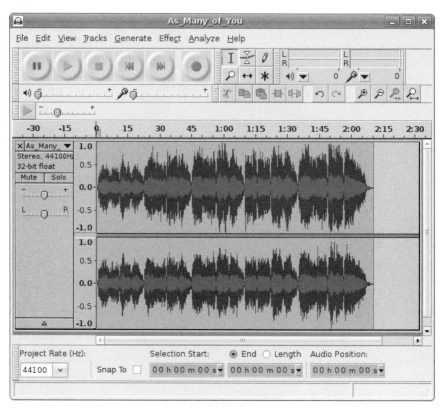

Figure 15-15: Audio recording and editing with Audacity

16

PLUGGIN' IN THE PENGUIN
Ubuntu and Your iPod

With all the talk in the previous chapter about ripping, encoding, and playing back audio files, you may be wondering whether or not you'll be able to transfer any of those files to your iPod using Linux.

Well, you will be happy to know that Ubuntu does iPods. You will also be happy to know that using your iPod on your Ubuntu system is quite easy. All you have to do is plug your iPod into one of your computer's USB ports, after which Ubuntu will automatically mount the iPod and place an iPod icon on your desktop (Figure 16-1). No longer do you have to mess around with mount and unmount commands or editing system tables. Just plug in your pod, and Ubuntu will do the rest.

Figure 16-1: A desktop icon for a mounted iPod

Knowing Your Limits

Although you can use your iPod in Ubuntu, you should remember that support for such devices is still relatively new. Because of that, there is likely to be the occasional odd moment while working with your iPod. I have been using mine without problems, but a friend did lose all his data when he managed to freeze his system while doing something bizarre. The same thing happened to me on a Mac, so I guess that's just the life of the Pod. Anyway, if you do happen to lose all the data on your iPod or somehow corrupt its system, you can just use Apple's iPod Updater while in Windows to bring it back to normal and repopulate its song library from your hard disk.

Assuming you downloaded and installed the codec packages mentioned in Chapter 15, you shouldn't encounter any problems if your iPod already has songs on it in either MP3 or iTunes' default AAC format (recognizable by the .m4a file extension) that you ripped using iTunes. As for the protected AAC files you might have bought from the iTunes store—well, forget about playing those back in Linux unless you're willing to do a bit of geeking around (https://help.ubuntu.com/community/restrictedformats/itunesmusicstore). Nevertheless, these playback support limits shouldn't prove to be a problem— you can still add protected AAC files to playlists, copy them to your hard disk, and delete them from your iPod in Linux. That said, however, you may find the world of AAC on your iPod in Linux a sometimes quirky one, so you might consider shying away from it as time goes on.

For a Linux diehard, however, there is one big problem with regard to encoded audio formats (and it isn't a limitation only in Linux): iPods do not support Ogg Vorbis files. There is talk that Apple might include support in future iPods, but I wouldn't hold my breath. In the meantime, you can convert your Ogg Vorbis files to MP3 format for use on your iPod, though there will be a bit of a loss in quality. (This is understandable, considering that both formats have their own, incompatible methods of compression, which require the throwing out of actual music data.) Of course, if you originally encoded your audio files in FLAC format, this quality issue will be moot. You'll learn more about this in "Converting Audio File Formats" on page 282.

iPod Filesystem Formats

All iPods have a formatted filesystem, just like your hard disk. In fact, with the exception of the Shuffle and the Nano, they actually have hard disks inside them. The filesystem format that is in place on your iPod depends on which system you originally used it on. Out of the box, all iPods except the Shuffle are in Apple's HFS+ file format. If you use your iPod only with a Mac, it will stay that way. If you use it with a Windows machine, it will be reformatted into Microsoft's FAT32 format.

Actually, in the short term, it doesn't matter which filesystem your iPod is formatted in; Ubuntu should automatically mount either one, allowing you to browse through all the files on your little white (or pink, or green, or . . .) beastie. If your iPod is HFS+ formatted, however, browsing and exporting tracks is most likely just about all you will be able to do without performing a minor tweak. The reason for this need to tweak is that HFS+-formatted iPods have journaling enabled. *Journaling* is an HFS+ feature that acts to protect the filesystem from damage due to power surges, power failures, or hardware breakdowns.

As fate would have it, however, the Linux kernel doesn't deal well with journaling-enabled, HFS+-formatted devices. Fortunately, the tweak to fix this is quite simple, and it isn't even particularly geeky: You just have to disable journaling on your iPod, a task you will learn to perform shortly.

Determining Your iPod's Format

How do you know whether your iPod is HFS+ or FAT32 formatted? Well, as I said, it is basically a matter of knowing which system you've been using your iPod with up until now. When you first plugged your fresh, out-of-the-box iPod into your computer, it really couldn't do anything yet. At that time, your Windows or Mac system popped up some wizard asking you to run the iPod Updater tool. That tool is primarily a formatter, which formats your device.

If you've been a two-OS sort of person up until now and have been happily using your iPod on both a Mac and a Winbox, then you can be sure that your iPod was formatted using FAT32, because Windows spews out chalk spittle when it tries to deal with anything that Microsoft itself didn't create. In other words, Windows can't read drives formatted as HFS+, while Mac OS can read both HFS+ and FAT32 drives. If you are using an iPod Shuffle, you can also be pretty sure that it is FAT32 formatted, because iPod Shuffles come that way.

Of course, if you're a prove-it-to-me kind of person, you can seek truth from facts by just plugging your iPod into your iTunes-equipped Mac or Winbox, and seeing what it says in the right pane of the iTunes window next to the word *Format*. If it says *Windows*, you're ready to go.

If you don't have a Mac or Winbox handy, you can check from within Ubuntu by right-clicking the desktop icon for your iPod and then selecting **Properties** in the popup menu. When the Properties window appears, click the **Volume** tab, and see what it says to the right of the words *File System*. If it reads *hfsplus*, as it does in Figure 16-2, well . . . you're going to have to disable journaling, as I mentioned earlier, if you want to transfer files to your iPod.

Disabling Journaling on HFS+-Formatted iPods

Disabling journaling on an HFS+-formatted iPod is a very easy task if you have a Mac nearby. Just plug your iPod into a Mac, close iTunes when it automatically opens, and then run Disk Utility (in the Utilities folder within the Applications folder). When Disk Utility opens, select your iPod (by name) in the left pane of the window, press the OPTION key, and then choose **Disable Journaling** in the **File** menu, as shown in Figure 16-3. (This menu is not available unless you press the OPTION key.) After a moment, journaling on your iPod will be disabled without any loss of data. If you connect your iPod to your Linux machine again, you will be able to use it more or less like normal.

Figure 16-2: Checking whether your iPod is HFS+ or FAT32 formatted

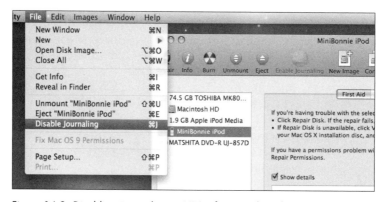

Figure 16-3: Disabling journaling in HFS+-formatted iPods (in OS X)

Reformatting Your HFS+-Formatted iPod

You may find that despite having deactivated journaling on an HFS+-formatted iPod, things still seem to feel somewhat quirky at times when dealing with your podster in Ubuntu. Such feelings would be understandable in that Linux still handles FAT32-formatted devices more smoothly. That said, if you want to go the smoothest route of all, you can just reformat your HFS+ iPod so as to make it a FAT32 one.

And how do you change your iPod from HFS+ to FAT32 format? Well, the easiest and most dependable way is to first find a machine running Windows 2000 or newer and a recent edition of iTunes. But, before you go any further, make sure that you have everything on that iPod backed up, because you are going to be reformatting it, which means wiping it clean.

Once you are ready to roll, make sure the Windows machine is connected to the Internet, start up iTunes, and then plug your iPod into one of the Windows machine's USB ports. A window should appear telling you that you have a Mac-formatted iPod that must be restored before you can use it in Windows. Click **OK**.

To bring your iPod to a comfy state of Linux usability, click the **Restore** button in the right pane of the iTunes window. A warning window will appear telling you that everything on your iPod is about to be removed (hence my warning about backing up everything first). Click the **Restore and Update** button, and then follow along with the brief wizard that follows. Once the wizard is complete, sit back and wait for your iPod to be restored (and FAT32-ized). This will take a couple of minutes, so enjoy the brief respite.

When the process is complete, a new window will appear asking you to name your iPod, and asking you whether you want iTunes to automatically synchronize your iPod with your photo and music collections. What you name your iPod is up to you (short names show up better on the GNOME desktop), but I strongly recommend unchecking the two auto-sync check-boxes; doing otherwise could lead to unwanted weirdness down the line. Once you're done, click **OK**.

Once the entire process is complete, you will have a properly configured, FAT32-formatted, and all-but-empty iPod that is ready for use in Linux, Windows, and Mac OS. You can even use your iPod now on all three systems interchangeably, though you should only do so if the auto-update function is disabled.

(Not) Auto-Updating Your iPod

When you enable auto-update on your iPod via iTunes, the function is set up within your iPod itself. With a FAT32-formatted iPod, you can use your iPod on a Winbox, Mac, or Linuxbox—or all of them interchangeably. An HFS+-formatted iPod can, likewise, be used interchangeably with Mac OS and Linux. If you set up your iPod to auto-update songs and playlists, however, you are leaving yourself open for trouble unless you have exactly the same music collection on all of your machines.

The reason for this is simple. While iTunes allows you to add files to your iPod, it does not allow you to copy files from it. The auto-update feature is thus strictly a one-way street. This means that whenever you hook up your auto-update–enabled iPod to an iTunes-enabled computer, iTunes will automatically add the tracks in its library to your iPod, and, more frighteningly, it will remove any tracks from your iPod that are not present in that machine's iTunes library. I learned this the hard way when I took my wife's loaded iPod to work and plugged it into my office Winbox with its completely empty iTunes library. When I brought the little Podster back home to her with nothing at all on it, well . . . what ensued wasn't pretty.

If you have an iPod that has already been formatted, either out of the box or from within iTunes, in either FAT32 or HFS+ format, it is best for you to disable the auto-update function on your iPod while it is connected to your Mac or Winbox, before bringing your iPod into the Linux world. To do this, start by connecting your iPod to your Mac or Windows machine. In the left pane of the iTunes window, click your iPod in the Devices section, and then in the Summary tab in the right pane, check the box next to the words *Manually manage music* (or *Manually manage music and videos* in video-capable iPods), as shown in Figure 16-4. Next, if you have a photo-capable iPod, repeat nearly the same process for your photos by clicking the **Photos** tab in the right pane and then unchecking the box next to the words *Sync photos from.*

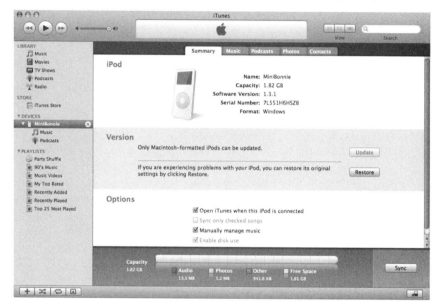

Figure 16-4: Disabling the auto-update function on your Windows-formatted (FAT32) iPod via iTunes in OS X

Managing Your iPod in Ubuntu

Normally in Windows and Mac OS, you load files to your iPod via iTunes, but, of course, since Apple has not created a Linux version of that popular application (and I doubt it ever will), you will have to find some other way to go about things. Fortunately, there are a few Linux applications that can work with your iPod to various degrees, including one you learned about in Chapter 15—Rhythmbox.

Managing Your iPod's Audio Files with Rhythmbox

Rhythmbox is set as the default application for iPods in Ubuntu, and as such it will automatically appear once your iPod is connected to your machine and mounted by your system. All you should have to do then is click the icon for your iPod in the left pane of the Rhythmbox window to see its contents. To copy a song from your library to your iPod, just click **Music** in the Library section of the left pane, and then drag the artists, albums, or single tracks you want from the right pane to your iPod's icon in the left pane. The copy progress will be shown in an orange progress bar in the lower-right corner of the Rhythmbox window.

Copying Files from Your iPod to Your Hard Disk

One feature that isn't available in iTunes (at least not without the installation of a special freeware plugin) is the ability to copy songs from your iPod to your hard disk (or even to an external USB drive). Luckily, Rhythmbox, and in fact just about all Linux audio players with iPod support, allow you to do this quite easily.

To copy music from your iPod with Rhythmbox, select the tracks you want to export (hold down the CTRL key to make multiple selections or use the tabs to select whole artists or genres if you like), and then drag the selected items to your desktop, music folder, or wherever you want them. The only catch with this seemingly simple approach is that you end up with files on your hard disk with funky filenames, such as ZPAD.m4a, rather than the name that appeared on your iPod or within Rhythmbox. This means you'll have to rename the files once they have been transferred to your hard disk, which isn't much of a chore unless you're dealing with lots and lots of files or if you just forget which file is which. In case of the latter, right-click the file, click **Properties**, and then click the **Audio** tab, where you will find the original filename. Once you know it, click the **Basic** tab, type the correct name in the Name box, and then click **Close**.

Ejecting Your iPod

When you're done working with your iPod in Rhythmbox, you can eject it by either clicking its entry in the left pane of the Rhythmbox window and then clicking the **Eject** button near the top of the window or by right-clicking its icon in the left pane and selecting **Eject** in the popup menu that appears. If Rhythmbox is closed, this right-click-to-eject approach also works from within a Nautilus window or with the desktop icon for a mounted iPod.

Managing Your iPod's Audio Files in gtkpod

While the latest version of Rhythmbox should be able to meet your typical iPod needs, there are other apps that can do the job. For example, the audio players Songbird and amaroK have iPod support capabilities. There are also a few other applications that are iPod-dedicated, one of which is gtkpod. Shown in Figure 16-5, gtkpod is a pretty straightforward application with a fairly large user base, which means you should be able to get a lot of questions answered in Ubuntu and other Linux online forums should you have any. It also handles most of the functions that one uses when dealing with an iPod, including album cover art and photos. However, gtkpod is not an audio player; instead, it uses XMMS as its default playback program, though you can change the settings if you have another player in mind.

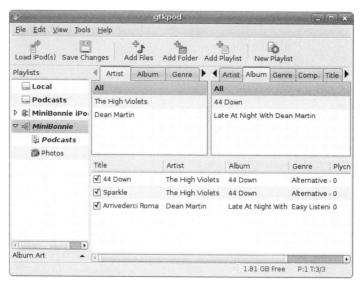

Figure 16-5: Managing your iPod with gtkpod

Downloading, Installing, and Running gtkpod

Of course, in order to use gtkpod, you first have to download and install it. You can do this via Synaptic by doing a search for *gtkpod* and then installing gtkpod-aac by following the installation steps in Project 5A on page 68. If you didn't install the multimedia codec packages in Project 15A on page 254, now would be a good time to do so. After that, plug your iPod into one of your computer's USB ports, if you haven't already. Once your iPod is mounted (once the desktop icon appears and Rhythmbox opens), go to the **Applications** menu and select **Sound & Video ▸ gtkpod**. You can close Rhythmbox if you'd like.

NOTE   *Be sure to install gtkpod-aac, not gtkpod. Both will work, but only gtkpod-aac provides support for aac files.*

Using gtkpod

When the gtkpod window opens, you should see three entries in the left pane: Local, Podcasts, and your iPod. To display the contents of your iPod, click the entry for your iPod in the left pane of the gtkpod window. The contents of your iPod will appear in the right pane. If you have any playlists on your iPod, click the small arrow to the left of your iPod's name in the left pane of the window to reveal your lists.

To add new songs or folders full of songs, click the **Add Files** or **Add Folder** buttons below the menu bar and then navigate to the items you want to add. You can also create playlists either by clicking **Add Playlist** to create a playlist of the contents of a particular folder or by clicking the **New Playlist** button to build your own playlist.

When you click New Playlist, a new list will appear in the Playlists pane at the left side of the window under the Local item. Drag the songs you want from the right pane to the new list in the left pane in order to build your list. (Just be sure to drag the files directly onto the playlist icon, as gtkpod can be a bit finicky in this department.) You can also add songs to existing lists in the same way.

NOTE   *While we're on the topic of dragging and dropping, it is worth noting that you can add songs to your iPod library by simply dragging them from your Music folder (or any other folder) and then dropping them in the right pane of the gtkpod window. To add a song to both your iPod's library and a specific playlist, drag a file or directory from your Music folder to the icon of the playlist in question. Pretty cool.*

Setting Album Art and Editing Tags with gtkpod

Tag editing, including album cover images, is another area in which gtkpod can prove quite useful. To edit a tag, right-click any track in the playlist and select **Edit Track Details**; the Details window for that track will appear (Figure 16-6). In that window you can edit all of the tag entries (artist, album, track title, genre, and so on), and you can set the album cover art for the track. Once you have finished making your changes, click the **Apply** button, and then click **OK**.

Figure 16-6: Editing tags in gtkpod

Copying Files from Your iPod to Your Hard Disk with gtkpod

Like Rhythmbox, gtkpod can copy tracks from your iPod to your hard disk. To do this, select the tracks or playlists you want to export (hold down the CTRL key to make multiple selections, or use the tabs to select all of the tracks by a particular artist or in a particular genre). Then click the **File** menu, click **Export Tracks from Database**, and choose one of the destinations from the submenu: Selected Playlist, Selected Tab Entry, or Selected Tracks.

Playing Tracks on Your iPod with gtkpod

You can use gtkpod to play the tracks on your iPod, though gtkpod must use a helper application to do so, as it has no playback capabilities of its own. The default helper app for this purpose is XMMS, which doesn't come preinstalled with Ubuntu. This means that if you haven't installed XMMS, you will need to either install it or choose a different helper app, such as Rhythmbox or Totem. To install XMMS, run Synaptic and search for *xmms2* (and if you want AAC playback support, *xmms2-plugin-mp4*). To change the audio helper application for gtkpod, open the gtkpod Preferences window by going to the **Edit** menu and selecting **Edit Preferences**. Once in the Preferences window, click the **Tools** tab, and then change the command in the uppermost box from xmms to **rhythmbox** or **totem** or whatever app you prefer (just be sure to leave the %s part of the command intact). Once your choice is made, click **Apply** and then click **OK** to record your changes and close the Preferences window.

Managing Photos on your iPod with gtkpod

Another feature of gtkpod is its ability to manage photos and other images stored on your iPod. In the left pane of the gtkpod window, just click the little arrow to the left of the icon for your iPod, and then click the **Photos** icon that then appears somewhat below that. A photo browser like the one shown in Figure 16-7 will appear. With that browser you can then add or remove images or photo albums on your iPod by clicking the appropriate buttons within the middle pane of the gtkpod window.

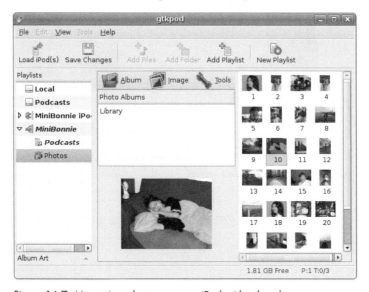

Figure 16-7: Managing photos on your iPod with gtkpod

Finishing Up the Job with gtkpod

Once you've done all you want to do with gtkpod, click the **Save Changes** button to save any changes you've made to the files on your iPod. Then right-click your iPod's icon in the left pane of the gtkpod window and select **Eject iPod**. If the desktop icon for your iPod does not disappear after that, right-click it, and select **Eject**. When the desktop icon disappears, you can disconnect your iPod from your computer.

Photo Transfer with GPixPod

It used to be that the only way to conveniently handle photos on an iPod was by means of an application called GPixPod (Figure 16-8). Now that gtkpod can do the same, however, the need isn't as great for GPixPod, but it is still out there for you to try.

You can get GPixPod via Synaptic by doing a search for *gpixpod*. Once it's installed, you can run it by selecting **Applications ▸ Graphics ▸ GPixPod**.

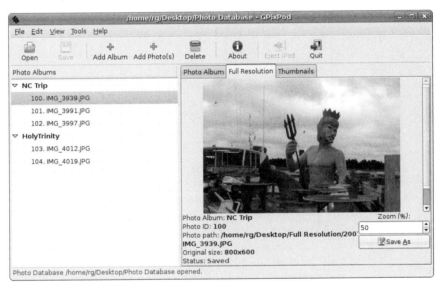

Figure 16-8: Adding photos to your iPod with GPixPod

NOTE   *You cannot add photos to the GPixPod interface without first connecting your iPod to your computer. You should also note that you cannot view images added to GPixPod's database in the right pane of the application window until you save your changes by clicking the Save button.*

Converting Audio File Formats

SoundConverter (shown in Figure 16-9) makes it easy to convert MP3 files to Ogg Vorbis format or vice versa. It can also convert AAC files to MP3 or Ogg Vorbis format, if that is of interest to you. Because SoundConverter does not come bundled with Ubuntu, you will have to install it if you haven't already done so. To do so, just run Synaptic, search for *soundconverter*, and install the application.

Figure 16-9: Converting audio file formats with SoundConverter

To use SoundConverter, just select **Applications ▸ Sound & Video ▸ Sound Converter**. Once SoundConverter starts up, add the songs you want to convert to the main pane by clicking either the **Add File** or **Add Folder** buttons. You can also drag audio files from your Music folder (or wherever else you store them).

Once you've chosen the files to convert, you need to choose which format to convert them to. You can do this by selecting **Edit ▸ Preferences** and then making your choice in the Preferences window (Figure 16-10). While you're there, it is also a good idea to tell SoundConverter to place your converted files in a location other than the folder where the original files are stored. Doing this prevents having to deal with duplicates in Linux audio playback applications that automatically scan your Music folder, such as Rhythmbox. You might also want to check the box next to the words *Create subfolders* in order to keep things organized.

Once you have set things up and are ready to convert, click **Close** in the Preferences window, and then click **Convert** in the main window. SoundConverter will then begin doing its stuff.

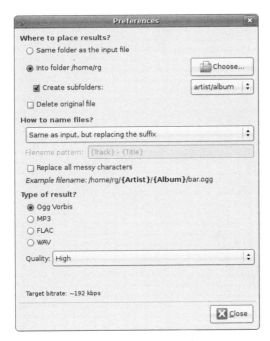

Figure 16-10: Setting conversion preferences in SoundConverter

Linux on Your iPod?

One thing you might notice if you do a Google search for information about using your iPod with Linux is that it is possible to actually replace your iPod's Apple-designed operating system with a form of Linux. Now, I am not advocating that you do this (and I most certainly have not done so myself), but some folks are interested in geeking around with whatever gadget they have in their hands. If you're such a person, or just curious, check out www.ipodlinux.org.

Other MP3 Players

Although Apple's iPod kind of dominates the portable audio player market-place, it is not the only kid on the block. There are numerous other players out there, many of which can be used in Linux with varying degrees of simplicity; more information is available at http://tuxmobil.org/portable_players.html. If you have one of Creative Lab's Zen or Nomad players, the Linux application Gnomad makes things easy for you. Gnomad is available via Synaptic, and can be run, once installed, from **Applications ▸ Sound & Video ▸ Gnomad 2**.

17

COUCH PENGUINS

Video and DVD Playback in Ubuntu

Now that we've covered much of what Ubuntu can do in terms of audio, let's turn our attention to what is arguably the second most important of its talents in our CNN/MTV–era world: video. Ubuntu is quite capable in terms of video playback, allowing you to view video files you download from the Internet or from your digital movie camera, video CDs (VCDs), unencrypted DVDs, and some Internet video streams. It even allows you to download movies from your digital video camera and then edit them.

Playing Video Streams with RealPlayer

In Chapter 15, we covered RealPlayer's role as an audio application that allows you to play Internet audio streams. Audio streams are not the only thing that RealPlayer can handle, however; you can use it to play video streams as well. If you would like to try out RealPlayer's capabilities for playing video streams, head over to C-SPAN at www.cspan.org/watch, and then click one of the **Watch** links for RealPlayer. If you click one of the

Stand-Alone Player links, Firefox will pop up one of its what-should-I-do-with-this-thing windows with RealPlayer listed as the default player. If you click the **OK** button, RealPlayer will start up and play the stream. If everything works as it should, you can set things up to bypass this step by checking the box next to the words *Do this automatically for files like this from now on.*, as shown in Figure 17-1.

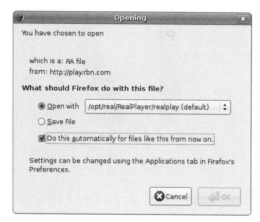

Figure 17-1: Telling Firefox what to do with the RealAudio stream

If you would like to view the video at an enlarged size, you have two ways of going about it. The first and easiest way is to double-click the title bar of the RealPlayer window, which will maximize it. The second, equally easy way is to go to the **View** menu and select **Fullscreen** or **Zoom ▸ Double Size**.

DVDs

Your system also allows you to play DVDs; however, due to licensing concerns, playback is limited to unencrypted disks. Unfortunately, this rules out a vast majority of the DVD movies you buy or rent at your local video shop and leaves you with a rather limited choice of movies that you can play on your computer. Of course, DVDs created on personal computers (such as the DVD slideshows that people create these days with applications such as iDVD on the Mac) pose no problem. Given the limited offerings in the unencrypted DVD world, you will no doubt want to enable your system to play back the encrypted variety, so you will learn to do so later in this chapter.

Can I Play Foreign DVDs?

Your computer can play DVDs of any broadcast standard (NTSC, PAL, or SECAM) and of any regional encoding. This is a better setup than that DVD player you have hooked up to your TV, because the vast majority of stand-alone DVD players in the United States (and I would venture to guess that the size of that majority is 99.9 percent) do not allow you to play anything other than Region 1 NTSC disks (NTSC being the broadcast standard in the

United States and what its televisions are designed to display, while the DVD region is 1). This information is usually provided on the back of DVD packages (see examples in Figure 17-2), though the packaging for most disks produced for the US market does not include it.

Figure 17-2: Examples of regional encoding labels on DVD packages

Despite the wonderful everything-goes nature of your computer in terms of DVD playback, there is a serious caveat to bear in mind. Depending on the manufacturer of your DVD drive, you will only be able to switch back and forth between DVDs of differing regional encodings four or five times. After that, the drive will be locked into the regional encoding of the disk you were playing at that time . . . *forever*. This is unrelated to your operating system— it is strictly a hardware matter. The only exception to this region-lock rule are those DVDs labeled *Region Free* or *ALL* (sometimes inaccurately labeled as *Region 0*), which can be played on any DVD player in any region, and thus do not register as a regional encoding switch when you plop one of them in your computer's DVD drive.

If your drive does eventually lock into one regional encoding, especially one for which you have few DVDs, there is some good news. That news comes in the form of Videolan's libdvdcss2, the library that you will be installing in Project 17, and which allows you to play back encrypted DVDs. In addition to that primary function, libdvdcss2 also, in theory, allows you to play back DVDs from multiple regions even if your DVD drive is already locked into one region. It does this by performing a *cryptic attack* (to use Videolan's term for it) on your drive until it can find the disk key for that drive. Of course, this process of cryptic bombardment can take several minutes, so it is not the optimal way of going about things. Better than being stuck, though. Whether or not this process of bypassing regional encodings is legal remains a subject of debate, so if you are concerned about such things, you should do a little research.

Project 17: Installing Support for Encrypted DVDs

As I already mentioned, Ubuntu does not allow you to play encrypted DVDs from the start. In order for you to watch such DVDs (and that would be the vast majority of them), you need to install a whole bunch of stuff, most crucially, the package libdvdcss2. Fortunately, if you installed the audio support files I mentioned back in Chapter 15, you're halfway there. (If you didn't install them, go back and do so now. Not having them is a show stopper).

In order to get the rest of the things you need for this task, you're going to have to turn to the trusty ol' Terminal (**Applications ▶ Accessories ▶ Terminal**), add a new repository to your current APT repositories, and then download the files you need. Once the Terminal is open, here's what you need to do:

1. Add Medibuntu to your APT repository lists by typing the following and then pressing ENTER:

   ```
   sudo wget http://www.medibuntu.org/sources.list.d/hardy.list -O /etc/apt/
   sources.list.d/medibuntu.list
   ```

2. When the Terminal returns you to your user prompt, add the GPG key for the new repository and update all of your repositories by typing the following and pressing ENTER:

   ```
   wget -q http://packages.medibuntu.org/medibuntu-key.gpg -O - | sudo
   apt-key add - && sudo apt-get update
   ```

3. It will take a minute (or less) for the update process to finish, but once you're back at your user prompt, install the files that you've gone through all this trouble to get by typing the following and pressing ENTER:

   ```
   sudo apt-get install libdvdcss2
   ```

Now, if you pop a DVD in your drive, Totem should open and start playing the DVD. Not that bad, was it?

Totem Movie Player

The default video player in Ubuntu is Totem, which, as you can see in Figure 17-3, has a very simple interface that makes using it equally simple. You can run Totem by going to the **Applications** menu and selecting **Sound & Video ▶ Movie Player**. You can also run it, as you have just learned, by simply placing a DVD in your drive, because Ubuntu is set up to run Totem any time you do so. If you don't happen to have a DVD on hand but you want to see Totem in action, you can also bring it up by double-clicking that Ubuntu video that comes with your system in the Examples folder (Experience ubuntu.ogg).

Using Totem to Play DVDs, VCDs, and Other Multimedia Files

As I already mentioned, you can play a DVD in Totem by simply placing your DVD in the drive, after which Totem will open and begin playing your movie. If you've got a copy of *Red Detachment of Women* on VCD that you're aching to watch, you can do so in the same way. Just pop the VCD in your drive; Totem should start up and begin playing it.

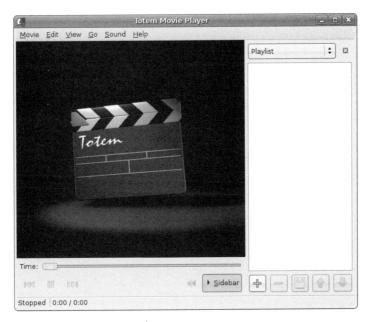

Figure 17-3: Totem Movie Player

Totem not only plays DVDs and VCDs, but it can also play MPEG files and, because you installed that big cocktail of packages I keep going on about, it can play WMV files too. You can play such files by either double-clicking them directly or going to the Totem **Movie** menu, selecting **Open**, and then navigating to the video file you want to view.

Making Things Look a Bit Better in Totem

One thing you may notice when playing a DVD in Totem is that videos seem to look a bit too dark. This can be easily fixed by going to the Totem **Edit** menu and selecting **Preferences**. In the Totem Preferences window, click the **Display** tab, and then raise the **Brightness**, **Contrast**, and **Saturation** sliders, as shown in Figure 17-4, until your picture looks the way you want it to. Once you're done, click **Close**.

Totem as an Audio Player?

You may have noticed while in the Display tab of the Preferences window that there was a Visual Effects section. Well, those visual effects aren't for the videos you play, but rather are visualizations to accompany your audio files when played via Totem (Figure 17-5). Yes, Totem not only does video, it does audio as well. In fact, it is, somewhat oddly, the default audio player for Ogg Vorbis and MP3 files in Ubuntu. Just double-click one of those files, and sure enough, Totem will be the application that pops up, blasting your ears out

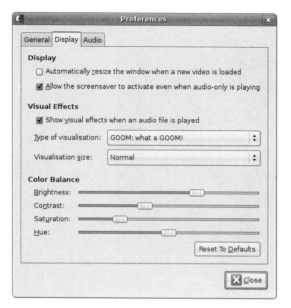

Figure 17-4: Adjusting brightness, contrast, and saturation
settings in Totem

with your favorite melodies. Of course, you can also play such files from the
Totem **Movie** menu, by selecting **Open** and then navigating to the songs you
want to play. If you have a CD in your disk drive, you can even use Totem as a
CD player by going to the **Movie** menu and selecting **Play Disc 'Audio Disc'**.

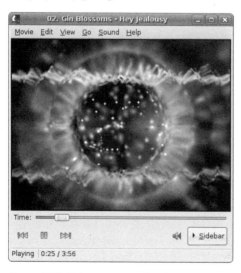

Figure 17-5: Totem as an audio player

A Couple of Other Cool Totem Features

There are a couple of other cool features in Totem that you might like to know about. One is its ability to perform screen captures of whatever video you happen to be viewing at the time. Just go to the **Edit** menu, select **Take Screenshot**, and you've got yourself a screen capture—a still image taken from a video file.

Another feature worth mentioning is Totem's Sidebar. As you no doubt noticed, at the bottom-right corner of the Totem window, there is a Sidebar button. If you click that button, a new pane will open at the right side of the Totem window. In that pane you can load, create, and save playlists. Such lists can consist of any combination of supported video or audio files, thus providing you with the whole multimedia banana. Any time you play a file in Totem, that file appears in the Playlist pane, but you can also add items to the list by simply dragging the files there from your desktop or any Nautilus window.

Using Your Digital Video Camera

Although they haven't achieved the ubiquitous status of digital still cameras, digital video cameras have become increasingly common in recent years. Likewise, while Linux support for still digital cameras is quite good, its support for DV cameras can be called . . . well, let's just say it's "progressing."

Don't be discouraged by my tone in that last sentence, though. You should have no trouble downloading video from your camera to your computer, editing those video files, and adding effects and even subtitles. To be honest, there are still some problems, especially in the area of file format conversions, but, as with all things Linux, it will only be a matter of time until the wrinkles are ironed out. There are also a couple of cool video editing apps that, while not quite ready for prime time, seem promising and are well worth keeping an eye on: PiTiVi and Kdenlive.

For the time being, however, the application of choice for the digital video camera user is Kino. Kino, shown in Figure 17-6, is an iMovie-like application with which you can capture video from your camera and then edit it. You can install Kino via Synaptic by doing a search for *kino*. Once it's installed, you can run it by going to the **Applications** menu and selecting **Sound & Video ▸ Kino**.

Setting Up Your System to Capture Digital Video

When you want to transfer a digital image from your digital still camera to your computer, you basically just download it. When you want to transfer a video clip from your digital video (DV) camera to your computer, however, you have to capture the video stream while you play it, which can be done rather easily using Kino. Before you can begin capturing video with Kino, however, there are a few steps you must perform the first time around. They are as follows:

1. Connect your camera to your computer using the FireWire (IEEE 1394) cable that came with (or you were forced to buy for) your camera.

2. Turn on your DV camera in play mode. Once you've done this, the raw1394 module will appear in your system's /dev directory (if it hasn't already).

3. After a few seconds, turn off your camera, but leave the cable connected.

4. Open a Terminal window, type `cd /dev`, and press ENTER.

5. In the same Terminal window, change the permissions of the raw1394 module so that everyone on your machine can read and write to it by typing `sudo chmod a+rw raw1394` and pressing ENTER.

6. Type your password when prompted, and then press ENTER.

If all goes without a hitch, you will be returned to your user prompt without any other messages appearing in the Terminal.

Capturing and Editing Digital Video with Kino

Once you have gone through the preparatory steps I've just mentioned, you are ready to capture video from your camera. To do this, connect your camera to your computer by FireWire cable (if it isn't still connected), turn on your camera to Play mode, and then start up Kino. Once Kino is open, click the **Capture** tab to the right of the playback pane.

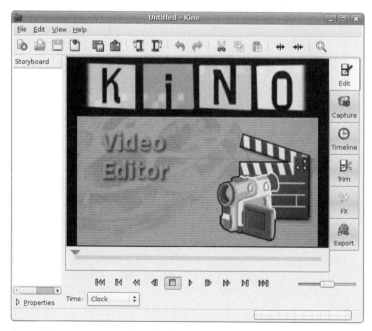

Figure 17-6: Using your digital video camera with Kino

To get started capturing video, you can use the playback controls located below the playback pane. These control buttons actually control the functions of your camera itself. Start out by clicking the rewind button until you get to the beginning of the video segment you want to capture. Once you get there, click the play button, after which the video on your camera will play back within the Kino window. When you reach the point at which you want to start capturing, click the **Capture** button just above the play back controls in the Kino window. Kino will then start capturing your video to disk (in your home folder by default). To keep things easy to manage, the captured video stream will be split into several files, the number of which depends on the length of the video played.

You will notice that after you click the Capture button, the video playback in the playback pane will stop moving. This being the case, you will need to view the action in your camera's viewer in order to know where you are in the capture process. When you get to the point where you'd like to stop capturing, click the **Stop** button. You can then view the captured video by clicking the **Edit** tab and then using the playback controls at the bottom of the playback pane. You can also view the video in Timeline view (as shown in Figure 17-7) in order to navigate between the various segments of the video; click the **Timeline** tab, click the segment you wish to view, and then use the playback controls below the playback pane.

Figure 17-7: Kino's Timeline view

If you feel like getting a bit arty, you can also try out the effects available in Kino (some examples of which are shown in Figure 17-8) by clicking the **FX** tab and then playing around with the various effects in the drop-down menu below the words *Video Filter*. Make your choice, specify the segment you'd like to convert (or at least experiment with) by typing the beginning and ending frame numbers in the boxes below the word *Overwrite*, and then click the **Play** button to see the results without saving the changes to disk. If you do want to convert the segment so as to keep the effect, click the **Render** button, and Kino will create a new file of just that segment. Those files, as well as the original captures, can all be viewed in Totem, which is a better application to use for video viewing, by simply double-clicking the files.

Figure 17-8: Examples of Kino's video effects, before and after

Other Video Apps

I've covered the main video applications in Ubuntu, but there are still others available that you might want to consider. One is gxine, a media player that is very much like Totem in looks and behavior; however, unlike Totem (which lacks DVD menu support), it handles DVD menus and subtitles the way they were meant to be handled. It is available via Synaptic by doing a search for *gxine*. Once installed, you can run it from **Applications ▸ Sound & Video ▸ gxine**.

Two other very popular alternative video/DVD players are MPlayer and VLC Media Player, both of which have significant followings, particularly for their ability to handle numerous video formats. Both are available via Synaptic by means of searches for *mplayer* and *vlc*.

Another cool application for video streaming enthusiasts is Miro (Figure 17-9), which allows you to search, download, and play online video streams. Again, you can download and install Miro via Synaptic by performing a search for *miro*.

If you are not only a video watcher but also a budding video artist, then you might want to consider a few handy video/DVD authoring and editing tools: the multiplatform video editor Avidemux; QDVD-Author, a DVD-creating application in the iDVD vein (albeit without the superficial polish of Apple's offering); and DVD:Rip, which, as you might imagine, allows you to rip the contents of a DVD to your hard disk. These applications are available via Synaptic by performing searches for *avidemux*, *qdvdauthor*, and *dvdrip*.

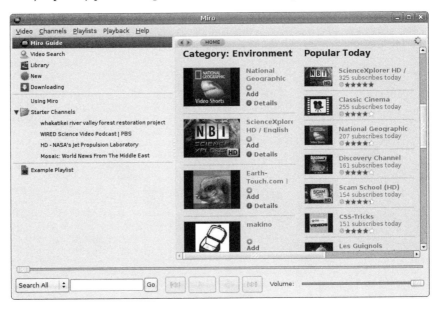

Figure 17-9: A video streaming enthusiast's dream: Miro

18

DEFENDING THE NEST

Security

Many a Windows user has entered the Linux fold after a host of bad experiences with *malware* in the Windows world—viruses, spyware, and all sorts of other malicious bits of software code, too numerous to imagine. Windows is also plagued by a seemingly endless array of security vulnerabilities, leaving the system easy prey to invaders with less than noble intentions. Every trip out into cyberspace thus becomes something like a run through the infectious diseases ward of a hospital. For a Windows user, it can sometimes seem that more time is spent ridding the system of viral pests and defending it from invaders than is actually spent getting things done.

Fortunately, Linux does not suffer greatly from such problems, leading to the much-touted claim that Linux is practically virus free and quite secure. There are numerous lines of reasoning proffered to explain Linux's malware- and exploit-resistant nature. One reason is simply popularity—or lack thereof. As Linux is not as widespread a system as Windows is, it is also a much less attractive target of digital evil-doers, who very often seem to be motivated by the challenge and headline-catching glory that comes with creating a truly global virus or finding a theretofore unknown back door.

Another reason is that Linux users, as a general rule, work on their computers in a non-privilege mode, one in which the user does not have the right to install software without a password. This is not the case, at least not by default, in Windows. A virus or other form of malware attached to an email or piggybacked upon another file or application cannot, therefore, install itself in your Linux system without that password . . . well, theoretically, at least. Of course, now that Windows uses its own privilege structure, this point is a bit less of an issue.

There is also the matter of structural design. Every system out there has security holes that can be exploited by digital and human foe alike. Windows might well be called the Swiss cheese of operating systems in this regard. Of course, Linux has its holes too, though far fewer of them than Windows does; and Linux plugs them up through downloadable updates faster, once they are found.

Finally, there is the defensive edge that Ubuntu's pre-configured security policy brings—there are no open incoming ports in Ubuntu desktop systems. This means that your Ubuntu Linux system is even less susceptible to unwanted intrusions.

Does My System Need Protection?

So with all this talk about Linux's great security, you may wonder whether you need to bother worrying about it at all. Well, if you take a look at the Ubuntu forums, you might find yourself a bit confused. When asked whether Linux users need to install antivirus software or firewalls, most users answer with an emphatic *no*. On the other hand, you'll find that there are an awful lot of people out there who have installed or are trying to install that software. Hmmm.

So what's a Linux user to do?

If you are on a network where you transfer a lot of files among a lot of Windows machines, you might want to think about installing some antivirus software, if for nothing more than the good of the Windows systems involved and the users of those systems—your unenlightened (i.e., Windows-using) email pals, for example. You might also want to give it a go if you are, by nature, on the cautious side of the spectrum. Basically, if it makes you feel safer to install some protection, go ahead. If it makes you feel safer to go whole hog and install the full line of defense mechanisms I cover in this chapter, go ahead. After all, either way you go, it isn't going to cost you anything, and it certainly isn't going to hurt you any.

The First Line of Defense

Regardless of the system you happen to be using (though I am assuming that you have become a Linux devotee by now), the first line of defense for any computer permanently hooked up to the Internet is a *router*—an electronic device that allows a number of computers on a local network (such as in your home or at your office) to connect to and share a single connection from your Internet service provider (ISP). While the router is connected to your modem via cable, the connection from the router to the computers on your local network can be wired, wireless, or both.

What has a router got to do with the defense of your computer? Well, most routers include a *firewall*, which essentially functions to keep all of the bad stuff out there on the Web away from your computer, much in the way that the firewall in your car keeps the heat, fumes, and noise from your engine out of the passenger compartment. This built-in firewall is one reason that even people with only one computer, who could just as easily connect their computer directly to their cable or DSL modem, use a router. Of course, just how much security the firewall in your router provides depends on which filters you select in the firewall setup software. For example, a very common and useful filter (particularly for those with a wireless network) limits Internet access to those machines specified on the firewall's access list. This prevents your next-door neighbors from hitching a wireless ride via your ISP connection. They aren't paying the bill, after all.

The setup software for a router is built in to the router itself, so you don't have to worry about software installation and system compatibility. Using your router with Linux is no different than using it with Windows. You can access the software and modify your settings via a simple web browser, as you can see in Figure 18-1. Just type the IP address of the router (usually provided in the owner's manual) in the browser's location bar, press ENTER, and you'll be ready to go.

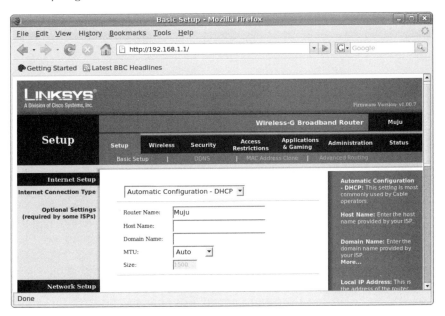

Figure 18-1: Setting up a router

Software Firewalls

If you don't have a router and don't plan on getting one, or if you have one, but you are bordering on paranoia, you might want to consider using a software firewall, in particular one of the most popular software firewalls available for Linux, Firestarter.

You can download and install Firestarter via Synaptic by searching for and installing *firestarter*. Once it is installed, run it by choosing **System ▸ Administration ▸ Firestarter**. You will then be prompted for your password, so type that, and click the **OK** button.

Firestarter will open with a pretty self-explanatory setup wizard the first time out. If the wizard doesn't seem all that self-explanatory to you, and you're not sure what to do, just accept the default settings by clicking the **Forward** button in each of the wizard screens until you get to the last one (shown in Figure 18-2). In that screen, make sure that the box next to *Start firewall now* is checked, click the **Save** button, and then click **Quit**. When the wizard is finished, the main Firestarter window will appear and, assuming the correct network device was detected and selected, the firewall will be up and running.

Figure 18-2: The last screen of the Firestarter setup wizard

If the wrong network device was selected, a warning window will appear telling you so. In that case, you can do a bit of trial-and-error manipulation by clicking the **Preferences** button in the main Firestarter window and then clicking **Network Settings** in the Preferences window that appears (Figure 18-3). In that window, select one of the other devices listed in the dropdown menu next to the words *Detected device(s)*, and then click the **Accept** button. Once back at the main Firestarter window, click the **Start Firewall** button, and see what happens. If you still can't start the firewall, repeat the process I've just described, this time selecting a different network device.

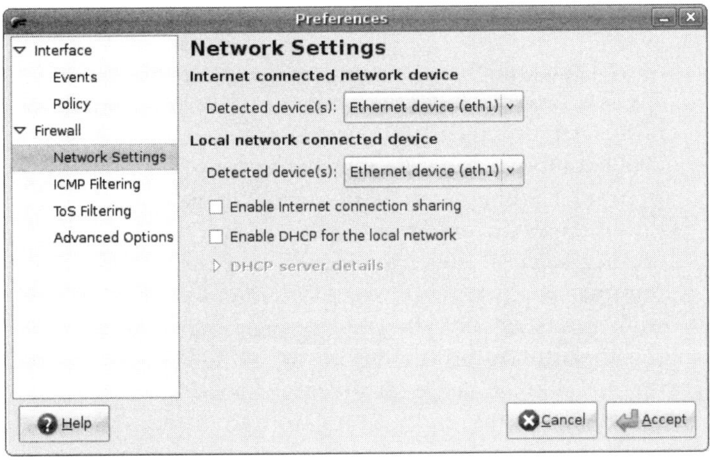

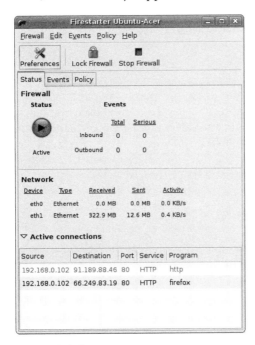

Figure 18-3: Selecting network devices in Firestarter

Once your firewall is up and running, there is nothing more that you really need to do. You can simply look at the Firestarter window (Figure 18-4) to see what is going on network-wise on your computer—what active connections you have, how much information has been coming and going, and if there have been any events in which, for example, the firewall has blocked an intruder. If you click the **Events** tab, you can then see the details of those events, such as what connection attempts were blocked, where they came from, and when they happened.

Figure 18-4: Firestarter in action

Taking Control of Firestarter

You can control how Firestarter deals with various network events by creating your own *policies*. The default policy set in Firestarter allows you to basically do whatever you normally do via the Internet, while it blocks new connections to your computer from the Internet or any other computer on your network.

To make things a bit more draconian, you can click the **Policy** tab, select **Outbound traffic policy** in the drop-down menu next to the word *Editing*, and then select **Restrictive by default, whitelist traffic**. If you just want to deny anyone working on your computer access to a specific website, for instance, simply click the **Deny connections to host** field to select it, and then click the **Add Rule** button. In the Add New Outbound Rule window, enter the domain name for the targeted site, click **Add**, and then click the **Apply Policy** button in the main Firestarter window.

Confirming That Firestarter Runs Automatically

After you run Firestarter the first time, it will set itself to automatically start up whenever you start up your system. Don't be concerned when you don't see the graphical interface you saw when you first started it up; Firestarter will be running in the background, silently protecting your computer.

If you are the doubting type, you can check to see whether or not Firestarter actually is running in the background by opening a Terminal window, typing `sudo /etc/init.d/firestarter status`, and then pressing ENTER. If Firestarter is running, you will see the message `* Firestarter is running...` in the Terminal window. Worries over. If Firestarter isn't running, the response will read `* Firestarter is stopped`.

Finding Out More

If the world of firewalls is new to you, you can check out the Firestarter home page to learn a bit more. To check out the online manual, just to go to the Firestarter **Help** menu, and select **Online Users' Manual**, which will bring up the page in your web browser. If you prefer to check out the manual before installing Firestarter, point your browser to www.fs-security.com/docs. You will also find a pretty good quick tutorial there.

ClamAV: Antivirus Software, Linux Style

Despite the lack of viruses out there that can wreak havoc upon your Linux system, your computer could still act as a transmitter of Windows viruses. As a result, there are a number of free antivirus scanners out there for Linux users interested in helping to protect Windows users from viruses. These include Panda Desktop Secure (www.pandasecurity.com/usa/homeusers/downloads/desktopsecure/), f-Prot (www.f-prot.com), and numerous others. For most Linux users, however, the virus scanner of choice is the open source contender—ClamAV.

Although it can be used on a number of operating systems, ClamAV is considered to be *the* Linux antivirus software package. It is open source, totally free, and you don't have to worry about licenses or suffer the bother of renewing them. Unfortunately, on its own, ClamAV is a command-driven application, which makes it a bit less user-friendly. Fortunately for all involved, there is also a graphical interface available, albeit a simple one, by the name of ClamTk. Both ClamAV and ClamTk are available via Synaptic—just do a search for *clamtk* and mark it for installation. Synaptic will then automatically mark ClamAV and all other applications it needs in order to run.

NOTE *If you do a Synaptic search for* clamav *and mark it for installation, Synaptic will not automatically install ClamTk, because ClamAV does not require ClamTk in order to run.*

Using the ClamAV/ClamTk Duo

Once ClamAV is installed, you can perform a virus scan by going to **Applications ▸ System Tools ▸ Virus Scanner**. This will bring up the Clam Tk Virus Scanner window (Figure 18-5). Before scanning, you probably ought to update your virus *scan signatures*, which tell ClamAV which viruses to look for. However, you can only check and install scan signatures while in root mode, so you have to run ClamAV via the Terminal to perform this particular task.

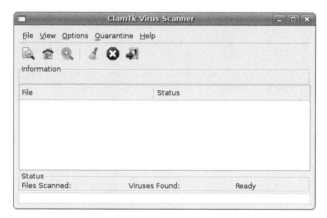

Figure 18-5: ClamTk—the graphical interface for ClamAV

To do this, close the ClamTk window if it's open, and then open a Terminal window. In that window, type `sudo clamtk`, and press ENTER. When prompted for your password, type it and press ENTER. After ClamTk opens, go to the **Help** menu, and select **Update Signatures**. ClamAV will download any new signatures it finds online. You can now quit ClamTk and open it up in user mode via the System Tools menu.

It is probably also a good idea to set things up so that ClamAV will automatically quarantine any viruses it finds. To do this, go to the **Options** menu, and select **Quarantine Infected Files**. Then go to the **File** menu, and select **Full Home Scan** to scan everything in your Home folder. If you just want to scan a single folder, select **Scan a Directory** (choose **Recursive Scan** if that folder contains subdirectories). When the Select a Directory window appears, find the icon for the folder or disk you want to scan in the left pane and double-click it. Once you've done that, click the OK button, and ClamAV will start scanning your system. ClamTk will let you know what it (or, rather, ClamAV) is scanning at any given moment in the empty space just below the button bar. If it finds anything suspicious, it will list that item in the main pane of the window.

As I mentioned before, the only viruses you are likely to encounter during a virus scan are those designed for Windows systems, and because those viruses cannot affect your Linux system, focusing your efforts where they are likely to do the most good seems a sound way of doing things. Although it won't hurt you any to scan your entire system for viruses, especially if doing so makes you feel better, it is probably better to focus your virus scanning activities on your Windows partition, if you have one, and on any files that you will be sending as email attachments, particularly to Windows users.

Project 18: Virus Scanning with avast!

While ClamAV may be the virus scanner of choice in the Linux world, my personal favorite is still avast!, which defended me during my Windows years. I think it is easier to use and, for what it's worth, nicer to look at. On the downside, it does require you to register every year so that you can get a license key, but that is hardly a monumental task, and it is still free—at least for home and noncommercial use, which, if my target audience for this book was correctly predicted, should include you. If nothing else, it is worth a try, so just go for it.

18-1: Downloading the avast! DEB Package and License Key

First you have to get the avast! file and license key. You can do this by opening your web browser and going to www.avast.com/eng/download-avast-for-linux-edition.html. Once you're there, click the **Download** button for the DEB package of the avast! Linux Home Edition.

Once the download is complete, double-click the DEB package, and when the Package Installer window appears, click the **Install Package** button. You will then be prompted for your password, so provide that, and click **OK**. The download and installation will then begin. When these processes are complete, close the notification window and the Package Installer itself. Once you've downloaded and installed avast!, you'll need a license key in order to use it. Just go back to the avast! Download page in Firefox, click the **registration form** link, and then fill out and submit that form. You should receive your license key by email a few minutes later, even though the page says it could take up to 24 hours.

18-2: Running and Using avast!

Once avast! is installed, you can run it by clicking the Run Application panel applet (or pressing ALT-F2), typing **avastgui** in that window, and then clicking the **Run** button. The first time you run avast!, a small window (Figure 18-6) will appear asking you to input your license code. Assuming you registered your free copy of avast! at the beginning of the project as I instructed you to do, your registration key should already be waiting for you in your emailer's inbox. Go have a look, copy the key, and paste it into the text field in the Registration window (you'll have to use the CTRL-V key combination to do this). Once the license key is in place, click the **OK** button.

Figure 18-6: Entering your avast! license key

The main avast! window (Figure 18-7) will now appear, but before you get started scanning away, it is a good idea to check for any updates to your virus database. New viruses are constantly appearing in cyberspace, so you should keep avast!'s virus database up to date so that it recognizes any viral newcomers. To perform the update, just click the **Update database** button, and let avast! do its thing.

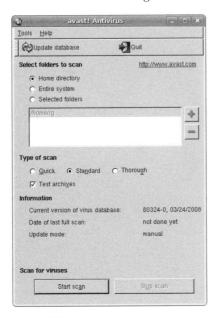

Figure 18-7: avast! virus scanner

When avast! is done updating the virus database, you can get on to the work of virus scanning by first deciding whether you want to scan just your Home directory, the entire system, or selected folders. You can also decide how thorough a scan you wish to perform via the three choices available in the middle of the window: Quick, Standard, or Thorough.

Which one of these sensitivity modes you choose depends on how thorough you want the scan to be. The Quick scan just scans files that end in certain extensions (.exe, .scr, .com, .doc, and so on), because these are the file types that are most often virus carriers. The Standard scan targets more files, ignoring extensions, but still limiting the scan to those file types that are usually associated with viruses. Finally, the Thorough scan scans everything and searches for every type of virus.

Once you have made your selections, click the **Start scan** button, and avast! will start doing exactly that—showing its progress within the same window, no less. When the scan is complete, a small window will pop up telling you, hopefully, that no viruses were found. (When was the last time you got a message like that on your Windows machine?)

A

UBUNTU DESKTOP CDS FOR AMD64 USERS

 As I mentioned in Chapter 1, the version of the Ubuntu Desktop CD that comes with this book is designed to work with i386 processors, either in PCs or Intel-based Macs. It will also work with AMD64 processors, albeit not in 64-bit mode. In order to use Ubuntu with AMD64 processors in 64-bit mode, you must get a different disk on your own. There are several ways of doing this: downloading an ISO (disk image) and then burning it to CD yourself, ordering the CD from Ubuntu (for free), or ordering it from an online Linux CD provider (for a nominal cost).

Downloading and Burning Ubuntu Desktop CD ISOs to CD

To download an ISO of the Ubuntu Desktop CD, go to the Ubuntu website at www.ubuntu.com, find the link to the download page, and then select and download the appropriate version for your machine. Remember that the ISO file you will be downloading is a heavyweight, weighing in at just over 700MB, so the download will take a bit of time. Don't count on getting it all downloaded and done before dinner . . . or, if you happen to be using a dial-up Internet connection, before dinner tomorrow. Yikes!

Burning the ISO to CD in Windows

Once the Desktop CD ISO has been downloaded, you need to burn it to CD before you can use it. Although Windows has built-in CD-writing capabilities, it does not have the ability to burn ISOs. To burn an ISO to CD in Windows, therefore, you must use a third-party commercial application, such as Nero. If you don't have a commercial disk-burning utility installed on your system, try the free and handy ISO Recorder.

To get ISO Recorder, visit to http://isorecorder.alexfeinman.com/v1.htm. Once the download is complete, double-click the **ISORecorderSetup.msi** file on your hard disk to install it.

After the installation is complete, burn your ISO to CD by double-clicking the Ubuntu ISO file on your disk and selecting **Copy image to CD** in the popup menu. A CD Recording Wizard window, like that in Figure A-1, should appear.

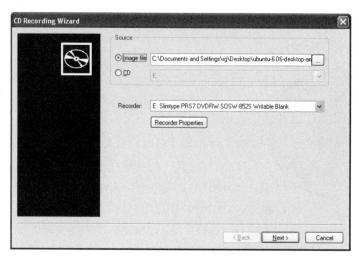

Figure A-1: Burning an ISO to CD in Windows using ISO Recorder

It is generally best if you burn installation or live CDs at a lower speed than the maximum speed allowed by your drive, in order to reduce the chance of error (with 2X to 4X speeds considered optimal). To do so, click the **Recorder Properties** button in the CD Recording Wizard window, and then drag the slider in the Properties window down to about 4X. Next, pop a blank CD into the drive and click the **Next** button. The CD burning process should begin. Once it's done, the CD should pop out of the drive, and if all goes well you'll have yourself an AMD64-compatible live CD. You can then use it by following the directions found at the beginning of Chapter 2 for using the live CD that comes with this book.

NOTE   *If your CD does not seem to work, there could be a problem with the ISO file you down-loaded. Find out by doing an integrity check as explained at https://help.ubuntu.com/community/HowToMD5SUM.*

Burning the ISO to CD in OS X

Although Ubuntu no longer comes in PowerPC editions, the i386 editions can be installed and run on Intel-based Macs. You can also, of course, download ISOs for other architectures on your Mac, and then burn them to CD for use on other machines.

To burn an ISO file to CD in OS X, first check to make sure the ISO image is not mounted by opening a Finder window and checking the disk area at the top of the left pane. If it is mounted, a white drive icon will appear in that location. If the drive icon is there, click the arrow next to that entry to eject, or *unmount*, it.

After that, click **Applications** in the same Finder window, and then look for and open the **Utilities** folder. In that folder, find and then double-click **Disk Utility**. If the ISO is not listed in the left pane of the Disk Utility window when it opens, go back to the Finder window, locate the Ubuntu Live CD ISO you just downloaded, and then drag it to the left pane of the Disk Utility window, just below the listings for your current drives. Once the ISO file appears in that list, click it once to highlight it. Your Disk Utility window should then look something like that in Figure A-2.

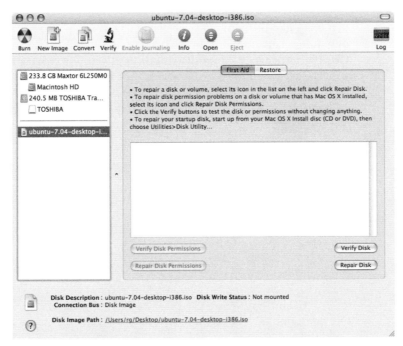

Figure A-2: Burning the Ubuntu Desktop CD ISO to CD in Mac OS X

To complete the process, click the **Burn** icon in the Disk Utility window's toolbar, and then insert a blank CD in your drive when prompted to do so. Once the blank disk is inserted and recognized, you will be able to adjust the burn speed from the drop-down menu next to the word *Speed*. Select as low a speed as your hardware will allow, which, depending on the age of your Mac, will probably be 4X to 8X. Finally, click the **Burn** button in that same window, and the burning process will begin.

Ordering an Install Disk from Ubuntu

The easiest and most foolproof way to get an Ubuntu Desktop CD is to simply order one (or more) for free from Ubuntu; you don't even have to pay shipping or handling. Ubuntu will not only send you one install CD for your particular machine architecture, but they will actually send you one for each of the architectures they support: i386 and AMD64. In fact, you don't even get to choose which you want; it's basically an all-or-nothing deal, which in this case isn't such a bad thing. Of course, the only downside to this approach is time. It can take four to six weeks for you to get the CDs in this manner, so if you're impatient, you might want to opt for one of the other methods.

To order your install CDs from Ubuntu, go to https://shipit.ubuntu.com and follow the directions there. It's easy.

Ordering an Install Disk from Other Online Sources

If you are in a hurry to get your install CD, you can also order a copy from one of the many online sources that specialize in copying and selling install CDs for a variety of Linux distributions at very low prices. For example, you can get an Ubuntu install CD from LinuxCD (www.linuxcd.org) for a quarter shy of two dollars. CheapBytes (www.cheapbytes.com) and UseLinux (www.uselinux.net) are two other well-known sources you might want to try.

B

RESOURCES

As Linux owes much of its growth and development to the Internet, it should come as no surprise that there is a wealth of information about Ubuntu available to you online. In addition to the usual news, how-to, and download sites, you will also find a variety of tutorials, forums, blogs, and other sources of useful information—all of which you can turn to as you use and learn more about your system.

Forums

When you are looking for advice, trying to solve a particular problem, or just looking for some general tips, online forums are the way to go. Fortunately, Ubuntu has a forum all its own, and since Ubuntu is primarily a desktop-oriented Linux distro, you are likely to find many fellow newbies and newbie-friendly posters there, rather than the hard-core geekiness you might find on some other sites. There are, of course, other newbie-friendly forums, which, although not Ubuntu-specific, should also be able to provide you with lots of helpful information.

Regardless of which forum you are posting in, just be sure to mention that you are using Ubuntu, which version you have (Hardy Heron, in case you forgot), and that you are new to Linux. And remember to always seek clarification when you get an answer you don't understand. The same poster will usually come back and clarify things for you. You should feel right at home at most of these sites, though you will probably come to like one or two more than the others.

http://ubuntuforums.org   The official Ubuntu community forum. Always a good place to start when you're in a fix, have a question, or just want to find out what's going on.

http://www.ubuntux.org/forum   Another slightly smaller Ubuntu-specific forum. A good place to turn if you find UbuntuForums.org a bit too much to wade through.

http://www.kubuntuforums.net   A forum dedicated to Kubuntu, an official Ubuntu edition based on the KDE desktop environment.

http://www.justlinux.com   If you can't find what you want in the previously mentioned forums, you can try this or the following two forums dealing with general Linux issues. You are sure to find many Ubuntu users on any of them.

http://www.linuxforum.com

http://www.linuxquestions.org

Linux Reference

These are sites, many of which are geared towards newbies, where you can learn more about using Ubuntu or Linux in general.

http://www.ubuntu.com/products/whatisubuntu/804features   An overview of what's new in the Hardy Heron (8.04) release of Ubuntu.

http://ubuntuguide.org/wiki/ubuntu:hardy   An unofficial Ubuntu startup guide.

https://help.ubuntu.com   Official documentation for the current release of Ubuntu.

http://www.tuxfiles.org   Lots of tutorials and information for Linux newbies.

http://www.linuxcommand.org   Learn to use commands in Linux.

http://www.linux.org   News, book reviews, downloads, and all sorts of other stuff—all about Linux!

Blogs

A lot of great information can also be found in blogs. In these, you can discover the findings of fellow users as they try new things, share tips, and offer solutions to problems.

http://ubuntu.wordpress.com   Ubuntu news with some tips thrown in.

http://www.ubuntux.org/blog   Mostly an Ubuntu-oriented news blog.

http://www.ubuntugeek.com   Despite having the word *geek* in the name, this is a pretty accessible set of mostly useful Ubuntu system and software tweaks.

Hardware Compatibility Issues

If you want to find out whether or not your hardware is compatible with Linux, or if you want to read up on other matters related to hardware support, take a look at the following sites:

https://wiki.ubuntu.com/HardwareSupport   Ubuntu-specific hardware compatibility information.

http://www.linuxcompatible.org/compatibility.html   Numerous compatibility lists, arranged by distribution.

http://www.linuxprinting.org   A great spot for reading up on printer compatibility issues.

http://www.linmodems.org   Find out if your modem is supported.

http://www.sane-project.org   Check to see if your scanner is Linux compatible, and look for fixes if it isn't.

http://www.linux-laptop.net   Have laptop, want Linux? Check it out here.

http://www.tuxmobil.org   Info for using Linux with anything that isn't stuck to your desk (laptops, PDAs, phones, etc.).

Wireless Connections

If you use a wireless card to connect to the Internet and have trouble getting your card to work, or if you just want to know where all the free wireless hotspots happen to be, the following sites should help.

http://www.linuxwireless.org

http://www.hpl.hp.com/personal/Jean_Tourrilhes/Linux

http://www.ezgoal.com/hotspots/wireless

Free Downloads

If you find yourself looking for more goodies to play around with, you should be able to find plenty of free stuff to download at one of these sites.

Applications and Other Packages

http://sourceforge.net

http://www.freshmeat.net

http://www.gnomefiles.org

Free Fonts

http://www.fontfreak.com

http://www.fontparadise.com

http://fonts.tom7.com

News and Information

These sites are mainly informational, keeping you abreast of what's going on in the Linux world. DistroWatch focuses on the various distributions available out there, whereas Linux Today and LinuxPlanet fit better in the online magazine/newspaper genre.

http://www.distrowatch.com

http://www.linuxtoday.com

http://www.linuxplanet.com

Magazines

If you are more of a tactile type who enjoys the feel of paper pressed between your fingers, then you might like to turn to some of the Linux magazines available at most major newsstands. All have a good deal of online content, so even if you're not interested in the pleasures of holding a magazine in your hand, their sites are worth checking out.

http://www.tuxmagazine.com

http://www.linux-magazine.com (European)

http://www.linuxmagazine.com (US)

http://www.linuxjournal.com

There are two (unrelated) magazines sharing almost the same name: One of these is from the United States, one from Europe. The newbie who wants some pizzazz in his or her reading materials, plus some useful tips, and some things to play around with should go for the European version. The US version is targeted toward business users and power geeks, not newbies.

Books

Once you've finished working through this book, you should be able to do just about whatever you want in Ubuntu. Still, your interest may have been piqued enough that you would like to find out a bit more about Linux. Here are some books that might help in that quest.

How Linux Works by Brian Ward (No Starch Press, 2004)

The Debian System by Martin Krafft (No Starch Press, 2005)

The Linux Cookbook 2nd Ed. by Michael Stutz (No Starch Press, 2004)

Running Linux by Matthias Dalheimer and Matt Welsh (O'Reilly Media, 2005)

Linux Multimedia Hacks: Tips & Tools for Taming Images, Audio, and Video by Kyle Rankin (O'Reilly Media, 2005)

Linux Pocket Guide by Daniel J. Barrett (O'Reilly Media, 2004)

Ubuntu CDs

To order an AMD64 version of the Ubuntu Desktop CD, get a replacement for the i386 version that comes with this book, or get the next version of Ubuntu when it comes out (if you don't want to or can't download it), just place an order with any of the following sites. Remember that those from Ubuntu will be free, while those from other suppliers will cost you a little ($5 to $10 or so) but will be delivered much faster.

https://shipit.ubuntu.com

http://www.cheapbytes.com

http://www.linuxcd.org

INDEX

W

Electronic Frontier Foundation
Defending Freedom in the Digital World

Free Speech. Privacy. Innovation. Fair Use. Reverse Engineering. If you care about these rights in the digital world, then you should join the Electronic Frontier Foundation (EFF). EFF was founded in 1990 to protect the rights of users and developers of technology. EFF is the first to identify threats to basic rights online and to advocate on behalf of free expression in the digital age.

The Electronic Frontier Foundation Defends Your Rights!
Become a Member Today!
http://www.eff.org/support/

Current EFF projects include:

Protecting your fundamental right to vote. Widely publicized security flaws in computerized voting machines show that, though filled with potential, this technology is far from perfect. EFF is defending the open discussion of e-voting problems and is coordinating a national litigation strategy addressing issues arising from use of poorly developed and tested computerized voting machines.

Ensuring that you are not traceable through your things. Libraries, schools, the government and private sector businesses are adopting radio frequency identification tags, or RFIDs – a technology capable of pinpointing the physical location of whatever item the tags are embedded in. While this may seem like a convenient way to track items, it's also a convenient way to do something less benign: track people and their activities through their belongings. EFF is working to ensure that embrace of this technology does not erode your right to privacy.

Stopping the FBI from creating surveillance backdoors on the Internet. EFF is part of a coalition opposing the FBI's expansion of the Communications Assistance for Law Enforcement Act (CALEA), which would require that the wiretap capabilities built into the phone system be extended to the Internet, forcing ISPs to build backdoors for law enforcement.

Providing you with a means by which you can contact key decision-makers on cyber-liberties issues. EFF maintains an action center that provides alerts on technology, civil liberties issues and pending legislation to more than 50,000 subscribers. EFF also generates a weekly online newsletter, EFFector, and a blog that provides up-to-the-minute information and commentary.

Defending your right to listen to and copy digital music and movies. The entertainment industry has been overzealous in trying to protect its copyrights, often decimating fair use rights in the process. EFF is standing up to the movie and music industries on several fronts.

Check out all of the things we're working on at http://www.eff.org and join today or make a donation to support the fight to defend freedom online.

ELECTRONIC FRONTIER FOUNDATION · 454 SHOTWELL STREET · SAN FRANCISCO, CA 94110 · 415.436.9333

More No-Nonsense Books from  **NO STARCH PRESS**

HOW WIKIPEDIA WORKS

by PHOEBE AYERS, CHARLES MATTHEWS, *and* BEN YATES

Wikipedia is one of the world's most trafficked websites, read by hundreds of millions of people in over 200 languages, with coverage of politics, science, the arts, technology, geography, pop culture, history, and more. *How Wikipedia Works* explains how this vast, collaborative site functions, condensing thousands of hyperlinks of documentation into an easy-to-use handbook for current or aspiring contributors. It covers the basics—such as navigating, searching, and editing—and dives deeply into difficult topics like advanced syntax, editor etiquette, and administrative policies and processes. The veteran Wikipedians behind this book share the secrets and profound success of this incredible, diverse, and unique community.

AUGUST 2008, 600 PP., $29.95
ISBN 978-1-59327-176-3

THE ESSENTIAL BLENDER
Guide to 3D Creation with the Open Source Suite Blender

edited by ROLAND HESS

Blender is the only free, fully integrated 3D graphics creation suite to allow modeling, animation, rendering, post-production, and real-time interactive 3D with cross-platform compatibility. *The Essential Blender* covers modeling, materials and textures, lighting, particle systems, several kinds of animation, and rendering. It also contains chapters on the compositor and new mesh sculpting tools. For users familiar with other 3D packages, separate indexes reference topics using the terminology in those applications. The book includes a CD with Blender for all platforms as well as the files and demos from the book.

SEPTEMBER 2007, 376 PP. W/CD, $44.95
ISBN 978-1-59327-166-4

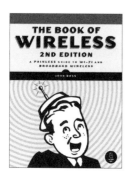

THE BOOK OF WIRELESS, 2ND EDITION
A Painless Guide to Wi-Fi and Broadband Wireless

by JOHN ROSS

This plain-English guide to popular wireless networking standards shows readers how to connect to wireless networks anywhere they go. After an introduction to networking in general and wireless networking in particular, the book explains all available standards, including all flavors of wireless Ethernet (Wi-Fi), along with new standards like WiMAX and 3G networks. *The Book of Wireless* offers information about all of the currently available wireless services for Internet access, with advice about how to understand the important differences between them such as cost, speed, and coverage areas.

JANUARY 2008, 352 PP., $29.95
ISBN 978-1-59327-169-5

FORBIDDEN LEGO®
Build the Models Your Parents Warned You Against!

by ULRIK PILEGAARD *and* MIKE DOOLEY

Written by a former master LEGO designer and a former LEGO project manager, this full-color book showcases projects that break the LEGO Group's rules for building with LEGO bricks—rules against building projects that fire projectiles, require cutting or gluing bricks, or use nonstandard parts. Many of these are back-room projects that LEGO's master designers build under the LEGO radar, just to have fun. Learn how to build a catapult that shoots M&Ms, a gun that fires LEGO beams, a continuous-fire ping-pong ball launcher, and more!

AUGUST 2007, 192 PP. *full color,* $24.95
ISBN 978-1-59327-137-4

STEAL THIS® COMPUTER BOOK 4.0
What They Won't Tell You About the Internet

by WALLACE WANG

This offbeat, non-technical book examines what hackers do, how they do it, and how readers can protect themselves. Informative, irreverent, and entertaining, the completely revised fourth edition of *Steal This Computer Book* contains new chapters that discuss the hacker mentality, lock picking, exploiting P2P filesharing networks, and how people manipulate search engines and pop-up ads. Includes a CD with hundreds of megabytes of hacking and security-related programs that tie in to each chapter of the book.

MAY 2006, 384 PP. W/CD, $29.95
ISBN 978-1-59327-105-3

PHONE:
800.420.7240 OR
415.863.9900
MONDAY THROUGH FRIDAY,
9 AM TO 5 PM (PST)

FAX:
415.863.9950
24 HOURS A DAY,
7 DAYS A WEEK

EMAIL:
SALES@NOSTARCH.COM

WEB:
WWW.NOSTARCH.COM

MAIL:
NO STARCH PRESS
555 DE HARO ST, SUITE 250
SAN FRANCISCO, CA 94107
USA

COLOPHON

Ubuntu for Non-Geeks, 3rd Edition was laid out in Adobe FrameMaker. The fonts are New Baskerville, Futura, and Dogma.

The book was printed and bound at Malloy Incorporated in Ann Arbor, Michigan. The paper is Glatfelter Thor 60# Smooth, which is made from 15 percent postconsumer content. The book uses a RepKover binding, which allows it to lay flat when open.

UPDATES

Visit **http://www.nostarch.com/ubuntu_3.htm** for updates, errata, and other information.

ABOUT THE CD

This software is released for free public use under several open source licenses. It is provided without any warranty, without even the implied warranty of merchantability or fitness for a particular purpose. See the license text included with each program for details. Source code for Ubuntu can be downloaded from http://archive.ubuntu.com or can be ordered from Canonical at the cost of the media and shipping. Ubuntu and Canonical are trademarks of Canonical Ltd. All other trademarks are the property of their respective owners.

Ubuntu's official documentation is online (https://help.ubuntu.com), and free technical support is available through web forums (www.ubuntuforums.org), mailing lists (www.ubuntu.com/community/lists), and IRC (#ubuntu). Commercial support is also available from Canonical (www.ubuntu.com/support/paid).

Ubuntu is sponsored by Canonical Ltd. For more information, visit www.ubuntu.com and www.canonical.com. To request free Ubuntu CDs, visit https://shipit.ubuntu.com.

The Intel x86 Edition packaged with this book will run on Intel x86–based systems (including Intel Pentium and AMD Athlon). See the section "Version Compatibility" on page 3 for more information. This and all other versions of Ubuntu are available for download at www.ubuntu.com/download.

No Starch Press does not provide support for Ubuntu. However, if the Ubuntu CD packaged with this book is defective, broken, or missing, you may email info@nostarch.com for a replacement.

You are legally entitled and encouraged to copy, share, and redistribute this CD. Share the spirit of Ubuntu!